THE
LAST
STORY

THE MURDER OF AN
INVESTIGATIVE
JOURNALIST
IN LAS VEGAS

ARTHUR KANE

WILDBLUE
PRESS

WildBluePress.com

THE LAST STORY published by:
WILDBLUE PRESS
P.O. Box 102440
Denver, Colorado 80250

Publisher Disclaimer: Any opinions, statements of fact or fiction, descriptions, dialogue, and citations found in this book were provided by the author and are solely those of the author. The publisher makes no claim as to their veracity or accuracy and assumes no liability for the content.

Copyright 2024 by Arthur Kane

All rights reserved. No part of this book may be reproduced in any form or by any means without the prior written consent of the Publisher, excepting brief quotes used in reviews.

WILDBLUE PRESS is registered at the U.S. Patent and Trademark Offices.

ISBN 978-1-960332-47-9 Trade Paperback
ISBN 978-1-960332-46-2 eBook　·
ISBN 978-1-960332-45-5 Hardback

Cover design © 2024 WildBlue Press. All rights reserved.

Interior Formatting and Cover Design by Elijah Toten, www.totencreative.com

THE
LAST
STORY

For Jeff

CONTENTS

A Note About Sources, Style, and Methods

As a journalist—especially an investigative reporter— you never want to make yourself part of the story or write about people with whom you have a personal relationship. It, however, would be impossible for me to tell the story of Jeff German's life and death without writing about friends and interviewing coworkers. For six years before Jeff was killed, I worked closely with him on the Las Vegas Review-Journal investigative team. We collaborated regularly on high-profile stories, consulted on each other's stories, and often went to lunch.

I would not say Jeff and I were close friends. I never went to his house before he was killed, and he never visited my house. He was definitely a colleague and close acquaintance whom I grew to like and respect. His murder was devastating for me and all of the RJ newsroom.

That work history and personal relationship, reluctantly, make me a supporting character in the story. After his murder, I broke a number of exclusive and significant stories for the RJ about the investigation into his slaying, the suspect in the murder, and the county government's culpability and failures before Jeff was killed. In the days after his death, I went on national television shows to talk about Jeff's life and work, and spoke about him at several investigative reporting conferences. I was also a named plaintiff/appellant in the Review-Journal's court case to protect Jeff's electronic devices, and therefore confidential sources, from search. by police and prosecutors, and was one of the people reviewing the devices for the newspaper to determine if there was privileged information on them.

With that history, I had to decide the best way to present the story. Instead of switching between the first and third person, which I felt would distract the reader, I decided to just write the whole book in the third person, with me, Arthur Kane, as one of the characters whose life intersected with Jeff's. I feel that was the best way to build a compelling, unbroken narrative. In the epilogue, I switch to the first person to cover a number of interactions while reporting the book and interviews I conducted.

In February 2023, I was promoted from investigative reporter to investigations editor at the RJ, supervising a team of four reporters, including one who filled the opening left by Jeff's murder. My current job is important to disclose. It is a particularly sensitive issue during the portion of the book that covers the controversial purchase of the RJ by casino mogul and Nevada's wealthiest person, the late billionaire Sheldon Adelson.

Objectivity is often touted as a journalistic virtue, but I believe it is a nearly impossible goal to achieve. The human brain, by definition, is subjective. Touting objectivity can deceive readers into thinking the author's biases, experience, and insights did not influence the story. That is never true. I think it's better to reveal your own interests and biases and allow readers to judge the work in that light.

For years, I have worked for the Adelson-family-owned paper, and, despite the views of outsiders and some former reporters, I believe the money and resources the family invested into the paper have significantly improved the RJ's journalism. Jeff, despite his liberal leanings, often said he felt the same way. I wasn't an employee during the tumultuous takeover and understand from my research that there were many mistakes made early in the process. But I can honestly say that I do not feel any stories I wrote were changed because of the Adelson family's interests. I was never asked to do a story because the owners wanted it. I wrote quite a few unfavorable stories about politicians that Adelson actively supported with his vast wealth. My editors never softened those stories and all of them appeared prominently on the front page.

I have never been a partisan person. I do not vote specifically because I do not want to actively support one party or the other when I may have to write about or edit a story about a candidate. I have, however, covered government for thirty years and witnessed the corruption, malfeasance, and waste in public agencies. I am skeptical, some would say cynical, of government intervention because, in many cases, it makes problems worse. For this book (and in my daily journalism), I worked very hard to be fair, complete, and tell the real story based on the facts. Only readers can judge if I succeeded.

Another challenge in reporting this book was that many of the sources were current and former work colleagues, friends, subordinates, and supervisors. I tried my best to come to each interview with the same quest for the truth that I would use in any story. I was pleased to find many people were open to answering all of my questions. I also was surprised and disappointed when journalists declined interviews or took the politician's tactic of wanting written questions. Of course, subconsciously, no matter how hard you try, professional and personal relationships can impact the story. I consciously thought about that the whole time I worked on this book and tried to understand and counteract any bias. Again, the reader will have to judge if I was successful.

THE LAST STORY is a work of non-fiction. I interviewed about eighty people who knew Jeff or understood the culture, politics, or journalism in Las Vegas. All of those interviews were on the record, and most were recorded when the interviewee gave permission. I do not like using anonymous sources but have in one or two places where people talked about ongoing police investigations that neither public records nor on-record sources would reveal. I attempted to interview dozens more who either turned me down or ignored my requests.

I reviewed gigabytes of records, news stories, video, and audio recordings. I read several books about Las Vegas politics, personalities, and history, which helped me understand what Vegas was like during Jeff's early years as a reporter. I reached out to every possible person I could think of who might have a story to contribute about Jeff's life and death and the journalism, government, and culture that prevailed in Sin City before I moved to the valley at the end of 2016.

To create a compelling narrative, I used conventions often found in fiction but only when I had incontrovertible evidence that the anecdotes were accurate. When I write that a character thought something, I obtained that information from the person in question, a trusted source the person confided in, or a public record. I used similar standards for direct quotes.

Another hurdle was that a significant amount of Jeff's work was based on his relationships with sources whom he agreed to protect from public disclosure. After his death, the RJ went to court to prevent police and prosecutors from accessing his phone and computers that they seized as evidence. I wanted to maintain his journalistic promises to confidential sources so I only revealed a person as his source if that person agreed to have his or her name made public for the book. The confidentiality of sources lies with the source and it is a bedrock of investigative reporting. If a person wanted to remain anonymous, I honored Jeff's promise to that person even if I learned the information independently.

In a high-profile murder case, facts and memories often contradict. Some sources discussed situations that happened decades earlier so memories were clouded by time. I tried every reporting tactic I know to verify what happened. If I wasn't sure an anecdote was accurate, I left it out. I tried to stick with the most logical scenario supported by a majority or all of the facts. If the points of view were so diametrically opposed that one narrative was impossible, I either put both people's perspectives in the story or included a footnote that provided the opposing (but usually the less credible) viewpoint. I hope this book does justice to both Jeff's life and his work, and his friends and family feel it accurately portrays the person they knew and loved.

Prologue: "Jeff's Dead"

The Saturday evening before Labor Day 2022, Las Vegas Review-Journal Executive Editor Glenn Cook received a call that provoked some apprehension. The caller, Las Vegas Metropolitan Police Sheriff Joe Lombardo, was not someone Cook expected to hear from in the middle of a long holiday weekend. He didn't know why Lombardo was calling him, but knew it likely was not good news.

Cook had spent the evening helping his son adjust to a bumpy freshman year of high school. Just weeks in, the thirteen-year-old was already struggling. Cook, naturally, wanted to make sure his son thrived. So he dedicated the evening to getting the teen back on track. He and his son sat at a large pine living room table, under a contemporary chrome chandelier. The Edison-bulb lights illuminated a pile of homework, papers, and computers as father and son planned out the coming year.[1]

Since 2015, Lombardo headed the Las Vegas Metropolitan Police Department made up of nearly six thousand civilian and police employees. It was the state's largest law enforcement agency and one of the biggest in the country. About three thousand sworn officers covered the city of Las Vegas and much of the sprawling Clark County, which stretches from the California border north nearly to Utah.

The Review-Journal and LVMPD, often known as just Metro, regularly clashed. The newspaper sued Metro repeatedly to obtain public records about crimes and police activities. After a madman massacred sixty people on October

1, 2017, from a comped suite at Mandalay Bay Casino, the paper, as part of a consortium of news organizations, went to court to obtain details of the mass murder and Metro's response. The newspaper regularly prevailed in court, forcing LVMPD to turn over the records and pay the paper's legal fees. But invariably, Lombardo and his staff denied subsequent requests, leading to more court battles and more squandered taxpayer money.

Despite the contentious court fights and adversarial relationship, Cook and Lombardo met regularly for coffee to discuss sensitive matters. Lombardo didn't hesitate to call Cook when police were upset about a story or angry at a reporter on his staff. Cook called Lombardo when his officers or public relations staff acted improperly towards RJ journalists.

Complicating the relationship further was that, months earlier, Lombardo had won the Republican nomination for Nevada governor. Polls showed he had a good chance to unseat incumbent Democrat Steve Sisolak in the November general election. Cook thought Lombardo's call could be about police work or politics, but it was clearly important enough for the sheriff to interrupt his time off.

His son coming first, Cook let Lombardo's call go to voicemail. He was at a key point in the mentoring. He also was sure his conversation with Lombardo—no matter the topic—wasn't one he wanted his son or the rest of his family to hear. When father and son reached a natural break in the study, Cook walked out of the sliding door into his backyard. The sun was starting to set but the temperature still hovered around one hundred degrees. Breaking a sweat, Cook sat under the beige stucco overhang of his house in the upscale Summerlin neighborhood about a dozen miles from the Strip. He called Lombardo, inquiring what prompted the call.

"I'm calling about Jeff German," the gruff thirty-four-year veteran of the department told Cook. "Do you know why I am calling about Jeff?"

Jeff German worked forty years as a journalist in Las Vegas and was currently one of four reporters on the RJ's investigative team. Cook racked his brain about what story German was working on that so upset Lombardo. Cook figured he must be onto a hell of an investigation about Metro or Lombardo's gubernatorial campaign. But Jeff German was obsessive about keeping editors—all the way to the top—updated on any major revelation he uncovered. He hadn't recently briefed Cook on any big stories that would explain the Lombardo call.

"Is it a story he's working?" Cook asked.

"He's dead," Lombardo blurted out.

Cook—tall with a runner's physique, closely cropped graying hair, and usually calm demeanor of a teacher or professor—was used to high-pressure situations. He had to be, as the top editor of the state's largest newspaper. But Lombardo's revelation sent his head spinning. Cook had known Jeff German personally for more than a decade, respecting his drive and dedication to the craft. He was a valued colleague at the paper. Cook also considered him a friend as the two spent time together outside work as competitors in the RJ's fantasy football league.

Jeff German started at the Las Vegas Sun in 1978, covering everything from the Mob and government corruption to the deadly MGM fire. After more than thirty years at the Sun, he was laid off. The RJ hired him, and he eagerly jumped on every big story like a cub reporter still trying to make his bones.

In 2016, he was moved from the courts beat to a new investigative team the newspaper formed after billionaire casino magnate and top Republican campaign donor Sheldon Adelson and his family bought the paper. Despite controversy over and some questionable actions during the purchase, the family funded a significant expansion of the paper's staff at a time of declining readership and revenue. The extra staff and new leadership significantly improved the paper's journalism.

Ten days before his death, Jeff German had turned sixty-nine years old. He recently suffered some health issues, including a tumor on his kidney. Sudden death from a medical condition would not be a complete surprise, Cook thought. Lombardo told Cook that German was found outside his house near a bush and that he was all scratched up. Desert plants—even ones used in residential landscaping—are usually covered with nasty spines and sharp thorns. Falling into a bush during a heart attack or a stroke could account for the injuries Lombardo described.

Lombardo asked Cook if the paper could provide German's next of kin so his officers could notify German's siblings. German lived alone but was close to his brother and sisters, who had moved to Vegas over the years to be near their eldest brother. As the call was ending, Lombardo said his officers did not rule out foul play but it was too early to determine what happened. German's body was on its way to the Clark County coroner. The coroner would make the final determination.

After hanging up with Lombardo, Cook immediately called RJ Publisher J. Keith Moyer. Moyer, a bear of a man with an intimidating demeanor but a deep love for his staff and the craft, had been a top executive at newspapers across the country. Starting as a reporter when Jimmy Carter was president, Moyer climbed to the top editor and publisher roles at the Fresno Bee in California and the Star-Tribune in Minneapolis, Minnesota. Then at sixty-three, he was lured out of semi-retirement and teaching at the University of Minnesota to head Nevada's largest news organization. Reluctantly, he accepted one last chance to reinvigorate and run a newsroom with a less-than-stellar reputation. He didn't mind telling staff that he was offered a lot of money to move from the Twin Cities to Sin City.

Moyer was naturally stunned by the call. He and German had built a close relationship in recent years with the veteran reporter coming to Moyer's office two or three times a week to discuss his latest story or talk fantasy football. German always liked to make sure his bosses knew he was hustling.[2]

Getting off the phone with his boss, Cook continued to work the phone. He called human resources director Kim Taormina to see if she had Jeff German's family contacts. Cook called Lombardo with the next-of-kin contact information. The RJ and police had the same goal of making sure the family didn't learn of German's death from media reports. Managing Editor Anastasia Hendrix, who joined the paper as assistant managing editor for features in 2016 but was quickly promoted to the second most powerful position in the newsroom, was next. Then Cook called German's direct boss, Assistant Managing Editor Rhonda Prast. Cook recounted the call with Lombardo, breaking the bad news.

Getting off the phone with Cook, Prast immediately started calling the rest of her team. Investigative reporter Michael Scott Davidson, blond and built like a linebacker, was dating and living with another reporter on the team, Briana Erickson. Erickson was slight, quiet, but a great writer and tenacious journalist. Both grew up in Florida, attending school and working there until Moyer, who graduated from the University of Florida, brought them to the desert.

For Labor Day weekend and Erickson's birthday, the couple had gone to Moab, Utah. Prast texted Davidson, who was at a motel watching home improvement shows after a day of hiking.

"Are you guys near a phone?" she texted at 8:30 p.m. "Need to talk to you and B."

Prast often called reporters at night, on weekends, and while staffers were on vacation even if the matter wasn't pressing. She lived alone in Vegas with her cat. When she took the RJ job, her husband remained in Idaho. Her adult children lived in cities on the West Coast so she talked about how she worked constantly.

Davidson and Erickson figured it was a typical, unnecessary interruption of their time off, but Davidson called her back. Prast told them German had been found dead. Health issues were the first thing that came to Davidson's mind.

Prast then called investigative reporter Arthur Kane. He was the first outside journalist hired for the new RJ investigative team in 2016. Kane, carrying an extra twenty pounds and shedding hair as he barreled toward his fifty-third year, had worked at newspapers and a television station across the Midwest and West before joining the RJ. He specialized in government accountability reporting and regularly broke stories that forced officials to indict or fire the bad actors.

Kane was drinking wine and enjoying the long weekend with his wife when the phone rang around nine p.m. He saw it was Prast and let it go to voicemail. Like Davidson and Erickson's initial reaction, Kane and his wife were irritated that she was calling on a Saturday night over a long weekend. Prast then texted, asking him to call her no matter how late. That was unusual, so Kane called her back.

"What's up?" Kane asked.

"Jeff's dead," Prast said, clearly distraught.

Kane had met with German about a week before his death, and had noticed his colleague becoming more frail. But he was still eager for more front-page bylines. The late-August meeting was to discuss a story idea Jeff German had and to determine if Kane had time to collaborate on it.

Kane and German often joked about the dangers of exposing graft and corruption in a city with a history of mob violence and quite a few officials who think nothing of taking bribes, hiring relatives, or threatening reporters. When one of them got on a good story, the other colleague would grunt a gallows compliment, telling him to watch his back. The author of the story would jokingly seek assurances that his colleague would investigate and write about the truth so the death was not in vain.

Jeff German had just published an investigation of an obscure elected official, Clark County Public Administrator Robert Telles. Telles' staff alleged he was abusive and unprofessional. They gave German video of a worktime rendezvous between Telles and a female subordinate in the back seat of her SUV. Telles lost his primary re-election bid a month after German's story ran. Kane, who hadn't met in person with German for nearly two years because they worked from home during COVID, joked that he should watch his back in case the five-foot, seven-inch tall, 143-pound, forty-five-year-old probate attorney would come after him. German laughed with his usually sarcastic "yeah ah." It was a silly thought but German knew Kane was complimenting his work and lauding the removal of another problematic government official. Their mutual lifelong passion was exposing and removing corrupt or incompetent bureaucrats and politicians.

Upon receiving news of the death from Prast, Kane's mind raced for possible explanations. Jeff German was nearly seventy, he reasoned. So a natural death was at the forefront of Kane's mind.

"Okayyyyyyyy, what happened?" Kane responded with his typical lack of emotion.

Prast said she didn't know. Cook had just called her and said Lombardo notified him that German's body was found outside his house. He was scratched up, but there were no other details.

Kane, who had collaborated with German on several high-profile investigations in the past half-decade, pointed out German's age and the brutal weather. Prast didn't sound convinced. They hung up.

Getting off the phone, Prast saw a news release from LVMPD announcing police were holding a briefing about a homicide later that evening. The homicide was in German's neighborhood—a fact Prast realized because she had just ordered condolence flowers to be sent to his house. She called Cook back around 9:30 p.m. and told him of the press conference because he wasn't on that email thread. Cook instantly called Lombardo, and the sheriff confirmed that the homicide briefing was about German. The paper's staff learned later that instead of being "scratched up," German had been stabbed four times in the neck, three times in the torso, and twice on the hands and arms in what appeared defensive wounds. The first slash cut German's larynx and carotid artery, but the assailant kept stabbing. The photo in the grand jury file showed a brutal and gruesome murder.

Cook called Moyer and Prast. Having trouble believing the news, Moyer wanted to hear it for himself. He quickly called Lombardo, who confirmed that police believed German had been murdered.

Prast texted the reporters on the team just after ten p.m. "Jeff was a victim of a homicide," she wrote. "Was killed by a guy unknown, caught on video."

German's death had gone from a potential medical fatality to something much more nefarious. Cook called Marian Green, the night editor on duty, to tell her about the news conference. They immediately assigned police reporter David Wilson and photographer *Erik Verduzco to the briefing with specific instructions: Do not let other reporters know German was the victim if police do not release the name.*

Wilson was working from home but drove down to the police headquarters building a few blocks from the newspaper. He thought it was strange that police were holding the briefing at HQ instead of at the scene of the crime. He wrote a quick online alert that police were about to hold a homicide briefing, then hurried to the news conference. When Wilson got there, he noticed that Metro

Captain Dori Koren, who at the time headed up the homicide and sex crimes units, was holding the briefing. That was also unusual, as more junior officers usually held the news conferences about routine homicide.

Koren told reporters that Metro received a call around 10:30 that morning from a neighbor, saying he found a body. "They determined early on that there were potential stab wounds that may have caused the incident," Koren said awkwardly. He said police had evidence that there was an altercation Friday morning that ended with the stabbing.

"Right now we believe that this is an isolated incident," he said. "There is no concern for the general public or anyone else at this time."

The next day, police would issue a news release that said: "At this time, it appears the suspect was potentially casing the area to commit other crimes before the homicide occurred."

If true, that would contradict Koren's statement that it was an isolated incident that didn't endanger the public. At the Saturday night press conference, Koren took a couple of questions and ended the briefing. Wilson, who had started at the RJ less than a year earlier, added a few lines to his original story from the news conference while sitting in a car in the police HQ parking lot.

As the news conference was going, Cook called Moyer back, conferencing in RJ Chief Legal Officer Ben Lipman. The three executives started going through possible scenarios. What was the likelihood German had been murdered for his journalism? Was anyone else at the paper in danger? What should they do next?

The murder of a reporter for doing his job was extremely unusual—at least in the United States. In the past three decades, fewer than a dozen US reporters were killed because of their work—always by criminals they were investigating. Five of those journalists were killed by a disgruntled reader in a mass shooting at the Capital Gazette in Annapolis,

Maryland, in June 2018. Police seemed to indicate Jeff German's murder was wrong place, wrong time, but they also didn't seem to have a suspect or motive.

To cover all bases, Prast emailed Cook a list of stories German was working. The email sent at 10:19 p.m., September 3, listed a profile of the head of the Oath Keepers. Stewart Rhodes had attended the University of Nevada-Las Vegas, which gave German a local angle to pursue the profile. He faced seditious conspiracy charges for his actions related to the January 6 riot at the US Capitol that attempted to overturn the 2020 election. Rhodes headed a violent far-right anti-government militia so maybe German's inquiries and interviews with Rhodes' ex-wife angered his followers.

"It was not a watchdog piece, more of a historical explainer timed to the Rhodes trial scheduled for Sept. 26," Prast wrote Cook. In her email, Prast also noted German's recent story about Telles.

After the story ran, Telles took to social media and his campaign page to criticize German's reporting. Telles' posts mocked German's reporting skills but did not seem threatening.

"I know that some may believe the allegations made in the article by the local rightwing paper," Telles wrote, slamming German's reporting and saying he was just carrying water for disgruntled employees.

Telles was a probate attorney who was just expected to return to private practice after losing his re-election campaign. Looking at Prast's email, Cook thought, surely someone might kill a reporter to stop a pending article but who would be insane enough to murder a journalist—and potentially face life in prison or even the death penalty—to exact vengeance for an article that was already published?

Prast also downplayed the Telles stories as a motive: "The most public criticism he got lately was from Robert Telles, the outgoing public administrator," she wrote Cook.

"He was outwardly pretty angry after the June stories but it would be crazy if he was connected to this in any way."

Davidson and Moyer were not so sure.

"That elected guy he wrote about at the county seemed pretty upset by the articles—but not to that degree," Davidson texted Prast Saturday night.

Early on Labor Day morning, Moyer texted Cook and Hendrix: "Just thinking out loud. You know, Robert Telles was the most recent person to lash out at Jeff."

It was all speculation at that point as the paper could only view the police investigation from the outside. What the paper could control was to break the news of German's death as soon as police notified his siblings. It was a huge, potentially national, story of a top Las Vegas journalist murdered in the front yard of his home.

The bosses wanted to let staff know about German's death but that was going to be difficult because most reporters, producers, and editors had worked from home for the past eighteen months of the COVID pandemic. It was also midway through a holiday weekend so Cook didn't expect many people to monitor their work email or news reports. The editors figured the best they could do was send a newsroom email.

Cook and Prast also started filling out Wilson's short police news conference story. Cook, his laptop balanced on a pile of his son's homework on the living room table, spent Saturday night updating biographical facts and inserting German's journalistic accomplishments into the piece. Cook dug out the award nominations the paper had written for German's work, using those to piece together the highlights of the veteran writer's career. Finally, about 12:30 Sunday morning, Cook received word that police notified the family. At 12:48 a.m. on September 4, 2022, the story went live on the newspaper's website.

"Las Vegas Review-Journal investigative reporter Jeff German, one of Nevada's most accomplished and trusted journalists, was found dead with stab wounds outside his home Saturday morning," the story opened.

"German, whose work in Las Vegas spanned four decades, made a career of breaking big stories about everything from organized crime and government malfeasance to political scandals and the Oct. 1 mass shooting.

"'The Review-Journal family is devastated to lose Jeff," Executive Editor Glenn Cook said (in the story). "He was the gold standard of the news business. It's hard to imagine what Las Vegas would be like today without his many years of shining a bright light on dark places."

The editors had done all they could for that night. Just after two a.m., the adrenaline started to clear from Cook's body. He caught a couple of hours. He was up at first light, knowing he would be working all weekend. At 9:07 a.m., Cook forwarded Prast's memo about German's pending stories to Lombardo.

"Sheriff, here is what we know about what Jeff was working on," he wrote. "In terms of hot investigations that could lead to threats against him, he wasn't involved in any that we know of. We've surveyed our leadership, and Jeff had not conveyed any concerns about his safety or any threats made against him to anyone in the RJ organization."

The homicide of one of its own put the Review-Journal staff in an unusual position. On a daily basis, journalists cover murder investigations, arrests, and homicide trials. It's also pretty well established that journalists do not cooperate with police investigations. They remain neutral observers unless they are victims of crime. In a sense, German's murder made the Review-Journal a victim—especially if the motive was one of his stories. Everyone at the RJ naturally wanted German's killer arrested. At the same time, journalists working on the murder investigation had to be skeptical enough to evaluate the police actions, making sure no innocent person was wrongly accused of the crime. Most

RJ staffers put emotion aside to report the story as fairly and accurately as possible.

Metro officers go out of their way to limit the information they release about crimes. Police were often reluctant to even release basic police reports or arrest warrants. When they do, the documents are heavily redacted, sometimes making it impossible to understand what occurred. For Jeff German's murder, it was different. There was a daily news conference where police asked for the public's help. They seemed to have absolutely no idea why German was killed or who brutally stabbed him.

On Labor Day, police announced that they had enacted Major Case Protocols which activates all of the department's resources to solve a high-profile crime. At that same news conference, police released a photo of a short, thin person wearing a large straw hat and a road-worker's reflective long-sleeve shirt walking down German's street before the slaying. Just north of German's house, road crews were tearing up a major thoroughfare. They all wore similar outfits to protect themselves against the brutal summer sun and heat. The figure in the picture, however, wore what appeared to be designer jeans and nice tennis shoes—something no construction worker would dirty on the job. The outfit, however, was enough to blend with the thousands of construction or landscape workers building the ever-expanding metropolis. No one looked twice at people dressed like the suspect. The outfit had the added benefit of hiding the suspect's face despite neighbors' houses with casino-style dome cameras covering the cul-de-sac where Jeff German lived.

Frustrated by the lack of leads, police continued briefings for the next two days. On the Tuesday after Labor Day, police released a photo of a red GMC Yukon. The license plates had been removed. They said the suspect had driven the Yukon into German's neighborhood right before the murder. The SUV photo was a key piece of evidence. Within an hour, a man texted LVMPD to let detectives know that someone with access to a very similar vehicle may have had a motive to harm German. Police quickly obtained search warrants and swarmed a neighborhood a few miles from German's house.

***

The murder of a journalist is always a big story as the job provides a public profile and a modicum of fame. Journalists also are driven to cover the murder of one of their own—it hits very close to home. In less stable countries like Russia and Mexico, journalists are regularly murdered by government officials and gangsters for doing their jobs. Citizens of the United States—with the First Amendment enshrined in the Constitution—like to think journalists are immune from powerful people using violence or influence to prevent them from exposing uncomfortable truths. It is still an uncommon occurrence but one that seems less and less unthinkable. When police made an arrest in German's slaying, the suspect's identity would propel the case to worldwide notoriety.

The slaying would show that the United States was not the civil and democratic land of ideas and discourse. Jeff German's killing also again highlighted the corruption and violent underbelly of Las Vegas's organized crime and government past. German built his career covering that and, to his last days, was never short of stories. It was a history that the current Vegas elite were trying to downplay and forget but that was on every corner bathed in neon. The setting of German's murder in the capital of sin, vice, and never-ending party would shine a harsh spotlight on the culture of Las Vegas, which for decades has been based on favors, nepotism, feuds, and questionable ethics of government and business officials—and sometimes even journalists.

His death highlighted biases in the national media and often wrong-headed narratives by the elite establishment that believed only stories on the coasts—not flyover country—mattered. The same biases resulted in national media getting the 2016 election so wrong without any journalist or pundit suffering consequences. During the Trump administration, pundits often said his rhetoric would incite violence against journalists from his fanatic, right-wing followers. As in many cases, when the pundits' prophecy came partially true it was a far different reality from the narrative they hoped to advance.

German's death serves both as a cautionary tale about what happens when government fails and a preview of a possible future where the country plunges into an autocratic and undemocratic future. German spent his whole life exposing graft, corruption, and waste, so there is some irony that the work he loved led to his high-profile death.

CHAPTER ONE: MILWAUKEE TO SIN CITY

Jeffrey Michael German was born on August 23, 1953, to Max and June German. June was in her early twenties and Max in his early thirties. The couple had just married on December 7, 1952, so they were clearly eager to start a family. Over the next eight years, the couple would welcome three more children. Julie was born a few months shy of Jeff's third birthday. In 1959, his brother, Jay, had to be delivered by paramedics because a March snowstorm in blustery Milwaukee prevented June from getting to the hospital in time. Two years later, the youngest and last child, Jill, joined the Germans' growing brood.

The close-knit family lived in a small white house on Milwaukee's west side, which at the time was a working-class Jewish neighborhood.[3] Max German initially taught music at public schools and played the violin.[4] He then took a job selling meat to restaurants, resorts, and hotels. June's life revolved around raising the children and the local synagogue, Temple Menorah. During Jeff's childhood, Rabbi Isaac Lerer led the temple. Rabbi Lerer had four children close in age to the German children. His son, Gil-Ezer Lerer, who took over as rabbi of the temple in 1982, and his siblings often played with the German children. The Germans weren't particularly religious but liked the community the synagogue provided. When the rabbi's children visited the Germans, they brought their own food because the Germans didn't keep kosher.

In her youth, June German attended the University of Milwaukee, which was not common for women in the 1950s. She loved to talk politics and closely followed current events. When the children were older and in school, June German started working part-time (and later full-time) as the administrator of Temple Menorah, handling the finances, scheduling, and correspondence. She also started June's Catering. The synagogue was her biggest client, serving meals for various social and religious functions.[5]

For a time, Max served as president of Temple Menorah when he wasn't driving around Wisconsin peddling meat. He was known for landing jokes without a smile. The humor was so dry that sometimes it was tough to know whether he was jesting or serious. Max loved to tell the story of what he found in some of the fanciest restaurant kitchens that he visited on his rounds. The kitchens were so filthy, they would turn off diners even with the strongest stomachs.

"You'd never eat in that restaurant if you saw what happened in the kitchen," he said, contrasting it with his wife's immaculate catering business.

Jeff met his best friend of his younger years, Gary Greenberg, in math class at Wilbur Wright Junior High School. Students were seated alphabetically so German and Greenberg struck up a friendship. Joining them was Allan Recht[6] to form a triumvirate that would last into college and beyond.

The three attended John Marshall High School in the late 1960s. At the time, Jeff was building a resume that easily could have led to a career in politics or government. He was a member of the National Honor Society, played in the senior orchestra, and was on the student council executive board. German took up his father's instrument, the violin, but was never able to proficiently master it the way his father did. Despite years of lessons, he quit playing the violin after high school, preferring to play basketball, baseball, or "chase a girl or two."[7]

His community involvement led to a meeting with Wisconsin Governor Warren P. Knowles when he declared December 26-31 Wisconsin B'nai B'rith Youth Organization Week. In the photo that appeared in the Jewish Chronicle, Jeff German stands at the corner of the governor's desk, mouth open, as Knowles signed the document with a big smile.

B'nai B'rith youth group took up considerable time outside of school for Jeff German. He was chapter president of youth organization and vice president of the regional conference. Friends and people in the organization were impressed by Jeff's organization and leadership skills. He always came in early and stayed late to make sure the five days of athletic and social events ran smoothly. When he wasn't volunteering in the youth group or in school, Jeff German found time to work in the shipping department of Sherkow Men's Formal Wear, a chain of a half-dozen tuxedo rental stories around Milwaukee.[8]

In June 1971, he graduated from John Marshall. At the time, it was the largest class in Milwaukee public school history with more than one thousand students. It was the early 1970s and German frequented parties, drinking beer and smoking a bit of marijuana. He and Greenberg saw Santana and Jefferson Starship play live, and decided to explore other parts of the United States.

Jeff German was eighteen when he and Greenberg flew to Florida to see the ocean for the first time. It also was both men's first airplane ride. They rented a cheap motel for nine nights on the beach in Hollywood, Florida. Money was tight. But Disney World had just opened that year to great fanfare so the buddies decided to take a nearly five-hundred-mile round trip to Orlando by Greyhound bus. Leaving in the morning and taking a redeye bus back so they wouldn't have to pay double for lodging, they still had the energy to check out the nation's newest attraction.

The autumn after the trip, the three friends began their freshman year at the University of Wisconsin-Milwaukee. Jeff German majored in political science. A few years into U of W, he started dating Sharon Maiman. She was seventeen and a freshman at the school. Jeff was a couple of years older and drove a sporty red car. He was quiet and kind, and she thought he was cute. They attended parties together with friends and talked about life and politics. She fit in with German's family and became friends with the siblings, often visiting the house that now included a small dog that Jeff German doted on.

Midway through his college years, the Watergate scandal broke. Washington Post reporters Bob Woodward and Carl Bernstein regularly broke revelations of corruption, illegal break-ins, and dirty tricks by top officials in the administration of President Richard Nixon. Nixon resigned right before German's senior year of college. A few years earlier, the New York Times, and other papers, published the Pentagon Papers that exposed the government lies that sucked the United States into the disastrous war in Vietnam. A cloud of cynicism and disillusionment descended on the nation. Those historic events turned the young German against government and affected him deeply. He started thinking of politicians as evil people, wanting to expose their corruption and lies.[9] He always loved to do research and to write so he started taking journalism classes. In a later newspaper column, he would credit his father, Max, as directing him to journalism when he was seeking a profession.[10] Maiman would type his papers for school because at the time that's just how it was.

German, Greenberg, and Recht discussed transferring to University of Wisconsin-Madison, but German decided to live with his parents to save money. He and Maiman even visited Greenberg, who moved there, sleeping in the same bed. Despite the sleeping arrangements, German did make a move on his girlfriend of two years. Their relationship never moved beyond the friendship stage. German maintained a close relationship with his family at a time when other twenty-somethings were openly rebelling against society and older generations.

If he was having trouble in his relationship with Maiman, he would tell his father. Max German would then call Maiman to try to work out the conflict. At one point, Maiman's parents went out of town, and she didn't want to stay home alone. She asked Jeff to stay at her house. He was planned to stay in her brother's room. Max German found out and called over to Maiman's house. Max German told Maiman to send Jeff home, and Maiman, who knew she was a bit of a handful, pushed back.

"He's an adult," she told Max German. "He can make his own decisions. And if he decides to come home, he decides to come home. It's not my decision or your decision to make."

Once Jeff learned about the call, he went home. Maiman thought: "Wow!" Jeff was not tough enough for her. She wanted a man with a spine and in their relationship, Jeff just did not fill that role.[11] Jeff German also displayed some insecurities that also bothered her. He did not allow Maiman to wear high heels when they attended weddings and parties because he was shorter than her. Heels would make the height difference even more pronounced.

Footwear also played a role in their breakup. The two were going to a Halloween party. Jeff dressed as a pirate. The couple got into a big fight because Maiman didn't bring enough safety pins to hold up the boots that were part of Jeff's costume. Maiman took the car and drove to a store to buy more safety pins but after the party, she told him they were through. It wasn't the safety pins. It was just how angry he got about it. She realized the relationship wasn't going to go anywhere.

Jeff earned his Bachelor of Arts degree in 1975 from the university's College of Letters and Science. He still wasn't set on career. He considered taking up law. German, Greenberg, and Recht all took the LSAT exams, figuring they might go to law school. Short on cash for preparatory classes, none of them scored high enough to get in on their first try. Greenberg retook the test, getting into law school. German decided to get a master's degree in journalism at Marquette University. Knowing he would need work samples—or clips as they were then known—German also started looking for writing opportunities.

German had connected with Carol Vogel, who was then working for a string of small papers covering the suburbs of Milwaukee. German approached her to write some freelance stories to get published clips. Vogel would be key in start of German's career and his eventual move to Las Vegas.

For fun and exercise, German played on the basketball team at the Jewish Community Center. He was a lifelong fan of the Milwaukee Bucks and the Green Bay Packers. He was tenacious and fast, going to the basket despite his five-foot-eight height and thin frame. But he was not one of the top players so he usually didn't make it to the regional championship teams. German found writing was a way to join his more athletic teammates for road games. In 1976, he traveled to the Midwest championship in Cincinnati—not to play but to cover the tournament.

German reported and wrote an article for The (Jewish) Chronicle. He decided to try his hand at the New Journalism style, then popularized by writers like Gay Talese, Hunter S. Thompson, and Tom Wolfe. New Journalism thwarted the objective, stolid writing of traditional, just-the-facts newspapers. Incorporating elements of fiction, the reporter's perspective and edgy, stream-of-consciousness writing, New Journalism filled the pages of top national magazines like Rolling Stone and Esquire.

"It's 10:35 a.m. Sunday," German wrote. "Things are looking good, just as planned. In the opening minutes of their second basketball game in 12 hours, the Milwaukee

Jewish Community Center Team I has stormed out to a 10-point lead over a strong Cincinnati team, the host of the tournament." The story ended with the Cincinnati team winning but the players were in good spirits, knowing they can't win every year.

In 1977, using clips from the suburban paper where he freelanced, German landed an internship at The Milwaukee Journal. Jim Romenesko had cobbled together part-time police and suburban gigs to earn a full-time paycheck at the Journal. Romenesko later gained fame for his media blog and he was hired by the non-profit Poynter Institute for Media Studies.

At the Journal, German was a month older than Romenesko and stood out both for his drive and his fashion sense. He had shed the shaggy hair and seventies' hipster look of high school for the disco style that was becoming popular with the release of Saturday Night Fever. While others at the Journal sported jackets and ties, German wore designer jeans and a button-up shirt that revealed ample chest hair. He accented the bare chest with a gold chain.

On Friday nights, German would call up Greenberg, who, half asleep, was planning to stay in and recover from a brutal week of study at law school.

"Hey, we got to go out to the bar," German cajoled. "We got to go out to the disco."

Clearly, Greenberg thought, German's journalism program wasn't as demanding as law school. But usually German could convince his buddy to head the club a few blocks from Greenberg's house for some cocktails and dancing.

His new "John Travolta look" seamlessly fit in places like Las Vegas but raised eyebrows in the conservative working-class city of breweries and factories set along Lake Michigan. At first, Romenesko thought, "This guy is a Playboy," but soon the two bonded over their mutual love of journalism. It didn't hurt that they both liked to hit the bars after work.

Drinking one night, they heard of a boat accident on Lake Michigan. German wanted to head to the shore to see if there was a story. If the boat sank, German thought it might get him on the coveted front page. After a while, Romenesko was ready to leave but German insisted they stay just in case. They were on the shore until two a.m. but the boat never sank. There was never a big story or screaming headline.[12]

At the Milwaukee paper, German was relegated mostly to intern-type stories—articles the experienced staff didn't want to do and that couldn't get the newspaper sued if an inexperienced intern screwed up. German covered a law enforcement conference at a local hotel that focused on vandalism. The story, in the May 25, 1977, edition is heavy on unnecessary details—like the t-shirts worn by officers. It shows a lack of writing experience, but it landed him on the front page of the local section. That was valuable real estate but not as valuable as the front page. Still, it was an accomplishment for a young intern. Two weeks later, he scored another local section story with a profile of an Eagle Scout who suffered from cerebral palsy.

"Fighting to hold back tears before his family and friends, Kevin Koehler officially became Troop 152's first Eagle Scout Tuesday night in an emotional ceremony at Gaenslen School for the handicapped," German wrote for the June 8, 1977, paper.

After the internship, German freelanced for the Journal while finishing his master's degree. In October 1977, he had a story that hinted at his later writing style. Datelined Oconomowoc Lake, German wrote: "You can't say that village officials were trying to kill two birds with one stone when they hired Police Chief Richard Riehle last December, but you could say they were going for five or six birds. That's how many jobs they gave Riehle, 48, who also has been the village administrator, building inspector, zoning inspector, health inspector and all-around government official for the last year."

Despite mostly feature and fluff, one of German's stories garnered a bit of unexpected controversy from the do-gooders and teetotalers of the area. He probably didn't care because it got him on the coveted front page. The story covered the happy-hour bars in Milwaukee that offered all-you-can-drink booze. The Journal published nearly half a dozen letters of complaint on February 26, 1978.

Readers raged that the story was promoting drinking, drunk driving, and providing publicity to liquor establishments. "I am amazed at the free advertising The Journal gave bars listed at the end of the article," Bleva M. Nerlien of Stevens Point wrote. "The Journal is an accomplice in corruption. Please stop and think!"

Patti Muehlbauer, of Milwaukee, chimed in with a similar theme. "The article by Jeff German 'Bottoms Up:' started as a very good putdown on the way drinking is given a sparkling attraction at many bars but at the end of the article, he sure defeated what appeared to be his purpose: All those bars just got free advertising of times, prices and locations!" she wrote. "Instead of discouraging people from joining the increasing number of drunken drivers, his article only made them more aware of all the places available!"

An editor's note at the end of the letters said that the story "pointed out that law enforcement authorities and people who deal with alcoholics were concerned about the danger 'happy hour' participants pose to themselves and others."

The minor controversy did little to kill German's love of newspapering. In August 1978, he wrote his last story for the Journal about neighbors clashing in court over the construction of a pier on Pewaukee Lake because it infringed on an easement. That story foreshadowed much of German's later career in Las Vegas covering courts. He had just graduated from Marquette in May 1978 with a Master of Arts in journalism.

During his internship, it was clear to German that he would not land a full-time reporting job at the Journal. Back then, reporters were expected to work their way up through smaller papers. If they had talent, they eventually landed on major metro dailies and then maybe the national papers. That journeyman process has recently been short-circuited as fewer people are going to journalism school to pursue a newspaper career because many newspapers are closing and jobs are few and far between. Now the few young people who graduate from a journalism program can often expect to land at a metro daily or maybe even a national paper. That wasn't the case in the 1970s and 1980s. Then newspaper jobs were sought-after careers especially after the fame and accolades that Woodward and Bernstein achieved by taking down President Richard Nixon.

As he was finishing his Milwaukee Journal internship, German called Vogel, who by then had moved to Las Vegas. She first worked for the now-defunct North Las Vegas Valley Times, then the Las Vegas Sun, and eventually the Las Vegas Review-Journal. Vogel had recently quit the Valley Times after a disagreement with its publisher and took a job with the Las Vegas Sun. There was bit of a pipeline from Milwaukee to Sin City in the 1970s as another later famous journalist, Ned Day, would move to the Valley Times and later, the bigger news organizations in Las Vegas like the Review-Journal and KLAS-TV. Day was known for muckraking and digging up stories on the Mob, which got his car firebombed in 1986. He died the following year of a heart attack while snorkeling in Hawaii. Some old Vegas hands think his death in 1987 at age forty-two might not have been a medical accident.

German told Vogel that the Milwaukee Journal wasn't going to hire him after the internship, and he needed a job. His timing was perfect. Vogel's editor had just asked her if she knew any good reporters because the Sun was looking to beef up its staff. Vogel handed the phone to then Sun City Editor Chris Chrystal who talked to German and basically agreed to hire him on the spot. [13]

Chrystal got off the phone and turned to Vogel. "He better be good," she said, adding that she was hiring German solely on Vogel's recommendation.

Within weeks, German was in Las Vegas for his first big-time journalism job. It would take German a while to get his bearings in the new town he had never even visited. He worked the courthouse sources and dug through documents, but he initially wasn't producing the steady stream of articles the Sun was expecting.

Chrystal went back to Vogel. "Hey, you know, he's not pulling his weight here," she said.

Vogel urged her to be patient, as German was in a new city with no sources or contacts and he was more of a guy who would dig and work on longer-term pieces. Even then German was interested in going deeper on stories and not just producing shallow, quick hits. Vogel went to German and told him, "You gotta get some stories," urging German to show Chrystal his skills. After the shaky start, German started building a thick Rolodex of sources and breaking big stories that would make him a journalism legend in Sin City.

***

Las Vegas started as a small mining community in 1905 after a train line was built linking Los Angeles and Salt Lake City. Within a decade, the mines went bust. Only the construction of the Hoover Dam in 1931 and legalized gambling propelled Vegas into the metropolis it is today. Fewer than thirty thousand people lived there before World War II. By the mid-1960s, the city had about 140,000 people and by 2023, more than 660,000 lived in Las Vegas proper. More than 2.8 million then resided in the metro area.

In the middle of the last century, mobsters saw Nevada as a natural extension of their illegal gambling operations out east but without having to look over their shoulders to see if police were on their trails. The gangsters moved to the desert valley to set up showgirl theaters and legal gambling halls for the men building the dam. Hydroelectric power from the dam lit up many of the casinos.

In 1946, gangsters Bugsy Siegel and Meyer Lansky laundered money through banks to build the Flamingo— the beginning of large hotel-casino resorts on the Strip. Organized crime groups quickly saw the potential. Teamsters Union President Jimmy Hoffa, who was connected to the Chicago Outfit, lent money from the union's pension fund to build the Riviera, Sahara, Sands, and Tropicana.

For decades, the freedom in the frontier desert valley attracted desperate and reckless people who got away with crimes that nowadays would land them in prison for decades or life. After serving in World War II, Hank Greenspun moved to Vegas eventually buying a small union paper that he built into the Las Vegas Sun. Greenspun would give German his first full-time reporting job. Greenspun's aptly named autobiography, Where I Stand: The Record of a Reckless Man, tells of his multiple indictments, including one for commandeering a yacht in California at gunpoint to run weapons to fellow Jews fighting the Arabs in Palestine. He is considered a hero in Israel to this day and always said that was one of his proudest achievements. Greenspun bought the paper that would become the Sun just days before going to trial in the gun-running case, facing Export Control Law and Neutrality Act charges. He only avoided prison in the case because of a sympathetic judge but received a hefty fine. In 1961, President John F. Kennedy pardoned him, restoring his civil rights and his right to vote.

A crusading journalist, Greenspun took on powerful US Senator Patrick McCarran, who then was supported by the Review-Journal. Greenspun blasted US Senator Joe

McCarthy, who became famous for falsely alleging the infiltration of communists in federal government. Greenspun sued McCarran and dozens of hotel owners, claiming they organized an advertising boycott of the paper. He won a settlement. He also was acquitted of a criminal charge that he was trying to incite the assassination of McCarthy after confronting him during a speech in Las Vegas. Greenspun had started as an attorney but worked public relations for Bugsy Siegel's Flamingo. Greenspun eventually built a media empire that included broadcast, cable, and print, and developed Green Valley Ranch in Henderson to an upscale suburban community.

Jeff German would get the benefit of Hank Greenspun's political connections, providing him sources and resources that an ambitious young reporter could only dream of in a city that was an amazing, sometimes unbelievable, news town. Within a year or two of starting at the Sun, Jeff German was the go-to reporter at the paper and proved that Vogel recommendation was a good one.

Chapter Two: The *Sun*

Before he was stripped, beaten with baseball bats and (possibly) buried alive in an Indiana corn field, Anthony "Tony the Ant" Spilotro ran rackets for the Chicago Outfit in Vegas. He was a big deal in the growing city where the Mob was skimming money from casinos. The skimmed money was sent to the Midwest bosses without taxing authorities getting their cut. No one in Vegas liked to get shorted.

In Sin City, Spilotro ran a crew known as the Hole in the Wall Gang for their tactic of breaking through exterior walls and ceilings to burglarize the homes of wealthy residents and local businesses. He also ran loan sharking, extortion, and protection rackets. And he planned and carried out murders. Joe Pesci's character in Martin Scorsese's 1995 film Casino was based largely on Spilotro. Covering characters like Spilotro attracted German from Milwaukee to Las Vegas. He wanted to write about crime and corruption in Sin City. And he often did anything it took to get the story—even if it risked angering some very, very dangerous people.

On Christmas Eve 1983, German was with friend and fellow reporter Scott Zamost as they drove past My Place Lounge. Stuck in a well-worn strip mall off at 4110 S. Maryland Parkway, the place was a known Mob hangout. My Place was next door to Upper Crust Pizzeria, which was partly owned by Spilotro associate and Mob hitman, Frank Cullotta. German and Zamost spotted a bunch of cars in the lot, which was unusual the evening before Christmas. The dogged journalists decided to stop by for a drink in case there was a story to be found.

Zamost and German became friends after taking jobs at the Las Vegas Sun at about the same time in 1978. German was covering organized crime and Zamost gaming, so at the time, there was a very strong nexus between their respective beats. They became friends, hanging out at TGI Fridays and grabbing lunches at downtown casino buffets that then cost three or four dollars. Zamost and German also shared apartments to save money on rent, moving from a two-bedroom at Lake Tropicana Apartments on Harmon Avenue to Park Terrace on Swenson Street. The two also bonded by their deep love of newspaper reporting that drove them day and night to search the city for scoops.

That Saturday before Christmas, the reporters hoped Spilotro was at the bar and thought maybe they could get an exclusive interview with the mobster. He had been indicted three months earlier so anything he said could be newsworthy. Spilotro never talked to reporters, but German and Zamost hoped for a Christmas miracle. Walking into My Place, they saw Spilotro in back holding court with actor Robert Conrad, who starred in The Wild, Wild West and had roles in the popular Adam-12 and Mission: Impossible television shows. The young reporters grabbed a table and asked the waitress to send the crew some drinks—on them. She talked to the mobster and returned with bad news.

"You don't send Mr. Spilotro drinks," she admonished. "He buys you drinks first."[14]

The reporters waited for what seemed like an hour, debating whether they should just leave. But sure enough, Spilotro sent some drinks their way and even joined the journalists at their table for a few minutes, engaging in small talk. German half joked about Spilotro doing an interview. Spilotro turned to Zamost, suggesting that maybe he should do the interview. German tried to be funny and charming but the breakthrough, exclusive interview wasn't going to happen—Christmas or not.

It wasn't always pleasant to run into the gangster, especially when he was drinking, or German wrote a negative story about the Mob enforcer. One night, German and Las Vegas Sun cartoonist Mike Smith were out to dinner with dates when Spilotro spotted German. Clearly drunk, the diminutive mobster starting screaming threats and obscenities at German as his crew held him back.

"I'm going to kill you!" he yelled as German and Smith directed their dates out of the bar. "I'm going to kill you."[15]

The FBI had recently convinced Frank Cullotta to cooperate with their investigation after he was arrested for a botched Hole in the Wall burglary of a furniture store. Cullotta also feared that Spilotro put out a hit on him. Using Cullotta's cooperation, Spilotro faced charges of conspiracy and obstruction of justice in a murder. Despite the indictment, Spilotro, that Christmas Eve that German and Zamost stumbled up on him, didn't seem to have a care in the world. He wished German and Zamost a merry Christmas and walked to the bar to greet other patrons. Within three years, Spilotro and his brother would be beaten to death and buried in a cornfield after his bosses tired of his antics and worried that he might rat on them. Such was life in Las Vegas in the early 1980s.

***

The Mob was just starting to lose its grip on Sin City in the early 1980s. A number of factors played into Vegas changing from Mob town to corporate-adult Disneyland. At the end of the 1960s, the Nevada legislature passed laws that allowed corporations to own casinos for the first time. Billionaire Howard Hughes had moved into the Desert Inn and bought the casino in 1967 after the owners tried to evict him. That was just the beginning of his casino-buying spree. Mobsters had built casinos using loans from the Teamster's pension fund and at the time, few legitimate sources of funding were available for gambling establishments that were illegal in most states.

Then, Steve Wynn started raising money with the help of Michael Milken's junk bonds. The Mirage, which became the Strip's first mega resort, opened in 1989. Milken, who in 1990 would plead guilty to securities and tax charges,[16] raised half a billion dollars for the Mirage in 1987.[17]

There was also a change in law enforcement. For much of Vegas history, the establishment—the people who owned or ran the town's biggest industry which was gambling— were either organized crime, criminals in their past lives or closely affiliated with criminals. Since gambling was illegal in most of the United States, only people who ran illegal gambling houses had the experience to run the Vegas casinos. The politicians and police were often beholden to them—if not directly at least knowing who holds the power in Sin City. Money corrupted police officers like former Metro Detective Joseph Charles Blasko. He was fired in 1978 for giving Spilotro intelligence and was convicted and sentenced in 1986 to two years in prison for participating in a failed Hole in the Wall gang burglary.[18]

In Washington, DC, the FBI was taking notice that Las Vegas was a rough city. FBI agents were apparently getting too close to the Mob and the politicians who befriended them. Special agents were taking security jobs at casinos after retiring from the FBI and were not particularly aggressive in weeding out public corruption, top federal officials believed.

On January 2, 1980, FBI Director William Webster called Joseph Yablonsky, who headed Cincinnati's FBI field office. "We've been unhappy with results in Las Vegas, and I feel with your background perhaps you could stimulate some activity," Webster told Yablonsky.[19]

Yablonsky's arrival shook Vegas' political and business environment almost as much as the nuclear testing sixty-five miles north of the city. Yablonsky made it clear that he would use undercover tactics to go after the bad guys and ignored any push back from the Vegas establishment.

"This town doesn't want to get straightened out," Yablonsky was quoted in the Review-Journal two years after his arrival. "It has a certain attitude, which is don't mess up our thing here."[20] Mess up "our thing" he did but not without controversy and blowback.

Soon after his quote in the RJ, Operation Yobo—named after the nickname locals used for Yablonsky—snared five top elected officials for accepting bribes from an undercover FBI agent. State Senators Floyd Lamb and Gene Echols, Clark County Commissioners Woodrow Wilson and Jack Petitti, and a Reno councilman, whose conviction was later overturned, all were found guilty of corruption.

Yablonsky then went after Federal Judge Harry Claiborne for bribery and tax evasion. President Carter had appointed Claiborne to the federal bench in 1978. The judge was definitely part of the old-guard establishment. Before taking the bench, he had represented the Horseshoe Casino owner Benny Binion, who had a long history of criminal behavior. Benny Binion and Claiborne apparently had lunch four or five times a week. Another high-profile client was Bugsy Siegel, who financed some of the city's first casinos and was killed in 1947 by rifle shot through the window of his Beverly Hills mansion.

Claiborne was ratted on by a brothel owner in rural Storey County, who faced prison for tax evasion. The brothel owner alleged that he bribed the judge to help him fix his own tax problems. The bribery charges did not stick after the brothel owner perjured himself by saying he paid a bribe to Claiborne in Nevada on a date that records showed the brothel owner was in New York. At retrial, prosecutors dropped the corruption charges but were able to convict Claiborne for failing to report $107,000 on his tax returns. There was outrage at Yablonsky offering to help the brothel owner with his tax problems in exchange for his flawed testimony, but Claiborne's conviction, two-year prison sentence and subsequent impeachment and removal in Congress indicated Claiborne had done something wrong.[21]

Claiborne's attorney was famed Mob counsel and future Las Vegas Mayor Oscar Goodman. During the 1970s and 1980s, Goodman would represent Spilotro and such high-profile gangsters and Mob associates as Meyer Lansky, Nicky Scarfo, "Fat Herbie" Blitzstein, and Frank "Lefty" Rosenthal. Rosenthal was another template for one of the main characters in Casino. Goodman had two cameos as himself in Casino. In the first, he walks Pesci's Spilotro-based character out of the courthouse and in the second he tries to argue in front of the gaming board for Robert DeNiro's character, who was based on Rosenthal, to get a license to work in a casino. The gaming commissioners refuse to hear Goodman out, and DeNiro's character starts a public airing of commissioners' corrupted laundry in front of television news cameras as the regulators flee.

At the time he was a Mob lawyer, Metro police were keeping tabs on Goodman, even though he was never charged with any crime. A police intelligence log showed there was a lot of surveillance on Spilotro, My Place Lounge, Mob-connected casinos, and the Columbo crime associates. On September 7, 1980, there's also a notation of Goodman flying to Kansas City on Frontier Flight 156. Other entries appeared to be purely antagonistic and harassing. Goodman regularly charged police were illegally harassing his clients but didn't know he was a target until well after his lawyer days.

"Pissed off Oscar Goodman," someone wrote in the log on January 25, 1980, with no other explanation. The next entry in someone else's handwriting says "(Oscar Goodman still pissed off.)"

And the log also showed the close relationship between Metro and some of the casinos that today would be unthinkable.

"At 1:00 am, I was requested to borrow $33,000 for a cocaine buy by Sgt Jolley. I borrowed the money at the Hilton. Narcs bought 1 pound of cocaine and arrested the suspect," a detective wrote on December 4, 1980.

When Goodman saw the intelligence log, which he received as mayor from a woman who came to his door, he found it to be a colossal waste of taxpayer money. He also thought it proved his allegations of police harassment of his clients. And he believes it should have been turned over during the criminal cases he defended because it may have provided alibis for gangsters he represented.

***

Goodman and German would have frequent interactions—some positive, some not—over the next forty years. At least one raised ethical questions for German. Goodman received his law degree from University of Pennsylvania Law School in 1964. Hating law school and looking for opportunity, Goodman heard that Las Vegas might be a good place to start a career.

"Sweetheart, how would you like to go to the land of milk and honey?" he asked his wife Carolyn.

"I love you, but I'm not moving to Israel," she responded before Goodman assured her, he only wanted to go to Nevada. He interviewed with prosecutors in Las Vegas and walked around near the courthouse where attorneys had hung out their tiles. Going from office to office, a young and lanky Goodman quizzed people whether he should move from Philadelphia to the desert. They unanimously told him Sin City was the land of opportunity, and he should take his shot.

There was, of course, a learning curve in the ways of the West. The couple arrived in August. Goodman didn't realize at the time that the bar exam was only given once a year and that was in July. He had missed it by a few weeks so he worked as a clerk in the district attorney's civil division and then in the public defender's office after becoming an attorney. Then he struck out on his own, buying a small piece of land and opening a law firm. Luck continued to shine on Goodman like the relentless desert sun. He filed a bankruptcy case for a card dealer at a local Mob-run hotel, and the dealer referred him to mobsters who need representation. His business spread by word of mouth.

Jeff German, by the late 1970s, was covering courts for the Sun, and Goodman had some of the highest profile clients and cases. They initially formed a close personal and source-journalist relationship. Goodman invited German and his sister, Julie, over for Passover Seder dinner one year. The Mob lawyer and rookie journalist also discussed writing Goodman's biography together. German complained he did not have the money to buy a computer with which he could write the book. Goodman gave him the money. The book never materialized. Goodman, figuring the computer was a gift, never asked for it back.

The First Amendment prevents government regulation of journalism in the same way agencies could enforce rules on professions like doctors, lawyers, and cosmetologists. But in the 1970s, voluntary rules were starting to come into practice for reporters. Years before Goodman bought German a computer, the Society for Professional Journalists made it very clear that shouldn't happen. In 1973, when German was an undergrad in Wisconsin, Chicago Tribune environmental reporter Casey Bukro almost singlehandedly updated the organization's 1926 code to bring them into the modern era. The update directly addressed gifts: "Refuse gifts, favors, fees, free travel and special treatment, and avoid political and other outside activities that may compromise integrity or impartiality, or may damage credibility."[22]

The gift apparently didn't influence German's reporting. Goodman's relationship with German eventually unraveled as German pursued stories that did not put Goodman or his clients in a positive light. Goodman also did not like crusading FBI agent Yablonsky despite all the defense work he was getting from the federal investigations and indictments. Yablonsky also wasn't popular with US Senator Paul Laxalt, who tried to get him transferred out of the state. German's boss, editor and owner of the Las Vegas Sun, was also not a Yablonsky fan, charging the undercover operations were entrapment. The establishment was starting to push back against the aggressive FBI agent, and there was enough smoke to raise questions about Yablonsky's ethics.

In 1983, Yablonsky would retire in a desert dust storm of scandal. He wanted to stay in Las Vegas but casinos, upset about his aggressive investigations, didn't give him the opportunities for security work that some of his predecessors received. Those were the same high-paying corporate casino jobs that Yablonsky criticized on his way into town but sought on his way out. He was censured by his Washington, DC, bosses for investigating the political opponent of a friend without finding any wrongdoing by the politician. And there were questions of about whether he accepted the same comps from casinos he criticized and whether he tried to help his wife sell seafood to the casinos. He was also investigated for bank fraud and other corruption but was never charged with a crime. Even with the federal crackdown, it seemed that Vegas still had the ability to corrupt even the most ardent reformers. The King of Sting, as Yablonsky became known, died in Florida in 2019 at the age of ninety. [23]

***

Just as Jeff German was starting to work for the Sun, Greenspun hired former Nevada Governor Donal Neil "Mike" O'Callaghan as his paper's executive editor. O'Callaghan had decided not to run for re-election in 1978 after two terms. O'Callaghan knew all the power players in Nevada and was happy to introduce German to sources. German referred to him as a second father.

O'Callaghan introduced German to Sig Rogich, who ran O'Callaghan's re-election campaign, early in the young reporter's tenure at the Sun. Rogich would later produce advertising for the Reagan-Bush campaign and serve as chief media advisor for Bush's 1988 election, working with future Fox News CEO Roger Ailes to produce devastating ads that attacked Bush's opponent Michael Dukakis. One ad showed a revolving prison door to raise questions about the Massachusetts governor's criminal justice record. Rogich used video of Dukakis visiting a military base and looking silly in a tank and helmet to undercut the Democratic opponent's credibility. After the election, Rogich worked as assistant to the president and was appointed as US Ambassador of his native Iceland.[24]

In Las Vegas, Rogich founded R&R Advertising in 1974 and built it into a powerhouse that helped politicians get elected. R&R also managed advertising and marketing for the Las Vegas Convention and Visitors Authority, a politically connected government agency whose job was to promote the city and attract lucrative convention business to Sin City.

Rogich came to Las Vegas from Iceland at age ten after his father landed a job in a metals factory. He befriended Paul Laxalt, who was a governor and US senator from Nevada, while working as a reporter at the newspaper now called the Reno Gazette-Journal. He started an advertising agency after leaving the newspaper business.

Rogich's advertising career had a shaky start as he initially worked for some of the Mob-connected casinos. He had invested in equipment to help with their advertising but was soon fired. He didn't know why until he realized the casino's new ad firm agreed to pad their invoices so that the Mob could skim more from the casinos but make it look like legitimate promotion. In the end, that firing was a good thing. The skimmers all went to jail while Rogich's star soared in Nevada and beyond. [25]

After getting into public relations, O'Callaghan recruited Rogich for his re-election campaign 1974 after Rogich ran an opponent's failed campaign four years earlier. Rogich's campaign removed O'Callaghan's from the ads, calling him simply Governor Mike or the People's Governor. He helped propel O'Callaghan to an overwhelming victory that is still the greatest landslide in Nevada history.[26]

German and Rogich met regularly after work for a beer and to talk about the events of the day or share latest the political gossip. O'Callaghan would call the young German into his office when Rogich stopped by to provide a key scoop or tip. Many of German's colleagues at the Sun felt German sometimes carried water for Rogich or his clients even when there wasn't legitimate news. Others contend German acted properly getting information from a source who helped him secure front-page scoops. Rogich concedes he represented his clients' interests, but German never took him at his word. He always checked out the story to make sure it was newsworthy and nailed down all the context and facts.

As his stature grew in Las Vegas, German thrived on the constant firehose of hot stories—many that went national— even if there were sometimes dangers in doing the job. Early in his Vegas career, German got on a story about court officer Seymour Freedman collecting debts for loan shark Jasper Speciale at the same time as he collected campaign contributions for the sheriff. Freedman was also collecting a paycheck from taxpayers for his court job. The storyline was, not surprisingly, unpopular with Freedman. After the columns, German's car window was smashed and air let out of the tires. He also received threatening anonymous phone calls, warning him to be careful about who he was writing about.

One evening in the fall of 1985, German was drinking at a retirement party at the Sands Hotel for Justice Court Chief Clerk Eileen Carson. German noticed Freedman, a former New York cop and boxer, at the event and confronted him about the threats and damage to his vehicle. German always prized the cars he drove, favoring upscale Volkswagen sedans and owning a black Mustang in the late 1980s. An attack on his always well-maintained vehicle was like an assault on his person.

"Sy, when are you going to call off the dogs?" German demanded. Freedman didn't blink. He threw the drink he was holding in his right hand right in German's face. With his left hand, Freedman sucker punched German. A ring Freedman was wearing slashed German's lip. German had to have four stitches, but the encounter didn't stop him from writing about corruption and organized crime.

After the assault, Metro Police Sergeant David Groover came to take a report at the hospital from German. Groover had been a target of German's reporting for a high-profile incident that dominated the local news and was even portrayed in Casino with some artistic license. On the evening of June 9, 1980, Groover, an intelligence detective at the time, and Sergeant Gene Smith were staking out the Upper Crust Mob-run pizza joint.

Spilotro and Cullotta were sitting outside the pizza joint shooting the shit when a Lincoln driven by Frank Bluestein pulled up. Bluestein went in, ordered food, and joined the mobsters outside while his dinner baked. Bluestein was a maître d' at the then-Mob-controlled Hacienda Hotel & Casino. His father was a member of the culinary union and was a subject of a search warrant related to the Spilotro investigation. The maître d' chatted with the mobsters until it was time to grab his food. Groover and Smith watched the exchange. Bluestein then took off at high speed, and Groover and Smith pursued him to determine who was associating with Spilotro.

The undercover car pulled over Bluestein for traffic infractions, and he exited the Lincoln gun in hand. The undercover officers shot him. In Casino, the portrayal of the incident shows Bluestein only had a hoagie wrapped in foil instead of a gun. Then the movie officers planted a gun to justify the shooting.

In real life, Oscar Goodman called the shooting a police execution, and German reported those allegations regularly. But at the coroner's inquest, Groover presented evidence that showed the gun was bought in Chicago by Bluestein's brother so it couldn't have been a plant. It was ruled a clean shoot. Despite that evidence, Bluestein's family sued, but the officers prevailed. The controversy only ended when the US Supreme Court denied hearing an appeal in the civil lawsuit. [27]

Groover and Smith had bigger things to fear than civil lawsuits. Authorities in Chicago notified Metro that the Mob had put out a contract on them over the Bluestein shooting. Police wanted a wiretap on Bluestein's father, but Clark County District Attorney Bob Miller didn't like wiretaps. Metro Intelligence Commander Kent Clifford, as he told a Las Vegas author before his death, got into an argument with Miller about associating with a person connected to the casino skim for the Mob so there was bad blood when Miller's office went to a judge for the wiretap. On the second day of the tap, the judge told police someone in the DA's office tried to get the wiretap closed down, but the judge refused.[28] When that failed, German received a tip about the wiretap, writing a front-page story in the Sun on August 21, 1981, titled "PURPORTED KILL PLOT LED TO BLUESTEIN WIRETAP."

The phones went quiet. Metro was pissed.

Miller, who would later be elected Nevada governor, contends he doesn't remember giving German a story on the wiretap, though he had "an off-again, on-again" relationship with German. Miller contends his only association with the

Mob was his father's business partner who went to prison for skimming from casinos. As DA, Miller thought wiretaps should be used sparingly since they were an invasion of privacy. He concedes he did not have a good relationship with the sheriff at the time and supported his opponent in the next election.[29]

Breaking the story of the wiretap put German into the hotseat. Clifford called German into his office on August 25, 1981, read German his Miranda rights against self-incrimination, and then grilled German on his sources for the wiretap story. Clifford told German he wasn't a target of the investigation but his cooperation was necessary to determine if someone broke the wiretap disclosure law, which was a felony punishable by up to six years in prison. German and his bosses refused to reveal the source of the story, citing the state's reporter shield law. Protecting sources was one of the bedrocks of journalism and one that German took very seriously. German had previously been subpoenaed by lawyers for Spilotro. US District Judge Harry E. Claiborne quashed those subpoenas citing the Nevada Shield Law and the First Amendment. The issue was so important to Nevada journalists that there would be a fight about German's sources that went to the state Supreme Court even after his 2022 death.[30]

The Chicago hitmen targeting Groover and Smith came to Vegas and were closely tracked by Metro officers. They left without carrying out the contract. Nevertheless, Clifford didn't like something like that hanging over his officers. He flew to Chicago and threatened Spilotro's bosses to get the contract cancelled.[31]

German wrote dozens of stories about the Bluestein shooting, often taking the side of the family as it was being represented by Goodman, who was then friendly with the young reporter. When Groover arrived at the hospital to take a report from German over the Freedman assault, German was crestfallen.

"Shit, I can't catch a break," German told Groover.

The reporter complained that not only was he punched in the face but now the officer investigating the incident had it out for him. German decided not to press charges in the case, and Groover thought it was because he was getting a lot of favorable publicity over the sucker punch.[32]

German, who later called the punch a "badge of honor," didn't let a little violence stop him from writing about Freedman or the incident. On September 30, 1985, German's column on the front page of the Metro section laid out the incident, harping again on Freedman collecting money for the Mob while also collecting campaign funds for the sheriff.

"Mom never told me journalism would be like this," the tongue-in-cheek column says. It's "going to take more than a sucker punch to scare me off."

John L. Smith, then a colleague at the Sun, congratulated German on his column about the incident, saying: "Great story. Somebody should punch you in the mouth every day."[33]

The incident became somewhat of a joke around the newsroom as German would detail in an October 2, 1985, column. German quotes city editor Bill Guthrie asking him to contribute to the Sun's blood drive and then reversing course to say: "Oh, I forgot. You've already done that."

Freedman's violence did not stop his name from appearing in Jeff German's columns. On October 9, 1985, German updated readers that he received an FBI report, apparently leaked to him, while recovering from his encounter with Freedman. He details Freedman's loansharking work for Speciale day by day as it is listed in the document.

That was the typical fearless German. He would often grill politicians mercilessly on the phone and when he didn't think he was getting the truth, it would turn heated. The whole newsroom would hear German repeatedly asking the same question until he beat his victim into submission.

Nevada remained a tough place throughout the 1980s. It wasn't just gangsters and their henchmen who practiced media criticism with personal attacks and even physical altercations.

In 1988, Nevada Attorney General Brian McKay called German a "venomous little man" during a television interview on KTVN-TV's Face the State program. He charged German had no credibility, failed to pay attention to the truth, and didn't "know fact from fiction." McKay had been traveling to national and western attorney general conferences. German started keeping a "McKay Mileage Meter," urging readers to contact him if they saw McKay or his wife outside the state. That really got under McKay's skin.

A Republican, McKay charged that German was doing the bidding of and working as a "hit man" for Bob Miller's supporters. Miller, a Democrat, had moved on from district attorney to lieutenant governor and would be elected governor for his first term in 1989. The Sun leaned Democratic, and the Review-Journal supported Republicans. McKay felt the Sun, and German, were attacking him based on partisan politics and not for substantial journalistic reasons. German responded to McKay's attacks in the United Press International article by saying he was pleased that the attorney general was an "avid reader" of his column. "I'm not little," he also told UPI.

Of course, when Miller was elected governor, German started writing about his travel, which also irritated Miller. Miller was traveling to Washington, DC, to confer with national leaders. He thought if the president of the United States and Congress would come to Nevada, he wouldn't have to travel, but they weren't going to do that.[34]

A year after McKay's televised comments, German was in Carson City covering the legislature for the Sun when he walked into Jack's Bar. The bar, near the legislative building, was a hangout where lawmakers hashed out deals with lobbyists picking up the tab. Reporters, naturally, frequented the bar to see if they could sniff out a scoop.

A fairly intoxicated German ran into an equally intoxicated John "Jack" Vergiels, a Nevada Assembly speaker who had been elected to the state senate. Vergiels was upset at something German wrote (no one can remember what) and called him a gay slur. That resulted in a shoving match and an informal ban by leadership from lawmakers hanging out at the watering hole.[35] Vergiels also lost his re-election bid two years later, though it's not clear if the spat had anything to do with the shoving match since his victorious opponent never heard of the scuffle. It apparently never made the news because even reporters who were covering the legislature at the time had not heard of it.[36]

German's scoops and column—with a photo of him with big glasses, even bigger hair, and a shirt open at well below the neck—were earning him a big profile in Las Vegas. The establishment taking was noticing. In the early 1980s, Marilyn Gubler had just been appointed state Republican chairwoman. She decided to start taking key members of the press to lunch to get acquainted.

The lunch with German led to a romantic relationship that lasted about a year. With her, German showed a softer side, hanging out by the pool and getting into rubber-band fights with her two young children. The couple would watch TV or go out to dinner. Later in life, German would often talk about a woman he almost married without naming her. His friends and sources were sure it was Marilyn Gubler. Most thought she was the love of his life, and he was heartbroken when the relationship ended.

She, however, doesn't remember the relationship being that serious nor can she remember exactly what broke them up. The breakup happened in 1986 around the time US Senator Paul Laxalt forced Gubler out of the chairmanship. She remembers getting kicked twice—out of a job and a relationship—while she was down. However, the conflict of a top reporter dating a major political player never occurred to Jeff German and Marilyn Gubler.[37]

During and after the relationship, German wrote repeatedly about Gubler without revealing they were dating, which nowadays would be a huge no-no. A September 23, 1985, column detailed her facing criticism for a remark she made about Republicans buying off politicians to switched parties. In the column, German defended her, saying most party officials view her as "a hard working, innovative strategist."

A March 5, 1986, German column bids farewell to Gubler leaving the GOP gig, saying she "singlehandedly rejuvenated the party." Two days later, he devoted most of his column to taking Laxalt to task for getting rid of a chairwoman who raised thousands for the party, calling her a "smart cookie." On March 17, 1986, German again started the column describing Marilyn Gubler's going away party, which she dubbed "I was 86'ed in '86" bash, and the flowers Laxalt sent her as a "peace offering."

"Gubler's light seems destined to be shining brightly again very soon," he wrote. In an October 26, 1986, column, German calls her a "razor-sharp former state GOP chief." Nowhere in any of those pieces does he reveal having a romantic relationship with the chairwoman.

In 1973, the Society for Professional Journalists updated their ethics code to warn reporters to "avoid conflicts of interest, real or perceived. Disclose unavoidable conflicts." Jeff German and his paper knew or should have known dating the subject of articles would have violated those though the codes were voluntary and had no enforcement mechanism.[38]

Outside his occasional dating, German built a close group of reporter friends at the Sun who would hang out at TGI Fridays or shoot pool at a local PT's bar. A dyed-in-the-wool reporter, he saw editors as the enemy. He kept a quote at his desk attributed to the Washington Post legendary investigative reporting team of Bob Woodward and Carl Bernstein: "Good work is always done in defiance of management."

The hottest bars and restaurants in Vegas change often and always have. In the 1980s, he was always up on the latest place to see sources and be seen. When Eighth Judicial District Judge James Bixler opened a bar in the city, German was the first to find out, urging friends that they had to go down there. German often annoyed friends during these drinking nights because he was always on the job. He would stop a conversation mid-sentence if he spotted a source or politician who might have a story or tip for him.[39] When he got on to a big story—or one he thought was big—he wasn't afraid of letting people know without giving out too much information that might get him scooped.

"It's big, it's big," he would say, to the point it became a running joke among colleagues.

"Jeff, is it big?" friends would mock him.

He either didn't understand his friends were mocking him or he didn't care. He always replied: "Oh yeah. Oh, it's big."

Sometimes it wasn't big but he pushed all his stories with the same level of enthusiasm. Geoff Schumacher was one of his editors at the Sun and believes Jeff German never wrote a story that he did not think was worthy of the front page— even if the editors disagreed. It was a delusion afflicting many—if not most—reporters.

George McCabe became friends with German when he interned at the Sun in the 1980s. Usually, German wouldn't give a minute of his time to an intern, but McCabe was brought in by O'Callaghan after they ran into each other at a University of Nevada-Reno football game. The connection to the paper's top editor gave McCabe an in with the high-profile investigative reporter and ornery veteran. McCabe introduced German to all his family and none of them liked German's brash style. German thought nothing of sending back a drink if it wasn't right or "dunking" on a journalistic competitor whom he had beat on a story. German appeared to delight in irritating people and didn't care whom he insulted.

While German turned off McCabe's family, McCabe loved his new friend's persona. He thought German was hilarious. He was a character, the prototypical reporter, which made him fun to hang out with, and interesting. McCabe would go on to work at the Review-Journal before moving to public relations, but he and German remained friends until his death. German also was close to two features journalists at the RJ. However, for most RJ reporters, German would have nothing but contempt during his Sun years.[40]

Looking for a lunch place with then Sun political editor Larry Henry, Henry suggested an Italian place he liked. German balked because there would be RJ people there. At the courthouse, German refused to even acknowledge the competition—unless he gained grudging respect for their work. He often slammed the door of his closet-sized office in the face of a competitor or walked away without acknowledging a greeting.[41]

With the Mob's influence waning, there was still plenty of corruption to cover for German because, well, it was Vegas. The courts had settled Claiborne's case years earlier, but he continued to collect a salary despite serving two years in prison for tax evasion. Claiborne refused to step down from his job so Congress stepped in. In 1986, Claiborne was the first sitting judge to be impeached by the House and removed by the US Senate. Oscar Goodman served as his attorney, and German covered the case and the impeachment trial. German, with bushy hair, beard, big glasses, and hideous sports coat, appeared on CSPAN to answer viewers questions about the case.

Goodman contends Claiborne was done in by bad bookkeeping and the judge's weakness for women. He had a thriving law practice, and Goodman once saw a $100,000 US Treasury refund check stuck in a drawer that Claiborne hadn't bothered to cash. He didn't need to short the IRS money, his attorney believed.[42]

German also sought out conflict—though not physical—with journalists he did not like and who didn't like him. Another big fish in the small Vegas journalism pond at the time was Jon Ralston. German and Ralston never got along. Ralston came from Michigan to cover crime at the Review-Journal in 1984. Within two years, he moved to covering politics. Neither had much respect for the other's brand of journalism. Both thought the other was in bed with certain politicians but felt they were independent.

There may have been a personal component to their mutual dislike. In the 1980s, Sarah Hoeveler was a pretty blonde reporter for KTNV-Channel 13 and later for KVBC-Channel 3. She had graduated from the University of Wisconsin and worked in Madison, which was a ninety-minute drive from German's hometown, before heading to Vegas. Hoeveler and German went out several times before Ralston swooped in and married her. Ralston maintains he did not know that his former wife dated German but that would not preclude animosity on German's part, which sometimes included attacks on Sarah by way of Ralston.[43]

The feud became very public in 1994 when it exploded over the airways. German and Ralston were on Nevada Week in Review, a local PBS television program that brought on reporters to discuss their stories and the topics of the day. German started subtlety needling Ralston, telling Ralston he was carrying water for his sources. Ralston exploded on air, jabbing his finger at German, and repeatedly yelling that he was pathetic.

Ralston was clearly embarrassed by his inability to keep his cool, writing in his newsletter, Ralston Report: "Usually reserved, cerebral columnist erupts on public TV program, spewing venom and vitriol. Mental patient performance frightens fellow guests, gives children nightmares ... TV career in jeopardy."[44]

After his eruption, Ralston went on the attack against German during a lengthy profile in New Times published on May 5, 1994. He calls German "vicious, unethical, doesn't do his homework, prints rumors and is not, in my mind, a journalist."

Three days after Ralston's remarks are printed in New Times, German devoted a column headlined "R-J columnist just flapping his yap" in response. He nicknamed Ralston the "Flapper."

"He has the manic demeanor of a Rosann Rosannadanna[45] on a caffeine high and the shrill voice of Pee Wee Herman," German wrote, referring to a popular Saturday Night Live character played by Gilda Radner. He charged that Ralston nixed German's appearance on a Las Vegas Chamber of Commerce forum and was promoting candidates with his thousand-dollar-a-year newsletter for friends like Billy Vassiliadis, who that year purchased R&R from Rogich.

"Recently, for example, the Flapper described Gov. Bob Miller's campaign commercials as 'marvelously produced'..." German wrote. "By no small coincidence, Vassiliadis is overseeing Miller's campaign. If the Flapper didn't use himself to promote his friends and the people who buy his newsletter, he probably wouldn't leave himself open for such heavy criticism... I think it's time to expose the Flapper."

Dana Gentry, who produced Ralston's television show in partnership with Channel 8, saw the German/Ralston feud firsthand and believed it stemmed from Ralston's insecurities and need to demean anyone he saw a competition. She remembered that he branded those people with nicknames—though many weren't particularly creative. Molly Ball, who was now a top national political writer at Time magazine before moving to the Wall Street Journal, was Molly Not On the Ball, and former Sun reporter Patrick Coolican was Patrick Not Cool. German was the diminutive Jeffie, which for a grown man competing in the hard-scrabble world of Vegas news did not sit well.

Ralston maintains he did not invent the nicknames and only heard one of them (he didn't specify which one and declined interview requests with author—only responding by email to some questions). He points out that he is friends with Ball, and Coolican donated to his current journalism project, The Nevada Independent.[46] Coolican remembered that he heard Ralston use the Jeffie nickname and the one about Molly Ball was familiar. "Nicknames were in his repertoire," he emailed.[47] The nicknames, history, and snipping made for a toxic feud that lasted until German's death.[48]

Two years after the 1994 blow-up, German continued his attacks on Ralston. In a September 28, 1996, column, German takes Ralston, Nevada Week in Review host Mitch Fox, and others to task for not upholding journalistic standards. He criticizes them for recruiting moderators who, German wrote, were not qualified to question candidates in a congressional debate between US Representative John Ensign and challenger State Senator Bob Coffin.

"After lengthy negotiations, Fox bowed to the wishes of Ensign and Coffin and put together a panel of questioners that includes two reporters who don't follow the race and a local columnist, Jon Ralston, who has a conflict of interest covering the campaign," German wrote, hinting that Ralston's then-wife Hoeveler worked on the Ensign campaign. "Ralston's family is closely tied to Ensign's rise to political power. Furthermore, Ralston, as reported in the Las Vegas City Life newspaper, recently got into a public tiff with Coffin. Some say the emotional columnist threatened Coffin's political career."[49]

Ralston maintained that despite his wife at the time working for Ensign's campaign, he did not "softball" Ensign or threaten Coffin's career. He said Ensign, who resigned in 2011 from the US Senate in the midst of an ethics investigation into his covering up an affair, blames him for ending Ensign's career.[50] [51]

Fox believes the column was sour grapes because German was not selected as a questioner on the debate, and appreciated that the column helped create "buzz" for the show.[52]

German called out his rival for ethical issues but didn't appear to see his own ethical lapses in the very same column. German again defended his former girlfriend, Marilyn Gubler, without revealing that they had a personal relationship. "Nevada Republican Party Chairman John Mason stunned party regulars Friday when he sent out a bizarre news release taking at cheap shot at former GOP leader Marilyn Gubler," German wrote. Mason's release said Gubler is not a spokesperson for the party or, in Mason's opinion, a Republican activist.

Jon Ralston also continued to fire back at Jeff German from his various platforms, including his Ralston Reporter newsletter and later his Twitter account. German "is not known as one of Nevada's most insightful or competent journalists," Ralston wrote in one newsletter, noting in another that German was "spoon-fed" information. Ralston's misguided attack about German's competence would later resurface and spark controversy after German's slaying in a letter written by the editor of Ralston's non-profit news organization, The Nevada Independent.[53]

Despite the attacks, German must have been doing something right as a journalist because police and criminal defense attorneys both felt he was targeting their interests. Both used the same derogatory nickname—Jeff the Germ— behind his back.

He also clung tightly to the Mob beat despite organized crime's waning influence by the 1990s. Steve Kanigher was interviewing for a job at the Sun in 1991. The managing editor interviewing him said he could write about anything except the Mob. That piqued his curiosity because Vegas was known for its Mob history, and Kanigher couldn't understand why it was off limits. It wasn't that the paper was protecting mobsters, it was that the Mob was exclusively German's beat and he was too territorial to let anyone else share in that big, juicy—if waning—story.

Editors found that Kanigher was well versed in the kind of research that wasn't exactly German's main strength. Editors started asking him to collaborate with German on stories that needed a lot of records or research. German would get a tip and the basic outlines of a story, and Kanigher would find the background, expert sources, reports, and any other supporting documents. Kanigher would write up a long memo that German used to write the final story. They would share the byline.

Kanigher often went to lunch with German, and his brother-in-law Mike Smith, who had married German's sister Julie on July 8, 1990, in Wisconsin.[54] Hazing was usually also on the menu during those lunches. When German would get too verbose, Kanigher and others would start talking about NASCAR because German hated car racing. He loved football and basketball but could never see the point of watching cars speed around a track.

Unprofessional behavior was rampant in the newsrooms of the early 1990s. When his colleagues found out that German had his multiple televisions hooked up to the Clapper, a device marketed on late-night TV by an elderly woman who could turn her lights on and off with a clap, friends mocked him mercilessly. When bored, Kanigher would amble by German's desk and clap in his face, drawing laughter from the room and his ire.

German's ego took a hit whenever he was not considered the best—or in some cases, the worst—reporter in Nevada. That all depended on who was rating the journalists. In 1995, President Bill Clinton's Energy Secretary Hazel O'Leary garnered a national scandal by paying $46,500 in taxpayer money to a consulting firm to rate journalists. When the scandal broke, the White House rebuked her but let her keep her job.

Las Vegas Sun environmental writer Mary Manning topped the list of bad reporters because of her hard-hitting coverage of the Yucca Mountain controversy. The feds wanted to store spent nuclear fuel and other highly radioactive nuclear waste in Nevada. Local politicians, naturally, didn't like the idea. When national media called to get comment from Manning, some ended up getting German instead. He insisted that he was really the worst in the country. Clearly it was a point of pride to have top national officials name reporters as bad. It showed a reporter was doing his or her job, holding government accountable and angering the people in power. German bristled that he wasn't the worst, which Manning found petty.[55]

Sources recalled German's long, drawn-out interviews with a level of detail that would pretty much start at prehistoric times and move at a glacial pace up to the twentieth century. Sussing out that level of detail, he often asked questions other reporters assumed or already knew. That, at times, made him appear naïve. It was hard to tell if he was so detail-oriented that he did not want to inadvertently introduce a mistake into his stories without knowing every fact explicitly. Or, as some surmise, he just didn't know what he was asking. Either way, there were times when German's questions backfired.

Bob Miller, by then Nevada governor, announced he was diagnosed with prostate cancer in 1996. Jeff German covered the news conference. When asked how the cancer was discovered, Miller responded by saying it was found during a digital examination. German followed up with: "What is digital examination?"

Miller didn't miss a beat, telling German that if he came back to his office after the news conference, he would show him. The room exploded in laughter.

Billy Vassiliadis remembers German grilling him about everything in such detail that it was "painful"—like a digital examination. But those tactics helped German understand the story, the back story, and make sure every detail was right and in context.[56]

German was not so gruff that he wouldn't notice if a pretty woman came into the Sun's offices. When Cathy Scott was interviewing for a reporting job at the Sun in 1993, German repeatedly—and she believes unnecessarily—kept coming into the room to make copies. It was a ridiculous amount of copying. He returned five or six times, leading Scott to conclude it was just to talk to her. Once she was hired, German asked her to lunch and brought her in to a group that regularly lunched together. The only qualifications had to be that the place was near the paper, fast, and cheap. German always drove his car, even if the spot was down the block because he never knew when he'd have to hurry back for a story.[57]

He sometimes roped Scott in when a story he was working on intersected with her crime beat. A few days into the new year in 1997, German received a tip about one of the last Mob hits in Vegas, breaking the story exclusively. Herbie Blitzstein was a top lieutenant of the late Spilotro. A source called German, saying Blitzstein was found shot to death at his three-bedroom Spanish-style three-bedroom ranch home at 3655 Mt. Vernon Avenue. German grabbed Scott, and they hurried to the scene. A television reporter was there but didn't know the significance of the police investigation. German, of course, didn't let on.

Blitzstein, who could have passed for opera singer Luciano Pavarotti, was found with a .22-caliber round in the back of his head—a weapon and method favored by Mob hitmen. Police initially theorized it was a robbery gone wrong. It was later learned that members of Los Angeles and Buffalo organized crime wanted to take over Blitzstein's rackets. And a month later, German broke the story that police warned Ted Binion, who was friends with Blitzstein, that his life might also be in danger.[58]

Ted Binion lost his casino license partly because of his association with Blitzstein, German reported the year before Blitzstein's murder. Ted Binion had been suspended for drug use but apparently still worked at the Horseshoe. Binion had agreed to refrain from casino operations in a 1994 stipulation. However, Binion signed at least thirty comps and signed a lucrative trademark agreement for the Horseshoe with fellow shareholders eight months after the suspension. The Gaming Control Board had a hearing to determine if he violated the terms of their agreement.[59]

While German and Scott never dated and he never attempted to take their relationship beyond the professional, Scott felt like German often invited her to places so people would think she was his girlfriend. UNLV basketball games were big draws before every conceivable professional sports team moved to Vegas in the 2010s and 2020s. The Greenspuns gave German great seats to the games. The who's who of Vegas elite occupied the courtside spots for the games, dubbed "Gucci Row." The Greenspun seats German obtained were not in the row but they weren't far away. He brought Scott to one of the games.

Kanigher spotted him with Scott at a UNLV basketball game and gave him no end of grief afterwards. A frustrated German, with his usual resigned embarrassment, would try to change the subject, but it usually didn't help. In fact, German's reaction to the ribbing would often make it worse. He would just have to ride out the harassment. The teasing did not prevent German from taking Scott to BBQs with family and other personal occasions but always on a platonic basis.

Newsrooms, like police precincts, hospitals, and other places that deal with life, death, murder, and rape, tend to be very politically incorrect. That was doubly true in the 1980s and 1990s when the word "woke" only meant that you were no longer sleeping. Inappropriate jokes and comments were commonplace. Hazing and breaking balls were considered an acceptable, almost necessary, ritual. Dating colleagues was also not taboo. German was so susceptible and reacted so hurt to people breaking his balls that he made an extremely enjoyable target. In the era of political correctness, it may seem inappropriate and a firing offense but often the gallows humor helped reporters cope with the horrific topics they covered.

***

During the 1990s, German's relationship with Oscar Goodman was also deteriorating. The former Mob attorney was looking for a new challenge and no longer represented the clients German was covering. Goodman felt he had done everything he could as attorney, but he also wanted to remain in the limelight. He decided to run for mayor, conceding he was the only person who thought he could win. In any other city, he knew he wouldn't stand a chance, having represented murderers, conmen, and crooked officials. But in Vegas, the worst thing you can do is be boring. Goodman was far from that.

The Review-Journal editorial page mocked his election campaign and urged readers to vote for anyone but him. But in 1999, Goodman was elected mayor with a healthy sixty-four percent of the vote. His popularity only grew, garnering about eighty-five percent of the vote in the two subsequent elections. His wife, Carolyn, was elected as Sin City's top politician the next election and voters also gave her the maximum three terms. Oscar Goodman always wanted to attract major sports teams to the city, but the Raiders and Oakland A's only fled California for Southern Nevada during his wife's tenure.

The Las Vegas mayor is not your typical big-city bureaucrat, just like Las Vegas is not Omaha or Sacramento.

Oscar Goodman's three terms were as bombastic and controversial as his arguments in court. His policy proposals included setting up brothels in Las Vegas, legalizing all street drugs to collect enough revenue to pay teachers six-figure salaries, and cutting the thumbs off people convicted of graffiti while broadcasting the punishment on television. Not surprising, none of his libertarian ideas were enacted into city ordinance.[60]

Goodman's administration was unlike any in the country. He was the first Las Vegas mayor to have his face on casino chips. He photographed a model for a topless pictorial for the Playboy website. Bombay Sapphire gin recruited him as its spokesman because he was never far from a gin martini, which he garnished with sliced jalapeno peppers and a glass of ice on the side. Oscar Goodman donated the gin endorsement honorarium to charity. In 2005, however, he faced nationwide controversy when fourth graders at a local elementary school asked him the one thing he would want with him if he was stranded on a desert island.

"A bottle of Bombay Sapphire gin," Mayor Goodman responded, adding that one of his main hobbies was drinking. He later apologized if anyone was offended by his remarks but was unapologetic about promoting alcohol to a room of pre-teens. This was Las Vegas, after all, and alcohol in a casino was like water in most restaurants—free to any gambling customer. Walking down the street with an open container was a big draw for tourists on the Strip and downtown. Alcohol abuse carried none of the taboos it did in the Midwest and Bible Belt.

After taking office, Goodman got revenge on the RJ for the "anybody but Goodman" editorial it published when he first revealed his intention to run. The Review-Journal, at the time, held awards ceremonies for top Vegas personalities and attractions. Newspaper staff invited the mayor. He didn't want to go to the event, remembering the past animosity, but was convinced to attend. Drinking heavily as he usually did, Goodman nearly fell off his seat when the paper named him the best politician. Despite the newspaper's attempt at good will, Goodman couldn't help but take a swipe at the RJ while accepting the honor. He told the crowd that when he was elected, he had two dogs but now he only had one.

"Now, I don't know what to do with the other half of the paper," Goodman said, making a reference to picking up dog feces with the paper. The crowd gasped as he left the stage to find his drink.[61]

That was Vegas in a quip: It was a rough town where you never forget to take revenge on your enemies. Vegas was also still a land of opportunity for anyone who wanted to seize it, and German was always looking for the next big story that would get him on the front page.

As the millennium drew to a close, he found probably the highest-profile story of his life. Ted Binion, who had been banned from running the family casinos, was found dead in his house. Law enforcement suspected his lover and her boyfriend. The trial would draw media from around the country and the world. German was at the forefront with every twist and turn. He saw it was an opportunity to achieve a career goal that he desired since the first days his feet hit the hot pavement of Sin City.

Jeff German continued to write about the Mob-connected court official who punched him, despite suffering four stitches during the attack.

Jeff German wrote favorable columns about Judge Harry Claiborne, who was close to German's publisher at the Las Vegas Sun. Claiborne would be convicted on tax charges and impeached.

CHAPTER THREE:
BINION BOOK

On September 17, 1998, Ted Binion, the second son of Horseshoe Casino and World Series of Poker founder Benny Binion, was found dead in his house. Pill bottles were strewn around his body. The Binion name dominated gambling downtown. Ted's father, Benny Binion, was a colorful and dangerous character who fled Dallas for Vegas to avoid prosecution. Benny Binion built a gaming empire in Downtown Vegas. The family was close to Judge Claiborne and other powerful people in Southern Nevada. Before his death, Ted had been arrested on drug charges. His friends and family knew he was addicted to smoking heroin. His gaming license was suspended in 1997. When the Gaming Control Board found out he palled around with known mobsters, like Blitzstein, the agency revoked his license to work in gaming.

With his professional life in jeopardy, Ted Binion's personal life was also coming apart. His wife filed for divorce in 1995. At fifty-five, he had been dating a pretty woman named Sandy Murphy, who was more than twenty years his junior. Ted Binion met Murphy at Cheetahs, a topless club. To complicate matters further, despite living with Binion, she kept a boyfriend named Rick Tabish.

Binion had used Tabish's trucking company to transport six tons of silver, Horseshoe casino chips, currency, and rare coins to an underground vault on a property he owned in Pahrump. Pahrump in Nye County was a rural outpost about sixty miles west of Las Vegas. It is one of the last vestiges of the Wild West. Pahrump's main street is lined with fireworks stands featuring items not legal in Clark County, like quarter sticks of dynamite. Legal prostitution was readily available in Nye County, just an hour's drive from Sin City. Three days after Binion's death, Tabish was caught by Nye County sheriff's deputies trying to dig up the stash worth many, many millions.

It wasn't clear how Ted Binion died, but the circumstances were suspicious. Clark County Coroner Ron Flud kept the case as a "pending" status as police and prosecutors worked for six months to determine what (or who) killed Ted Binion. The coroner's office found strange details—like heroin digesting in Binion's stomach before he died. That made no sense. Addicts smoke, snort, or shoot heroin—they don't swallow it.[62]

Binion's family thought it was murder and quickly pointed at Ted Binion's young girlfriend, whom they never really liked. The family hired retired Metro Homicide Detective Tom Dillard, who worked as a private investigator, to look into the case. Dillard, like many, had a frenemy-type relationship with Jeff German. While Dillard was still a homicide investigator, German had taken Dillard to task in a column for receiving free perks at taxpayer expense. He wrote that the Clark County sheriff gave Dillard special treatment by having his car painted, but the car was a seized undercover vehicle that had caught fire and needed repairs. It was all for official police business.

After the column ran, Dillard bumped into German on the street one day, grabbing him and lighting him up about the column. Instead of avoiding Dillard after the encounter, German used the interaction to recruit him as a source. Dillard would play a key role in one of German's last stories. Dillard found that despite the erroneous column about his car, German was hardworking and fair. German would sometimes call Dillard two or three times a day, trying to confirm a story or a tip after the Binion case broke.

At the time of Ted Binion's death, David Roger was an ambitious prosecutor in the Clark County District Attorney's Office. Because of Ted Binion's drug addiction and criminal connections, Roger felt like the police were not very excited about the case and it would go nowhere. For example, homicide detectives, who usually want to be on the scene before the body is moved to collect evidence, weren't assigned until a week after the death.[63] Roger lobbied to get on the case. He worked with Dillard, impeached Judge Claiborne, who by then had his law license reinstated[64] and represented the Binion family, to determine if there was foul play.

Adding to the intrigue was that Murphy and Tabish were spending Binion's money after his death. Right before his death, Ted Binion received eighty thousand dollars in sequentially numbered hundred-dollar bills from his safe deposit box. He was planning to use them for a campaign contribution. Police found Tabish and Murphy spent some of the bills paying for dinner at a local restaurant.[65]

Once German realized Roger was assigned the Binion case, he started calling him and his investigator daily. He also badgered Coroner Flud about the delays in getting a cause of death and was miffed that Flud never would explain the delay. The coroner just sent German to the police, which compounded German's frustration.

Some people, however, were apparently talking to the persistent reporter. Whenever Roger heard his usually boisterous investigator whispering on the phone, he assumed he was talking to German. German had an uncanny, almost psychic ability to know just when Roger arrived at work. He regularly called him just as he was sitting down at his desk.

"What do you have for me today?" German demanded.

"Nothing," Roger replied.

At first, Roger refused to talk, but German's persistence paid off. Roger maintains he never gave German a story, but he would confirm one if German had the facts. Getting nothing on most morning calls, German would call at the end of the day so Roger could confirm what he learned or waive him off an inaccurate story.

On May 5, 1999, the Clark County Coroner's Office reclassified Binion's death from "pending" to "homicide." Dillard had hired New York pathologist Dr. Michael Baden to review the case. Baden's theory was that Binion was suffocated by Murphy and Tabish when he did not die from the drugs the couple forced him to swallow. Murphy and Tabish were charged with murder and burglary for trying to take the desert loot.

German was writing almost daily about the case and would write more than three hundred and fifty articles. He often used a well-worn reporter tactic to keep himself in the paper. He would find a small bit of news and lead off the piece with that. Then he padded out the rest with already reported background. German was also gathering material for a book. The case would take the twists and turns usually reserved for a thriller. It would be made into a TV movie based on German's book. Ted Binion's death drew national and international media to Las Vegas, including Court TV and the Geraldo show. That put the case and German in the limelight.

***

The Binion family was Vegas gambling royalty. Benny Binion was the patriarch. Benny ran gambling operations in Dallas as head of an organized crime syndicate. He was accused of killing at least three people in Texas but inexplicably served no prison time. For the first murder, he received a suspended sentence; for the second, he successfully claimed self-defense; for the third, he just was never indicted. But when a new sheriff was elected in 1946, he lost his law enforcement protection. He wisely fled to Vegas.

In Nevada, Binion purchased a casino and hotel. He rebranded it: Binion's Horseshoe. His gaming innovations included providing free drinks to playing customers, offering two-dollar steaks from cattle raised at his Montana ranch, and removing betting limits on table games. The free alcohol and cheap eats were adopted by many casinos in the coming years after they brought the Horseshoe quick success. Like many famous gangsters, Binion may have been able to avoid answering for violent crimes but not for cheating the IRS. In 1951, Binion was sentenced to a five-year prison term for tax evasion. He lost his casino license. Binion had to sell the Horseshoe, but the family regained the controlling interest in the downtown property in 1957. His sons, including Ted Binion, took over the gambling license. But Benny was in charge until his death on Christmas Day in 1989 from heart failure.[66]

His greatest lasting contribution to Vegas is arguably the founding of the World Series of Poker in 1970. After a few years of holding the tournament, Benny Binion predicted the ten thousand dollar buy-in Main Event tournament would be popular enough to draw more than fifty participants in the coming years. In 2023, the Main Event at the WSOP, which was purchased by Harrah's Entertainment two decades earlier, drew a record of more than ten thousand players from around the world. First place paid $12.1 million that year.

Metro Lieutenant Wayne Petersen (now retired) headed up the unit that investigated homicides when Ted Binion was found dead. Initially, given his reputation and well-known drug use, it was no surprise that Ted Binion had overdosed. A New York Times reporter once told Petersen that every time he interviewed Ted Binion, the casino boss would admit to at least one felony. Becky Binion and Binion attorney Richard Wright both approached Petersen, saying they didn't believe Ted overdosed. Petersen did not sense any lack of motivation from his subordinates despite Roger's contention that the police were not too enthusiastic about the investigation. It was just a tough case to investigate because it was purely circumstantial.[67] Flud concurred that the detectives who received the case tried to work it hard.

One break in the case came when Dillard found Murphy's manicurist. She told police about a conversation with Murphy where Ted Binion's young girlfriend said she would inherit three million dollars and Binion's $900,000 house if he died. Binion had also instructed one of his attorneys to take Murphy out of his will the day before his body was found, raising questions about whether Binion suspected Murphy was cheating on him or had it out for him.[68]

The case was a roller coaster ride for prosecutors. Roger, not usually one given to anxiety, felt like he was having a stroke during the preliminary hearing. Baden seemed to undercut the prosecution's theory that Murphy and Tabish forced Ted Binion to overdose by giving him drugs. Instead, to justify the homicide charge, Baden provided a murder history lesson. He theorized Murphy and Tabish suffocated Binion by "burking" him—or sitting on his chest while holding their hands over his mouth. The term refers to a method used by William Burke and William Hare in the early 1800s to obtain (really, create) corpses for sale to medical schools. When caught, Burke was hanged.[69]

Baden pointed to abrasions on Ted Binion's chest and wrist along with hemorrhages in blood vessels in his eyes often created by suffocation. He testified the physical evidence was proof the lovers held Ted Binion down while sitting on his chest to suffocate him.

Tabish and Murphy were charged with first-degree murder, grand larceny, and burglary. The trial started in March 2000. From the beginning, the sex, drugs, and a ton of buried treasure drew readers and viewers to the often-tawdry case. Murphy's fashion senses and clothes played to the tabloid aspect of the trial. She was twenty-eight years old during the trial and wore a different, flattering outfit each day. Someone stole her panties while she was in the county jail, leading to articles about the scandal of the "purloined panties."

While German prided himself on scooping others and basically owning the Binion case, he sometimes got beat. Then-Channel 13 television reporter Glen Meek scooped German on a key story. Meek had determined that the jail log of who visited Tabish should be public record. He requested it, and the Clark County District Attorney's Office agreed he had a right to see it. In the log, Meek noticed that a guy connected to the Chicago Outfit had visited Tabish in jail. He went on air with the revelation.

Getting scooped sent German ballistic. German scrambled to confirm the story and find a new angle. He wrote that another mobster with film connections had also visited Tabish. Without crediting Meek's scoop, German published an article with the new tidbit and the information Meek uncovered.[70]

Another scoop came from the Pahrump newspaper. Doug McMurdo, who then was the editor of the Pahrump Valley Times, received a two-a.m. call from a source, saying sheriff's deputies caught Tabish and his associates digging up Binion's treasure trove off the main drag in Pahrump. German started recycling stories that McMurdo broke under his byline with no credit weeks or months after they ran in the Pahrump paper. That upset McMurdo, but it was just standard practice at the time not to acknowledge the competition. Such were the newspaper wars.[71]

Murphy and Tabish were convicted of murdering Ted Binion in a seven-week trial. In May 2000, District Judge Joseph Bonaventure sentenced Tabish to twenty-five years in prison and Murphy to twenty-two years. Roger's successful prosecution of Tabish and Murphy gave him the name recognition to win the election as Clark County District Attorney three times. In 2006, Roger was floated as a possible replacement for US Attorney Daniel Bogden. Bogden was dismissed as Nevada's top federal prosecutor by the George W. Bush administration as part of a group of seven federal prosecutors removed for questionable reasons. German pushed Roger to take the job. German acted like he was just supporting a friend, but in the back of Roger's mind, he figured the dogged reporter really wanted a good source in the federal prosecutor's office. Jeff German just wanted more scoops.

Roger declined to be considered for the federal prosecutor's appointment because he was not fully vested in the state pension system. Federal prosecutors often serve a year or two before a new president puts his own person into the job. In another example of how the state's lucrative pension system impacts qualified office holders, Roger resigned about a year into his third term as district attorney to take a job representing the Las Vegas Police Protective Association. He was by then vested in his state pension and could collect monthly payments while getting a paycheck from the police union. He started collecting more than one hundred thousand dollars a year from PERS the day after his January 3, 2012, retirement, pension records show.[72]

After Murphy and Tabish were convicted, the judge agreed to an unusual request of sitting for an interview with German for his book. Bonaventure met German for lunch at a bar. Bonaventure told him he would give him an hour. Bonaventure had agreed to an interview because he respected German's reporting so much that he was willing to give him his perspective of the initial trial. Unlike some media, Bonaventure felt German never twisted his words and reported the story down the middle—as factually as he could.[73]

Judges almost never talk about cases and this one was particularly sensitive. Unknown at the time, the Nevada

Supreme Court would overturn Tabish and Murphy's convictions. The state's high court found Bonaventure allowed prejudicial and hearsay evidence. He would have to preside over a second trial.

With his interviews in his notebooks, German scrambled to get the book out while the story was still hot. Working with HarperCollins editor Sarah Durand, he quickly submitted a manuscript and immediately completed any needed rewrites. She found him extremely efficient when he called her back to answer questions. With the sounds of the newsroom in the background, German gave her everything she needed in a few minutes. German was used to being edited—something he submitted to nearly daily for two decades—so revising the book was a breeze. Murder in Sin City: Death of a Las Vegas Casino Boss, written more in German's newspaper style than a narrative approach taken in many non-fiction books, was published only in paperback on July 31, 2001. He would have been paid less than twenty-five thousand dollars for the advance, and it's unclear if he made any more above that from sales.

After the book was published, Bonaventure and his clerk, Al Lasso, heard German was signing Murder in Sin City at the Horseshoe. Lasso rushed down to Binion's casino because the book contained a revelation that Murphy and Tabish engaged in sex in their attorneys' office when they should have been discussing the case. Bonaventure was upset that might have happened, Lasso remembered, and wanted to see what German had written.

German's book detailed Tabish's cushy jailhouse lifestyle, including smoking cigars and eating BBQ ribs with his attorney and corrections officers. Tabish's "most enjoyable privilege might have been having sex with Murphy right under the noses of the guards," German wrote in Murder in Sin City. "At one session, while the lawyers and other defense-team members were talking with the two defendants, Murphy was observed slipping to her knees under the table and giving oral sex to Tabish. Defense-team members could hardly believe their eyes… The corrections officers, sitting outside the boardroom, apparently never saw Murphy disappear under the table."

Bonaventure remembered that he and Lasso just went to the Horseshoe to support German's book. He had previously heard the sex allegations. They were titillating but not that significant to the judge. At the Horseshoe, Bonaventure was swept up in the spirit of the event. He even signed a few— actually about one hundred—copies of German's book. The judge got some heat for doing that as it could have been perceived as not being the most objective thing to do, but he just wanted to support German's project. German also autographed a copy for Bonaventure with the inscription: "Joe, the best judge in the world and a good friend. Great job with the trial. Jeff German." Bonaventure still keeps the autographed copy prominently on his bookshelf.

German was thrilled to have written a book, but the case was far from over. Murphy found a wealthy benefactor to fund an appeal. The defense brought in the big guns. Harvard Law Professor Alan Dershowitz argued an appeal before the state's top court. In 2003, the state Supreme Court gave Tabish and Murphy a new trial.

The second trial did not go well for the prosecutors. Murphy and Tabish's new defense attorneys knew the prosecution case and were able to undercut it. Murphy hired Las Vegas attorney Michael Cristalli, who clerked for Bonaventure, figuring it would help her to be represented by an attorney with a relationship with the judge. The defense set to undercut the prosecution's scientific theory and their witnesses. A defense pathologist testified that the depression on Binion's chest, which Dr. Baden believed was from burking, looked more like a carcinoma. Since Ted Binion had long been buried, experts on both sides were relying on coroner photos instead of looking at the skin lesion under a microscope. Each side could only present its own theory for the jury to decide.[74] The defense attorneys also demonstrated that key prosecution witnesses were paid tens of thousands in reward money, undercutting their credibility.

Going on the offensive, the defense pushed on the fact that Ted Binion bought a dozen balloons of heroin and filled a prescription for one hundred and twenty Xanax the night before his death. The defense argued away the contention that heroin in his stomach proved he was being poisoned by saying he had a ritual of licking the drug off his fingers after smearing the drug on the foil to smoke. In the end, a jury acquitted Tabish and Murphy of killing Ted Binion. The second jury found the couple was guilty of burglary and larceny for thefts of Binion's valuables. Murphy was sentenced to time served, but Tabish stayed in prison until he was paroled in 2009.[75]

Murphy felt she was not portrayed fairly in news reports or German's book. The allegations of being a stripper and gold digger stuck in her craw. She was just in town with a friend, gambling and partying. A friend of hers would go to Cheetahs to sell lingerie to the strippers, and that's how Murphy found herself at the topless club, her attorney contended. She may have danced for Ted Binion the night she met him, but she never had the sheriff's card that exotic dancers in Clark County are required to maintain. She was never paid as a stripper. Murphy and Cristalli felt that German's book was basically a recitation of the prosecution case and had none of the defense's rebuttal—though that is somewhat understandable since the book was published after the conviction and before the retrial and acquittal.[76]

Roger ran the district attorney's office during the retrial so he didn't argue the case. Christopher Lalli, who prosecuted the second case and was eventually promoted to a top deputy in the office, tried to spin the failure to reconvict the pair for murder. He told Roger that Tabish received the longest sentence for larceny in recent memory. Roger wasn't buying it, knowing that failing to convict on the murder charge was a huge embarrassment for his office.[77]

German was also in a bit of pickle. His book was titled Murder in Sin City, and the Lifetime channel had optioned it for a made-for-television movie. It was tough to claim there was a murder when the suspects were acquitted of homicide. German's book had been published years before the second trial so he was generally safe from a libel lawsuit. But Cristalli put Lifetime on notice, saying calling it a murder would be legally problematic.[78]

Will Kemp was another attorney whom German befriended. Kemp reviewed the contracts for German's book. There was no negotiation for the movie rights which Kemp believes were sold in the fifty thousand dollar-range. The network was basically take it or leave it. Then German's agent, who Kemp believes did nothing to secure the rights, came back, demanding payment for the Lifetime deal. He had to be paid his percentage.[79]

The Lifetime movie, starring Matthew Modine and Mena Suvari as the lovers, was titled Sex & Lies in Sin City: The Ted Binion Scandal. The kicker line on the cover said: "Someone is about to make a killing." The movie featured a reporter who likely was based on German, but he had few lines. He asked a few questions at a news conference. In a scene in the middle of the movie, he and two television journalists debate how Ted Binion died and Murphy and Tabish's involvement. After Murphy is acquitted in the second trial, the television reporter asks the German character whether he thinks she did it. He responds that the jury acquitted her but walks away like he doesn't believe it. The credits just call them Reporter #1 and Reporter #2.

In 2008, when the movie aired, German held a viewing party at his modest, single-story house on a cul-de-sac in the northwestern part of Las Vegas. German and his guests were universally underwhelmed by the adaption of his book. It was one of the few times his friends didn't give German a hard time. Emotions were just too raw after seeing the movie for any ritual hazing.[80]

German wrote a disappointed column about the process and his brush with the movies. He questioned the changes Sandy Murphy and Rick Tabish pushed to soften their roles in the case but realized there was little he could do given the circumstances.

"You've sold them your baby," German wrote in the column.

On the upside, the actor playing him was a "handsome devil" and "snazzy dresser to boot," but German wrote that Hollywood's reputation is well earned.

"During this lengthy process, I learned that many of the stereotypes about the movie business are true.

"—It really is cutthroat.

"—Agents won't call you back unless they smell money.

"—Back-stabbing is the norm.

"I also learned that life is much simpler as a reporter— and life as a reporter can get pretty complicated."[81]

Despite the disappointment, German still had big stories to cover for the Sun—a gig he thought would last forever.

Chapter Four:
Career Disaster

Less than a month before the 2006 gubernatorial election, a cocktail waitress accused the Republican candidate, Jim Gibbons, of drunkenly groping her in a parking garage near a popular, off-Strip restaurant. Gibbons was having dinner with political guru Sig Rogich at McCormick & Schmick's on October 13, 2006, to discuss the possibility of bringing an NFL team to Sin City. Chrissy Mazzeo, then thirty-two years old, and her friend approached Gibbons' party and had some drinks with them. Rogich left to go to bed and the next day received a call that Mazzeo alleged that Gibbons had accosted her. She accused Gibbons of throwing "her against a wall" and "threatening to sexually assault her," according to a story Jeff German wrote.[82]

It was big news, especially for the Democratic-leaning paper that supported Gibbons' opponent, Dina Titus. Gibbons, a former pilot for Delta Airlines, previously ran for governor in 1994 but was defeated by Bob Miller, the former Binion prosecutor. Two years later, Gibbons was elected to Congress, serving five terms before again vying for the state's top elected office. Gibbons had weathered several scandals during the 2006 campaign, including allegations he hired an illegal immigrant as a housekeeper. The Wall Street Journal also reported that he was under federal investigation for bribery.[83]

The groping incident showed how the RJ and Sun saw some stories very differently. At the time, the Sun was ramping up hiring and holding itself out as the investigative newspaper while the RJ was the paper of record. During the incident, Gibbons' attorney Don Campbell also represented the Review-Journal.[84] Campbell called a news conference disputing the woman's credibility and telling reporters to look into her background. Sure enough, the RJ had a story about her foibles on the next day's front page. In the 2000s, the Sun had been hiring dozens of reporters and editors from out of state, using a windfall of cash the paper received from a revamped joint operating agreement (JOA). In 2005, the Sun and Review-Journal signed a new version of the 1989 JOA that was very lucrative for the smaller paper. Court records contend the Sun paid twenty-five million dollars to the RJ and relinquished its printing press and other property in exchange for profit sharing that some years was as much as twelve million dollars a year and never less than $1.3 million during the 1990s and early 2000s.[85] The new and veteran Sun troops were pressed into duty on the Gibbons incident.[86]

Brian Greenspun, Hank's son, and his editors hired Drex Heikes from the Los Angeles Times in 2005, where he had worked as the paper's magazine editor, and in the Washington bureau. He had done everything there was to do at the Times and saw a move to Vegas as an inexpensive place to live and an opportunity to do great work. The big salary they offered him to be deputy managing editor also helped.

Heikes recruited young talent from around the country, directing them to dig deep. He also activated grizzled veterans like Jeff German for big stories, like the Gibbons groping allegation.[87] He needed someone with German's sources on the case because the establishment was trying to make the accusation go away. Sheriff Bill Young and DA Roger supported and donated to Gibbons. Police didn't seem that interested in finding the truth, saying Mazzeo would not sign a complaint. Police said there were no cameras in the location of the alleged incident, but the Las Vegas Sun sent one of its reporters to the garage. The reporter found there were eleven cameras, including one directly in the area of the encounter. However, when the videotapes were released days before the election, they were inconclusive. Experts questioned whether times and date stamps could have been altered.

Richard Wright, who was Ted Binion's attorney, also represented Gibbons' accuser. The attacks on her in the Review-Journal emboldened her to keep the case alive. For the reporters like German, Sam Skolnik, and J. Patrick Coolican, who were on the story for the Sun, it was a frustrating dead end—one German would face repeatedly in his career. Key video that would have resolved disputing stories was deleted, altered, or inconclusive when a high-profile political figure was involved.[88]

At Heikes' direction, German refused to give up on a story that threatened to derail Gibbons' candidacy. German had an incredible Rolodex of sources, a bulldog attitude, and a tough skin that allowed him to continue when others might back off. As was typical, German was the source guy—not the records guy. Returning from reporting, he dropped a two-foot-tall stack of documents at fellow reporter Mary Manning's desk on deadline and demanded Manning determine who Gibbons called the most. She found eight calls between the embattled gubernatorial candidate and the sheriff but realized that German only obtained Gibbons' cell phone calls. He did not have any calls Gibbons might have made from the Paradise Road Motel room phone where the candidate was holed up on the night of the alleged assault. She yelled over to German, asking where those records were, and he had to admit he didn't have them for her to analyze. On February 10, 2007, German and Sun reporter Sam Skolnik published a story detailing the calls between political consultant Sig Rogich and Sheriff Bill Young, quoting experts who said the contacts appeared to be inappropriate.

No criminal charges were filed. Instead, Mazzeo filed a civil suit against Jim Gibbons in 2009, charging battery, false imprisonment, and second-degree kidnapping. It was settled for an unimpressive fifty thousand dollars four years later. Gibbons survived the scandals and was elected governor. Some other politicians were not so lucky.

The same year the Gibbons groping scandal broke, five Clark County commissioners were guilty in a bribery scandal focused on the Crazy Horse Too strip bar. The owners wanted no-touch laws removed so patrons could interact more intimately with dancers and paid off county commissioners to get the change. Three went to prison for between two and five years on various charges, including bribery and filing false statements. It was yet another case of county officials benefiting themselves through their public offices.[89]

German was on top of those stories, invariably obtaining secret grand jury transcripts before anyone else. The same year, German also started looking into an institute at the University of Nevada-Las Vegas that was set up to prevent terror attacks like the ones on 9/11. The 2006 stories about the Institute for Security Studies questioned the spending and performance of the center. A lab at the center was supposed to develop "a sensor device to seek out snipers," perform tests that measure "electromagnetic waves" from a nuclear blast, and build "concealed weapons that could see through walls." None of those innovations apparently happened. The stories prompted an audit that "found shoddy record-keeping and an overall lack of oversight at the center." The following year, the institute cut its ties with a secretive lab that was supposed to be a cornerstone of the institute.[90]

German also led the way on a sex scandal involving US Senator John Ensign. The Nevada Republican had been carrying on an extra-marital affair with his campaign aide and was under an ethics investigation for potentially paying off and helping her husband, who was also a staffer, find lobbying work.

German got on a story about Fox News sitting on information about the affair for days before it broke. German reported that the network gave Ensign a heads-up that the scandal was getting out so he could hold a press conference. German worked day and night to confirm that Fox had buried the scandal and, with his editor at the time, Patrick McDonnell, finally had enough to post it at two a.m. McDonnell drove home after the story was online, but German called just as he was pulling into his driveway. German started talking about how the story went and began a post-mortem on the piece. They discussed potential follow-ups for the next day's story. The two ended up talking until the sun rose. German was so pumped up with his scoop that he couldn't sleep and didn't let McDonnell get any rest before getting back at it. That was the drive that kept Jeff German going for thirty years.

That same year, the Sun scored a major national victory. The hiring of young talented reporters and experienced editors paid off big. Alexandra Berzon, then twenty-nine years old, won the Pulitzer Prize for Public Service reporting for an investigation into the high rates of death for construction workers building Strip projects. The story detailed the lax regulation that contributed to the fatalities and sparked policy changes that improved work conditions. The Sun still touts that they're the only Las Vegas newspaper who won print journalism's top prize. Despite the prestigious award, within six months, the paper's leadership took actions that made a repeat win very unlikely.

By 2009, the JOA money was drying up at the Sun. Nevada's economy tanked during the real estate market crash and the Great Recession. Las Vegas, always sprawling with new housing projects, was arguably hit the hardest when home prices plummeted. Work stopped on major

Strip projects like City Center and the Fontainebleau Las Vegas, leaving metal skeletons that marred the glitzy Strip. Tourism, which is the city's main lifeblood, also dried up. Travelers didn't have money to drop on expensive meals, lavish suites, and high-stakes gaming tables. The Sun, which had been on a hiring spree, changed course.

Like the satirical comedy movie Office Space, a consultant was brought in to help. John Temple, often sporting a casual mountain-town look and greying bowl cut, was editor of the Rocky Mountain News in Denver when Scripps closed the paper earlier that year. Previously, Temple traveled and talked to Brian Greenspun about Denver's JOA, revealing what he learned to help negotiate one between the RMN and The Denver Post.[91]

When the Sun decided to cut staff, Sun leadership called Temple again to help decide the best way to unify a very divided newsroom.[92] Temple found a newsroom basically at war. There was a top editor for print and another one for digital who weren't on speaking terms. He found a bunch of reporters who wanted to stick with the print product when clearly the future of news—something newspapers were mostly late to discover—was online. Years later, Temple can't remember if he specified cuts and doesn't remember German. But he is sure he had a hand in what happened to him.[93]

On December 1, 2009, German, sportswriter Ron Kantowski, and Manning were called into the executive suites and each directed into separate rooms. There, they were told they would be laid off immediately. In the room where Manning was meeting, the human resources executive was crying and offered Manning tissues. Manning resolved to show no emotion.

As German, Manning, and Kantowski reconvened in the common area, they were stunned. The veteran scribes had trouble understanding how three experienced reporters had just lost their jobs after decades of loyalty to the Sun.

"They've got a hundred and twenty years of journalism experience here," Kantowski offered.

German started crying—something that surprised Manning as he always presented a tough-guy exterior.

"I'm ruined," German cried. "What am I going to do? I've never done anything else. What am I going to do now?"[94]

Dillard ran into German on his last day at the Sun, carrying a Bankers Box. He made a smartass comment, asking if the Sun had finally canned him. They had, and Dillard quickly had to apologize.[95]

The next day, the Sun ran German's last story for the paper—a short explainer on how mediation helps settle court disputes instead of expensive litigation. He had written nearly one hundred stories in 2009—or nearly two a week of varying length and complexity.

About forty other Sun journalists lost their jobs the same day. Some, like Kantowski, were quickly picked up by the rival paper, the Las Vegas Review-Journal. German's path to the RJ, with his prior hostility to the paper, competitive nature and propensity to rub it in when he scooped the competition, was much rockier.

CHAPTER FIVE: THE REVIEW-JOURNAL

In the winter of 2010, Jeff German's life was at a crossroads. He had dedicated more than half his life to the Las Vegas Sun, but the managers at the paper turned around and fired him. He had no income; no significant savings; no spouse whose job could support him. Four months before the layoff, he had turned fifty-six years old, which made job hunting considerably tougher.

The years of meager pay at the Sun always had him living on the financial edge. He told acquaintances that the house he bought in 1996 for $93,000 was under water, which was not uncommon in Las Vegas, especially during the 2008 housing crash. Between 2002 and 2014, he repeatedly refinanced his house and had liens placed on his property by the trash company for failure to pay.[96]

As a journalist, he had few job prospects. Newspapers around the country were contracting and laying off staff. He didn't think he could go into broadcast. Except for appearances as a journalist on public affairs shows, he had no on-air experience. German found a few freelance gigs, but they didn't pay enough to meet his expenses.

A few Las Vegas Sun journalists who had been laid off in 2009 quickly found jobs at the competing newspaper, the Las Vegas Review-Journal. The Sun and the RJ had a long rivalry driven by competition for scoops and a deep political divide. The Sun was known as the liberal paper backing Democrats, and the RJ was known for a conservative editorial position that backed Republicans. The RJ, the state's largest news organization, was founded in 1909 as the Clark County Review and renamed the Las Vegas Review-Journal in 1926. While Sun and RJ reporters competed aggressively to beat each other, German had gone out of his way to antagonize the competition. Some reporters there had long memories and felt German got what he deserved when the Sun canned him.[97]

After his layoff at the Sun, German called his friend, Carol Vogel. She had helped him land the Sun job in 1978, and he thought maybe she could provide another lifeline. He was clearly upset by the turn of events and at a loss. She told him to apply at the RJ.

"I would never go to the RJ," he told her.

"Never say never," she responded.

Vogel thought German seemed open to joining the state's largest newspaper but his pride got in the way. Vogel sensed that he wanted the RJ to reach out to him. He had made a name for himself in Vegas and felt like that should count for something.

Vogel also counseled German to look at national papers. She thought he was good enough to land at the New York Times or the Washington Post if he wanted to move east. The Los Angeles Times was another option if he wanted to stay in the western parts of the United States.[98]

German didn't want to leave Las Vegas. His sisters, Julie and Jill, had moved to Las Vegas. His brother was planning to join his siblings after retiring. Jeff German had a house, a life, and, until recently, a job he loved.[99]

He reached out to friends and sources who tried to help.

Political guru Sig Rogich called Las Vegas Review-Journal Publisher Sherm Frederick on German's behalf. "Jeff is a really good reporter," Rogich told the controversial publisher. "And he got a chickenshit deal at the Sun. I think he'd be a great asset."[100]

Frederick was receptive. He had competed with German as a young reporter and kept a close eye on his work at the Sun as Frederick rose to editor and publisher of the competing paper. He thought German was a "cocky son of a bitch" but also a great reporter with impeccable sources. He saw some stories that raised questions about whether German was doing the bidding of the Greenspuns but understood that reporters often have to take assignments and orders from their editors and publishers.

Frederick's fiery conservativism made him a firebrand in Nevada and nationwide—particularly in liberal circles. In 2009, Frederick wrote a column in reaction to US Senator Harry Reid (D-Nevada) saying that he hoped that the RJ would go out of business. That column brought a withering attack from former RJ columnist Jon Ralston, who moved to write for the Sun before quitting over another Reid controversy. The Sun killed Ralston's column on Reid.

"If you want to know the truth about the sad sack suffering from Pulitzer-envy who needs to engage in demagoguery to prop up his failing enterprise, the facts speak for themselves," Ralston wrote about Frederick.[101]

The following year, MSNBC left-wing talk show host Keith Olbermann named Frederick the "Worst Person in the World" for a column he wrote taking President Obama to task for not reacting quickly enough to terrorism attacks.[102]

To do his research on German, Frederick approached RJ staffers who knew the former Sun scribe. Many were still bitter. But some, even ones who clashed with German, grudgingly knew he was a good enough reporter that it was worth forgetting past slights.

Doug McMurdo covered courts for the RJ, competing with German when he was at the Sun. They worked in closet-sized courthouse offices, but the close quarters initially did not breed camaraderie. In fact, it was the opposite. McMurdo would try to talk to German only to get a door slammed in his face or have the surly Sun reporter turn and walk away without saying a word. Other reporters recall German walking past them at parties without even a gruff hello.

Eventually, German and McMurdo found a mutual respect. When Frederick asked his court reporter what he thought about hiring German, McMurdo gave a thumbs up.

"You can be an asshole and still be a good reporter," McMurdo thought.[103] Some would argue being an asshole helps develop the thick skin needed to be a good reporter. German's skin was about as thick as they come. German did have some friends at the RJ, as long they were not on beats that intersected with his. He was close to features editor Frank Fertado, who died in 2014, and Art Nadler.[104]

But there were many other staffers at the Review-Journal who were apprehensive about German joining the RJ. A.D. Hopkins, who ran the bigger paper's investigative team, was sore that German's stories tried to undercut his investigations.

In 1991, Hopkins uncovered that a gambler, who was convicted in a Boston College basketball point-shaving scandal, was palling around with University of Nevada-Las Vegas (UNLV) basketball players. NCAA prohibited of players from associating with gamblers. The RJ even published a photo of the gambler in a hot tub with three UNLV athletes.

German's bosses at the Sun were close to UNLV, especially the sports teams, which at the time were the only game in town if you wanted to attend live sporting events. Greenspun College of Urban Affairs and Hank Greenspun School of Journalism and Media Studies are prominent on the UNLV campus. He wrote stories to undercut Hopkins' point-shaving stories and defend towel-biting coach Jerry Tarkanian. That did not sit well with Hopkins. But even Hopkins' grudge was tempered by German's work on a story about the UNLV terrorism center. The RJ had heard the same rumors at German but couldn't confirm a scandal. Hopkins was impressed when German got the scoop.[105]

In March 2009, Frederick went to the paper's managing editor, Charles Zobell, asking him to talk to German about an RJ job. Zobell also had some concerns about hiring German because of stories he wrote that he thought carried water for the Greenspuns or their friends. Zobell took German to lunch. He grilled him about the suspect stories, and German answered all his concerns. The only thing to do was to come with a salary. The RJ wanted to make sure the paper was paying German more than the Sun.[106]

German started work at the RJ on April 21, 2010. He hustled to gain the respect and trust of his new bosses and colleagues. He also jumped on the chance to join the RJ's fantasy football league, which happened to have a rare opening in 2011. German had few interests or hobbies outside of work except for religiously following sports. Fantasy football allowed him to indulge his one non-journalistic interest and make friends with some of his former competitors. He jumped into the fantasy league with the same gusto that he reported a story.

Each year, German would take a few days off before Labor Day to research the players. The league met on Labor Day to make draft picks. He named his team "Oscar's Mob," a reference to Oscar Goodman and Vegas' Mob history. Participants warned German that this was a tough league and not to expect stellar results in his first year.

However, Oscar's Mob got off to a great start. German won the title and seven-hundred-dollar prize pool the first year. The league had been around for a decade and no one had won back-to-back titles so everyone figured German's luck would run out in 2012. It didn't. German also won the top prize that year. He won again in 2016, grabbing hundreds of dollars more in prize money but, more importantly, bragging rights. Never one to be humble around his victories, German approached another member of the league and inquired: "I thought this was a tough league?"

After German's death, David Ferrara, who worked with German covering courts at the RJ, took his spot on the team. Ferrara, a husky Chicago-area transplant, worked at news organizations around Chicago and in Mississippi before moving to Vegas in 2011 to play poker and freelance. Realizing the hard work it took to support himself at the poker tables, Ferrara decided to jump back into journalism full time. They say playing poker professionally is a "hard way to make an easy living."

Ferrara joined the RJ first as a reporter in 2014 and was later promoted to assistant city editor. He is arguably the paper's most dedicated gambler, often spending his free time at the Strip poker rooms or playing online. There are surprisingly few people at the RJ who gamble regularly or even know much about the games offered by the industry that drives Southern Nevada. Ironically, Ferrara's first year as owner of Oscar's Mob, the team came in last. German would not be happy, but Ferrara defends his poor showing by admitting he knows very little about football. After the first year, Benjamin Lipman, the Review-Journal's chief legal officer, took over Oscar's Mob.[107]

When German joined the RJ, Nevada's economy, heavily based on housing, was in the middle of a long dive into the Great Recession. The newspaper was quickly losing ad revenue and subscribers. Frederick looked for any niche that could make the paper additional revenue, coming up with an idea for a website that would provide inside information and gossip to lawyers, judges, and other members of the area's legal community. The Chicago Daily Law Bulletin and the New York Law Journal had dedicated subscriber bases eager to get the inside information about their profession. German and McMurdo were assigned to the new venture and asked to use their court sources and experience to fill up the legal wire.

In Las Vegas, however, there were just not enough attorneys willing to pay the hefty subscription fees to make a legal publication work. German and McMurdo tried to file stories for the wire but also developed them into print stories. That way they made sure they were valuable enough to stay at the paper when the wire inevitably went kaput. At its peak, the wire attracted about one hundred and fifty subscribers, which wasn't nearly enough to sustain two reporters' salaries. German and McMurdo were absorbed back into the Metro desk, covering courts for the print newspaper and digital website.

Three months after German joined the Review-Journal, James G. Wright came in as an editor. Like many in the business, Wright had worked at papers all over the country, from Albany to Seattle to Denver and Colorado Springs. He was running a small paper in Idaho and decided it wasn't for him when he heard about the opening at the Review-Journal.

Wright loved working with German because he required very little direction and found his stories independently. Wright would check in with him in the morning about what he planned to cover. He would have that story finished by afternoon. At the RJ, Jeff German wasn't by title an "investigative reporter," but he was always ready to dig. He got his chance when law enforcement uncovered a fraudulent scam involving lawyers, police, and HOA boards.[108]

Attorneys were bribing HOA boards and fixing their elections to gain control of the community groups. The corrupted boards would then file construction defects lawsuits on behalf of the HOA using the corrupt attorneys and steering construction contracts to certain firms that were in on the scam. Federal prosecutors dismantled the scheme, leading to a long line of arrests and even a few suicides. Nancy Quon, an attorney German knew well and who would talk only to him after her arrest, killed herself in March 2012 in the bathtub of her Henderson, Nevada, home. Another attorney implicated in the case was found hanged in California that same month.[109] Retired Metro Lieutenant Christopher Van Cleef shot himself after being linked to the scandal.[110] Soon, like in many Nevada scandals, federal prosecutors were also implicated in the corruption. German broke a story that employees of the US Attorney's Office were under investigation for leaking information to one of the suspects that would have allowed her to destroy or alter evidence.[111]

If he wasn't researching his fantasy football team, German was working the phones either to find a story, confirm a tip, or talk to people about a story he already published. Most reporters move on after their story is published, but he liked to call people who knew about the issue or were quoted to see whether they liked the piece. His follow-up calls were both a way to get affirmation for his work and to see if there were any follow-ups he could write. He regularly quizzed sources: "What else? What else you got? What else do you know?"

German led the coverage of the HOA scandal with his typical scorched-earth style. One day at the federal courthouse, German ran into Glen Meek with whom he competed on the Binion case when Meek was a television journalist. Meek, who moved between journalism and government jobs, was then working as an investigator in the federal public defender's office.

"Listen, I need the 302s on that case," he queried Meek, referring to the FBI investigative reports detailing an interview with a suspect or witness that are known by that number. "Can you get me copies?"

Meek demurred, saying he didn't feel comfortable providing the records. Meek was shocked that German would make such a blunt approach. They were never friends and had no professional relationship. They were just occasional competitors. He felt there was no subtlety.

However, German's take-no-prisoners approach worked, allowing him to out-report any competition. Colleagues and supervisors remembered that the Sun just gave up covering the HOA scandal because they couldn't compete with

German.[112] About forty people eventually pled guilty or were convicted as part of the wide-ranging probe, German reported in 2015.[113] By the time it ended, he wrote hundreds of stories for the RJ about the HOA scandal over more than four years.

Jeff German's work started to appear often on the front page of the Review-Journal and his colleagues warmed to him, respecting his hard work and newly found collegial attitude. But the Review-Journal was undergoing the same turmoil German had witnessed at the Sun and that was impacting newspapers around the country. Ad revenue and subscriptions declined and layoffs were a regular minefield that all journalists scrambled to avoid.

Newspapers are filled with quirky and eccentric people, and in Vegas, it was no different—or maybe more so because of the crazy location. There were a series of assistant managing editors who Wright was pretty sure hadn't worked in years and were just required to hide in their offices to receive a paycheck. Another top editor was sure the internet was a fad. That editor would tell anyone who would listen that the internet is just one credit-card-leaking scandal from being shut down, Wright recalled.[114]

About six months after hiring German, Frederick was ousted as publisher. He was named a consultant and columnist. Executive Editor Thomas Mitchell went from the top spot in the newsroom to a senior opinion editor. Less than a year later in 2012, more cuts came, with Zobell, Fertado, City Editor Mary Hynes, Sports Editor Joe Hawk, Art Director Ched Whitney, and Editorial Page Editor John Kerr getting the ax. Wright, then the business editor, had his job consolidated with Hynes' position to make him deputy editor of the paper.[115]

The Review-Journal went through a series of owners, some of whom were very cheap and others who were just cheap. They often didn't care much about the local content, leaving the staff to their own devices. At times, however, the news staff would win a surprise journalistic jackpot. Wright's reporters were investigating a series of shootings by Metro officers—many of which did not appear justified. The reporters needed key records to complete the investigation. Metro put up its typical roadblocks to transparency and accountability by demanding thirty-three thousand dollars for the documents. The reporters talked the cops down to ten thousand, which was still an obscene amount for one records request. Surprisingly, Bob Brown, the publisher at the time, agreed that the newspaper would pay it.

Brown rarely interfered in the newsroom, except when he needed to please an advertiser. He approached Wright with a story about a car dealer and advertiser who claimed he owned the tallest cow in the land. Wright found a freelancer to do the story and it actually was funny enough to attract significant readership. Wright was willing to assign a story that had little journalistic merit once in a while if he could also get ten thousand dollars for a speculative, hard-hitting piece. The shooting investigation would win the Nevada Press Association's Award for Community Service and Freedom of the Press Reporting in 2012.[116]

The paper hummed along for a few years with German part of a team that covered the courts but there was a big change in the air. GateHouse Media purchased Stephens Media in February 2015, taking over the RJ and other papers in Nevada and Arkansas. Stephens had owned the paper for more than two decades.[117]

In November 2015, the RJ's three court reporters (German, Ferrara, and Carri Geer Thevenot) were given a strange assignment directly from corporate. The three were directed to pick a judge and cover everything that came before that court docket, no matter how minor and not newsworthy. One of the judges specified by top executives was District Court Judge Elizabeth Gonzalez, who had been hearing a wrongful termination lawsuit against the Las Vegas Sands Corporation. Former Sands executive Steve Jacobs alleged Sands managers directed him to do inappropriate things in Macau and had fired him when he protested. The case prompted the SEC and Justice Department to look into whether Sands was bribing foreign officials.[118] Sands responded in court papers that Jacobs was fired for failing to prevent the situation. Sands was owned by billionaire Sheldon Adelson, a controversial figure in Las Vegas and on the national political scene, where he contributed millions of dollars to get Republicans elected.

Adelson was born in 1933 into extreme poverty in South Boston and worked hard to become one of the country's wealthiest men. In his early teens, Adelson bought a license to sell newspapers on certain corners and eventually started a business selling candy in vending machines. Throughout his career, Adelson tried everything from venture capital investing to condo sales to charter travel. He hit it big when he organized a computer tradeshow, Comdex, that would bring computer enthusiasts annually to Las Vegas. He also bought the old Sands Hotel, famed playground of Frank Sinatra and the Rat Pack, to build the Sands Expo and Convention Center. Eventually, he sold Comdex, demolished the Sands Casino and built the luxury Venetian resort and later a twin property named Palazzo. He also made a foray into Macau, China, casinos. A staunch supporter of a Jewish homeland, the Adelsons made investments in newspaper in Israel, the home country of his second wife, Miriam Adelson (née Farbstein).

Adelson worked his way up to become the richest man in Nevada. His fortune roller-coastered from twenty-six billion to thirty-eight billion dollars and back over the past decade, according to Forbes. Drawing the ire of liberals everywhere, Sheldon and Miriam Adelson contributed more than half a billion dollars to federal conservative causes and Republican candidates, starting in the early 1990s. When Donald Trump ran for president in 2016, the Adelsons flooded his campaign with money. Over approximately three decades, the couple contributed $26.3 million to state Republican candidates and anti-drug initiatives, mostly in Nevada but also in other states, records from Opensecrets.org and Center for Responsive Politics show.[119] Sheldon Adelson had also tried and previously failed to buy the Review-Journal.[120]

During the Jacobs wrongful termination trial, Judge Gonzalez had clashed with Adelson while he was on the stand. Sands attorneys attempted to get her removed from the case, saying she showed a bias. That was thwarted by the Nevada Supreme Court.[121]

During that contentious case, strange things were happening. A story published under a pen name that criticized Gonzalez's rulings appeared in two papers in the suburbs of Hartford, Connecticut—thousands of miles from Las Vegas.[122] The Connecticut paper's publisher was Michael Schroeder, a disheveled man—shirttail hanging out of his ill-fitting suit and known by his staff as loud and boisterous but close to advertisers, according a New York Times story.[123] About the same time, GateHouse directed German, Geer Thevenot, and Ferrara to keep close tabs on Gonzalez and other judges.

"You've got to be shitting me," German told Wright when he broached the assignment. Geer Thevenot and Ferrara (who was chosen for the Gonzalez assignment) were confused, angered, and concerned. But an assignment was an assignment so they relented, filing a fifteen-thousand-word summary of the day-to-day workings of the three judges that found nothing untoward. It was sent off to GateHouse corporate, where it promptly was never heard from again.[124]

On December 10, 2015, employees at the Review-Journal were called to an all-staff meeting. RJ Publisher Jason Taylor would regularly hold what Wright dubbed "rah, rah" sessions, but this one was different. Las Vegas Review-Journal editor Mike Hengel had just been in a meeting where top newspaper supervisors were told the paper was sold again. Hengel caught up with Wright as he was walking to the internal event and told him that he would want a reporter and photographer cover it.[125]

Wright looked at Hengel and said: "They've sold us again?"

At the "rah, rah," Taylor took his time getting to the point, discussing advertising and some minor awards the paper won. Then he introduced Michael Schroeder,[126] who would discuss some changes in the paper. Schroeder told the staff that the RJ had been sold, and he was the new manager. His name was the only one on the corporation that bought the RJ and related papers.

Hengel raised his hand to ask who bought the paper.

"They just want you to focus on your jobs, and not worry about who they are or what they do," Schroeder responded.[127]

Howard Stutz, the RJ's gaming reporter, leaned over to Wright and said: "It's Sheldon, isn't it?"[128]

Wright, not knowing anything more than the rest of the staff, just had to shrug. After the meeting, Wright and Hengel met in Hengel's office. They decided they had to get to the bottom of who bought the RJ.

Wright selected three business reporters—Stutz, James DeHaven, and Jennifer Robison—to dig into the new owners. German and the others who were given the strange judge-stalking assignment wanted on the team, but Wright felt the people investigating the ownership should be independent of that assignment. He also sought staff who were looking to leave anyway in case there was retribution for the assignment.

A week after the announced sale, the reporters confirmed that the one-hundred- and forty-million-dollar purchase, which experts said was far above the market value of the RJ and related papers, was funded and orchestrated by Adelson and his family. They had the story ready to post and were just waiting for Taylor's approval.[129] Hengel kept trying to get his sign off but the publisher was atypically difficult to reach. Finally, at about seven p.m., Hengel sent Taylor a message saying he would post the story if he didn't hear from him. He didn't. The story ran on the RJ website to much interest in Las Vegas and around the country.[130]

The New York Times, NPR, New Yorker, the Atlantic, and CNN all covered the purchase of a metro newspaper in Las Vegas, and the reporters who had broken the story of the secret ownership. Review-Journal writers and editors were awarded the James Foley Medill Medal for Courage in Journalism in 2015 for breaking the story of Adelson's purchase.[131] Glenn Cook, who wrote an editorial saying the ownership is free to change the editorial page but should stay out of interfering with news content, was part of the team that won the award.[132] After being promoted to managing editor, Cook would come under criticism by some of the anti-Adelson journalists who left the paper for allegedly letting Adelson impact coverage. But after the exposé ran, the reporters involved were treated as heroes who took on the conservative Goliath. The Review-Journal reporters were quoted widely in national news stories (Robison, DeHaven, and Stutz either declined or did not respond to requests for comment for this book). Wright was surprised by the widespread coverage, figuring the issue wouldn't have national interest beyond Nevada.

But the new RJ top editors thought it was the perfect storyline for the liberal East Coast elite media: a conservative billionaire Republican megadonor purchases the largest newspaper in the glistening party town of Las Vegas and uses it to push his own interests and attack his detractors while a small group of journalists at the paper battle their corporate ownership to reveal the truth.

Adelson was not considered press friendly. He had a history of filing libel lawsuits against journalists. There were clearly indications early in the purchase and maybe even before that Adelson hoped to use the paper to influence and undermine opponents. As a business owner, Adelson didn't always abide by the standards of transparency and accountability that journalists expect of everyone they cover.

Adelson clearly made serious mistakes in the purchase of the RJ and early in the family's ownership. But it also appeared that much of the liberal media acted like they didn't believe conservatives should own major papers. When Rupert Murdock bought the Wall Street Journal, there was mass outrage. Not so much when Amazon billionaire Jeff Bezos bought the venerable Washington Post, or Warren Buffett wanted to keep his hometown paper in Omaha, The World-Herald, from collapse. The national media—either from liberal bias or laziness—would return to the Adelson and RJ storyline even when the facts didn't match reality.

The Adelson family had no experience with newspapers in the United States and were shocked at the universal condemnation of the purchase.

"By the way, newspapers are the first of over 50 companies that I started where my employees tell me how to run my business," Adelson told The New York Times.

Keith Moyer, brought in from Minnesota as executive editor, said Adelson's "hair was blown back by the reaction to their initial mistakes."

Many of the journalists—Hegel, Wright, DeHaven, Robison, and Stutz—involved in uncovering the Adelson purchase would soon be gone. German, Geer Thevenot, and Ferrara would stay as a whole new group of journalists who would take jobs at the Review-Journal.

Jeff German would never throw his lot in with the journalists who were concerned about Adelson purchasing the paper. He was happy that someone was going to fund his journalism instead of looking for cuts and layoffs. "It's like the old days for me," he told Slate.com after the purchase. "I never thought I'd have this much fun in the journalism business again."

CHAPTER SIX: ADELSON ERA

In 2016, former USA Today Publisher Craig Moon called J. Keith Moyer. The two had worked at the Arkansas Gazette in the early 1990s. Moyer, born in 1952, went into journalism to be a sportswriter but never ended up even covering one game for a newspaper. Instead, he worked his way up from covering transportation and city government at small Florida newspapers to the top editor and then publisher of some of the major metro and regional papers in the United States, including the Fresno Bee and the (Minneapolis) Star-Tribune. In 2006, Moyer, as publisher, helped to orchestrate the sale of the Star-Tribune, known colloquially as the Strib, to a private equity firm. After the sale, he retired to teach at the University of Minnesota.

Moon had just been appointed the new publisher of the Review-Journal, and he wanted to know if Moyer would move to Vegas and run the paper. Moyer's first response was that Moon was on his own for this one. Adelson's purchase had been a mess, and Moyer wasn't about to damage his reputation by stepping into that steaming pile. But Moon persisted.[133] Moyer, who was in his early sixties, thought this might be one last challenge to turn a mediocre newspaper into a journalistic powerhouse.

Moon promised there would be no Adelson interference in the news product, and a flood of money to hire reporters, including the formation of a six-person investigative team. A team of that size for a newspaper with the Review-Journal's circulation during the collapse of the industry would be unheard of and historic. Moyer yearned to go back to journalism as he didn't really consider being a newspaper publisher a journalistic endeavor. A publisher was a businessman. An editor shaped news and content, which was Moyer's first and enduring love. A big investigative team was like a military special forces unit that he could unleash on any corrupt and wasteful agency that came to his attention. That made his decision.

Before taking the job, Moyer met with Adelson and his family, getting assurances they would not meddle. They even promised not to go to the newspaper's dingy, windowless offices and printing facility that the family now owned. The family also repeated the promise of additional resources to beef up staff. By all accounts, Adelson had overpaid for the newspaper, but the family was going to pour more money into the unprofitable enterprise. For billionaires, a few hundred million were a rounding error. Moyer got the sense that the Adelson's wanted their hometown to have a good newspaper and were willing to spend what it took to do that.

Moyer knew it wasn't going to be easy. The Review-Journal, at the time, was not considered a great metro paper. He had friends calling to demand, "Are you fucking crazy?" The MinnPost, a non-profit journalism website in the Twin Cities, headlined a story: "FORMER STRIB PUBLISHER KEITH MOYER JUST SIGNED UP FOR THE MOST SCRUTINIZED JOB IN AMERICAN JOURNALISM." The story said Moyer was stepping "into the roiling cauldron of suspicion" and the paper was "shedding newsroom leaders like a drunken frat boy spilling chips in a cheap casino."

It was a rocky start and one of the most stressful jobs of Moyer's career. The newspaper appeared in open revolt when he arrived to take the helm on February 5, 2016. And the national media supplied internal critics with regular negative coverage of the paper and the conflict over the ownership.

In April, the New Yorker dedicated more than 2,300 words to the paper under the headline "HOW THE *LAS VEGAS*

REVIEW-JOURNAL UNMASKED ITS OWNERS." The Atlantic and Mother Jones published pieces with nearly identical headlines. "WHY DID SHELDON ADELSON BUY NEVADA'S LARGEST NEWSPAPER?" wondered an Atlantic story by former Las Vegas Sun writer turned national Time Magazine reporter Molly Ball. That story ran in December 2015. Two months later, Mother Jones published a timeline of the events under the headline: "WHY DID SHELDON ADELSON BUY NEVADA'S BIGGEST PAPER?" National media dug into every little aspect of the controversy, including a nearly 1,300-word story in the New York Times about Schroeder's role in the purchase. CNN posted a 4,300-word treatise by Slate.com titled, "INSIDE SHELDON ADELSON'S JOURNALISTIC GAMBLE." NPR repeatedly weighed in, including focusing on Adelson's propensity to sue journalists for libel.

On January 14, 2016, NPR's media writer David Folkenflik published nearly 2,500 words about an ongoing battle between RJ columnist John L. Smith and Adelson. Adelson sued Smith in 2005 over a passage in a book that tried to connect the casino mogul's rise to organized crime gangs in Boston.

Adelson's lawsuit bluntly laid out the mistakes. "John L. Smith deceptively manipulates language, quotations and sources in order to concoct the smear that Adelson had dealings with the Boston Mob when Adelson was in the vending machine business," Adelson's lawyers wrote. The lawsuit notes a $3.1 million prior jury verdict against Smith's publisher that was reversed due to erroneous jury instructions and says the reversal that emboldened Smith. The lawsuit charges Smith's timeline in the book is decades and miles off. Smith tried to link Adelson to Mob-vending businesses in Boston in the 1970s when Adelson's involvement in the vending business was in a city twenty-five miles away from Boston and twenty-five years before the Mob entered the business. The lawsuit also claims Smith's book erroneously said Adelson had to answer questions before the Nevada

State Gaming Control Board about forgiving loans to "underworld characters" when there were neither such loans nor questions from regulators.

Smith, according to Folkenflik, conceded the problems with his book. He and his publisher, Barricade Books (which is probably most famous for publishing The Anarchist Cookbook that provided recipes of bomb and drug manufacturing for budding anarchists), offered to make corrections in unsold copies of the book. Smith offered to write a column in the RJ with the corrections (Smith declined repeated requests for an interview for this book and the owner of Barricade named in the lawsuits has since died).

Smith also inexplicably played on emotions in the Folkenflik story without addressing the allegations in the lawsuit of inaccuracy, libel, and intentional malice. "I was sued at a time when my daughter was in the hospital being treated for brain cancer," Smith was quoted in the NPR story. "I thought it was particularly cruel, quite frankly."

Smith is quoted in the NPR story saying Adelson's representatives offered a settlement where Smith would "admit that I meant to malign him, and libel him, and paid a [one] dollar judgment, which would have ended my career." Adelson also offered to pay up to two hundred thousand dollars of his daughter's medical bills, Smith said, but he chose to fight the case and go into bankruptcy. Adelson dismissed the case, according to the NPR story, though the court docket doesn't show the resolution and attorneys involved in the case were either deceased or could not remember what happened. Other news stories say Smith won the case.[134]

Folkenflik was drawn to the Adelson controversy after noticing a small news item that the owners of the largest newspaper in Nevada were unknown. He thought it was a ridiculous lack of transparency, calling it "crazy, comical and alarming." Through the reporting he learned that Adelson sued one Smith before buying the paper.

"Jesus, that's a story," he thought. "How better to illustrate the potential tension or conflict between personal and corporate interests on one hand and the notion of service the public on the other."

It took weeks to convince Smith to talk to him, but Folkenflik didn't press Smith on whether he really had a grudge against Adelson and why his work was the focus of so many libel claims from Nevada's top casino owners.

"To me the story is about how Adelson reacts," Folkenflik said. "I'm not saying everything Smith did was right and he acknowledged to me there were shortcomings.

"To me the question for a national audience with a local stake is what is the nature of this new proprietor of the state's most important news outlet."[135]

On January 28, 2016, RJ publisher Moon informed Smith he could not write about Adelson because he had a conflict of interest because of the libel cases against him. Newspaper management felt that since the lawsuits were about publications outside of Smith's work for the Review-Journal, there would be an appearance of conflict about Smith writing about Adelson. Smith stayed with the paper for three months until Moyer discussed the ban at a journalism forum. Moyer also learned that Steve Wynn also filed a lawsuit against Smith and Barricade over advertising for Smith's book about Wynn. Smith was dismissed from the case as he proved he did not participate in the advertising campaign that Wynn claimed also attempted to link him to organized crime.[136] Moyer told Smith he also couldn't write about Wynn since the other casino mogul also sued him for outside work and not something he wrote for the newspaper.

After Moyer told Smith he couldn't write about Wynn either and the ban became public, Smith quit, writing if "you don't have the freedom to call the community's heavyweights to account, then that 'commentary' tag isn't worth the paper on which it's printed." The New York Times, Politico, Salon.com, the Guardian, and NPR all wrote stories about the resignation of a columnist, who most of their readers probably never heard of before the controversy.

The pieces pushed the angle that Adelson was behind the Smith writing ban without any proof. The stories also downplayed the fact that Smith stayed at the RJ for months after the Adelson ban and only quit after the Wynn ban and the Adelson ban became public. Headlines like "COLUMNIST QUITS OVER BAN ON HIM WRITING ABOUT BILLIONAIRE SHELDON ADELSON" in the Guardian and NPR's "LAS VEGAS COLUMNIST QUITS AFTER BAN ON WRITING ABOUT ADELSON" would have been more accurate if they said: "COLUMNIST QUITS MONTHS AFTER BAN ABOUT HIM WRITING ABOUT BILLIONAIRE SHELDON ADELSON." Those facts, however, would get in the way of the prevailing narrative.

Moyer explained that the appearance was the problem. Media ethics experts like Folkenflik and Poynter's Kelly McBride agree that Smith's position at the paper was untenable for him and management.[137]

"I never suggested or believed John would use his column to settle a personal score, but if his writing on Adelson and Wynn created even a perception of score settling in the minds of readers, then it would have reflected on the credibility of the institution," Moyer was quoted in Folkenflik's NPR story. "Invoking 'conflict of interest' restrictions might not be common in Nevada, but they are elsewhere... The real question reporters should be asking is: 'Did Sheldon Adelson order the ban?' But I suspect they're not asking that because they've already made up their minds that he did. Shame on them."[138]

Smith joined the Nevada Independent, founded by Jon Ralston.[139] Stutz also joined Ralston's Indy. Wright became Investigations Editor at the Louisville Courier Journal in Kentucky. In 2016, Robison took a public relations job at Pacific Gas and Electric Company—a company whose CEO would plead guilty to eighty-four involuntary manslaughter charges for negligence in sparking a 2018 fire that nearly wiped out a small town in the Sacramento Valley. It was not the only time PG&E faced criminal charges for killing residents with its negligence, but Robison still worked for the company in 2023, her LinkedIn profile shows. (She did not respond to emails sent to her work, outreach by a colleague, a LinkedIn message, and phone numbers that public records sources linked to her.)[140]

Reporters who remained at the RJ and new hires continued to vigilantly look for an undue influence from Adelson. When marijuana reporter Colton Lochhead was sent to Denver to cover how cannabis legalization impacted Colorado, he perceived that editors were steering him to show that drug legalization damaged the region. Adelson, who lost a son to a cocaine and heroin overdose, was vehemently against Nevada legalizing the drug. After his purchase, the editorial department changed from supporting legal pot to opposing it. Lochhead felt editors were trying to influence the direction of the story without knowing what his reporting showed. He wrote what he found out about Colorado's legalization. The piece ran without major changes.[141]

The Jacobs lawsuit continued to be a journalistic thorn. Top editors, according to Wright, required that sections from an exclusively obtained filing in the case be published verbatim. Sands settled the lawsuit with Jacobs for an undisclosed amount in 2016.

But Jeff German, still sore from his Las Vegas Sun layoff and accustomed to strong-willed owners who may push their agendas, appreciated the new resources that a billionaire owner provided the Review-Journal. In 2016, Moyer started putting together the investigative team that the Adelson money would allow him to form. He hired a headhunting firm to look for an editor, and they reached out to Chicago Tribune investigative reporter Karisa King. King had never been an editor, but she was attracted to the opportunity of building her own team in a vibrant, news-rich place like Las Vegas.

Joining the staff in September 2016, King talked to Moyer about whether anyone currently on staff should be considered for the new team. Moyer suggested one person: Jeff German. Within an hour of leaving the meeting with Moyer—probably more like fifteen minutes after—German was in King's windowless, cramped office pitching his experience, sources, and knowledge of the city. He clearly wanted to get on the team. When King asked German for investigative story ideas, the one that stood out to King as the most likely to have wide-ranging impact was questionable spending and conflicts of interest at the Las Vegas Convention and Visitors Authority. Sources had been telling German about abuses and spending at the government agency for years, but the paper had surprisingly never done a deep dive into the politically connected authority and its long-time CEO Rossi Ralenkotter. After meeting German, King was convinced he should join the unit, and he was quickly moved from courts to investigations.

In the fall of 2016, King was having trouble filing the rest of the openings with qualified reporters. Under any other circumstances, an investigative reporting job opening at a major metro daily would have been flooded with applicants. But the controversy over the Adelson purchase and Vegas' reputation for being less-than-family friendly created a dearth of qualified candidates.

In Denver, long-time journalist Arthur Kane was working for a non-profit that was losing its funding. Kane had moved to Denver sixteen years earlier to work for the Denver Post covering city hall, the statehouse, and eventually working as an editor. When he was hired, the Post was quickly increasing staff and circulation, but seven years later, regular layoffs were instituted and morale plummeted. Kane left to work as a producer and executive producer for investigations at the local ABC affiliate. There he was part of a team that won two duPont-Columbia Awards—known as the broadcast Pulitzer—as well as a Peabody, the award for the best television. Then—when the station was bought by the same company that closed the Post's competitor, the Rocky Mountain News—he took a series of jobs at shakily funded non-profit investigative reporting websites. Throughout his career, Kane had interest from national publications like the New York Times and Wall Street Journal. But he had fallen in love with the western part of the United States and couldn't see moving to New York, Washington, DC, or Atlanta, which would have been required to take those jobs.

Despite working at smaller publications, Kane had built a strong reputation as an investigative reporter. He saw King's posting on the Investigative Reporters and Editors website and sent her a resume and story links. The two exchanged emails, and he told her he was traveling to Vegas in November to play some poker tournaments. She asked if he would stop by for an interview. The week before Christmas, Kane started as the first outside hire on the RJ's investigative team. King eventually hired three more reporters for the unit, which set out to make its mark on Southern Nevada.

As part of the purchase, the newspaper was undergoing a redesign for its print and digital editions. Moyer wanted to make a big investigative splash that showed off the paper's new design as well as highlighting the investigative unit. In mid-December, Moyer, Cook, King, Kane, and German met to discuss a story to anchor the redesign, which was scheduled to be finished in April.

It was Kane's second day at the paper. He had already started working on an investigation of public officials who collected taxpayer-funded salaries at the same time they collected government pensions. He pitched that story for the redesign not knowing his reporting would later kick up controversy in the corporate offices. One of the prominent double-dippers was notoriously thin-skinned Sheriff Joe Lombardo. Kane found that Lombardo collected a $163,000 pension on top of his $161,000 salary in 2016. Kane also backgrounded Lombardo as would-be standard practice for a reporter looking into one of the county's top politicians. Kane dug into divorce records, property filings, and financial disclosures. He found the expensive house where Lombardo lived, rental properties, cars, and other goodies Lombardo could afford with his double-dipping of public money. When Lombardo refused to do an interview that spring for the story, Kane let Lombardo's spokesman know that he would try to find the sheriff at a public function to discuss the pension and pay. Lombardo, not used to being questioned aggressively, went to Moon to complain. Moon told Moyer that he needed to fire Kane because Lombardo was upset at his tactics.

"You can fire Kane but you'll have to fire me first," Moyer told Moon.

That ended the matter, but Kane only found out about his close call with unemployment years after Moon "retired" from the paper in 2018. Moon's departure was suspicious and Moyer said he was fired despite the newspaper story that labeling it as "retirement."

A year later, despite a career change flacking for corporate felons, Robison again wrote about the RJ in Columbia Journalism Review. She described allegations of sexual harassment against Moon and Moyer.[142] Moyer was described in the piece as making crude jokes, but Moon was alleged to have attempted to kiss a subordinate. Robison wrote that she planned to publish the story in Ralston's Indy but the Indy backed out, fearing a financial hit from potential RJ litigation.

Moyer and Moon denied any wrongdoing and their attorneys maintained the former employees were disgruntled and made up the claims.[143] Around that time, Moyer was called to a meeting at the Venetian on a Sunday afternoon.

He thought the ax might fall on him, but instead, he was offered the publisher's job.[144]

Vegas media has a long history of allowing top officials and connected businessmen to influence their coverage, which is abhorrent to reporters but happens at publications around the country. It just seems more blatant in Vegas. Ralston quit the Las Vegas Sun after Brian Greenspun killed a column he wrote on Harry Reid.[145] After the Wall Street Journal reported allegations of sexual harassment against casino owner Steve Wynn, RJ city editor Carri Geer Thevenot, who was a court reporter at the time, dug into her archive to show that the RJ killed a story about similar allegations against Wynn filed in a 1998 lawsuit.[146]

Editors assigned Kane to write the mea culpa for the paper's misdeeds in the Wynn case. But the national media again couldn't write about the RJ without insinuating— without proof—that Adelson was behind the piece because of his "on-again, off-again" rivalry with Wynn. With an unbelievable straw-man headline—"VEGAS NEWSPAPER STAFFERS REJECT CLAIMS THAT WYNN STORY WAS A HIT PIECE"—CNN writers Tom Kludt and Hadas Gold suggested the story was more about Adelson attacking Wynn than what it really was—a journalistic exercise of transparency to reveal past journalistic sins at the Review-Journal.

CNN's main evidence of Adelson's influence was Cook's denial that Adelson had anything to do with the story, and Ralston wondering (with zero proof) whether Adelson's relationship with Wynn had something to do with the story. Then the story quoted Steve Friess, a freelance journalist who covered the Vegas gaming industry and briefly wrote for the Review-Journal three decades earlier. Friess "told CNNMoney that he finds it hard to believe Adelson did not know the story was coming... Friess said he thinks that 'somebody talked to somebody talked to somebody.'" Gold called Kane for comment but failed to even leave a phone number or contact email on his work voicemail. Kane tried to contact her through Twitter because CNN reporters are insulated from direct calls by viewers, but she did not respond. (Kludt couldn't remember what happened with the story, referring Kane to who he thought was the editor on it; that editor also couldn't remember specifics; Gold could not be reached for comment.[147])

***

In December 2016, as the RJ editors were figuring out what would lead the redesign, Kane's PERS story was deemed not broadly interesting enough for the spot. (The double dipping story eventually ran on Sunday, July 7, 2017, on the front page.) German brought up the LVCVA story. At the Denver television station, Kane had produced a number of stories about a Colorado government agency—this one, the worker's compensation provider of last resort—that was also spending massive amounts of money wining and dining board members at fancy resorts. Kane loved the government misspending stories both because they generated outrage from taxpayers and because there were often very compelling details of lavish, unnecessary spending of tax money to write about. He thought those kinds of stories concretely demonstrated the waste and lack of accountability often found in government.

Jeff German, always relying on sources, wanted to call around to former employees and people who might know about the LVCVA misspending. Kane, often overbearing and just as cocky as his older colleague, insisted that the only way to do it was with public records. Over the years they worked together, the two men often clashed. Sometimes it was about minor things like who would be the first name on a byline, but other times there were serious strategic differences about how to report a story or when it should run.

At first, Kane bristled at German's failure to keep up his skill set, relying almost solely on a phone, lunch meetings, and his contacts. While not an expert on advanced techniques, Kane attended conferences and training sessions, developing extensive skills in public records' research, computer-assisted reporting, and website scraping. German couldn't even open a spreadsheet. Editors were concerned about the conflict, but the healthy competition often drove the reporters to uncover better stories or dig deeper on issues.

Eventually, the two found mutual respect especially when German started to see the value of some of the records and data techniques that Kane and other team members used to produce stories that just couldn't be written by making phone calls. Kane also found German's encyclopedic knowledge of Vegas and vast network of sources very useful. Why spend hours digging through clips when German could give a briefing of the history of an issue or person in a few minutes? Before taking the job, Kane had only been in Vegas for vacations and poker tournaments, so he had zero sources in his first few months.

He started collecting sources after breaking a story about then-Henderson Constable Earl Mitchell using public money to gamble and travel to see family. Mitchell's indictment sparked by the work attracted gadflies, disgruntled government officials, and even law enforcement to secretly tip Kane on significant stories because they knew he would be able to get the story out and have an impact. Kane and German's divergent styles, preferences, and skill sets complimented each other and significantly improved the Review-Journal's journalism.

Kane also quickly learned the pleasures that many of German's friends and former Las Vegas Sun colleagues found in teasing and giving him a hard time. German handled the ball busting so badly that he made an irresistible target. It was almost like he went to a high school with no bullying because he just never had a good response or witty comeback to the ridicule. German often inflated his importance and stroked his ego by discussing his past successes and long history of reporting in Nevada, so he was definitely a target who needed to be brought down a peg or two, Kane thought.

At one point, German unfathomably announced that he was a fan of Katy Perry, a style of "music" almost exclusively enjoyed by prepubescent girls who think that Britney Spears and Miley Cyrus are too hardcore. Kane could hardly believe his luck at such an opening. Since his early teen years, Kane had been a dedicated devotee of heavy metal bands like Black Sabbath, Judas Priest, Slayer, Motörhead, and later, Tool and Pantera. He attended shows whenever he could and collected memorabilia from the bands of his youth. It was a way to stay connected to a different but important time in his earlier life. Kane had very strong opinions about what qualified as artistically significant music and what was not. He may slam a fan of a band he loved if that person favored an inferior album of the group. Not a sports fan, Kane ignored the often-heated debates German would have with other members of the investigative team and newsroom about the latest basketball game or chances of victory for the football team. Art and music were Kane's obsessions.

Kane enjoyed debating a band, album, or song's merits with anyone who would engage though he never found a target as easy as a Katy Perry enthusiast. German, seeing the fatal unforced error he had committed, tried to play his comment off by suggesting that he just found Perry physically attractive. No one was buying the unconvincing justification.

For months, German would never hear the end of his faux pas. Leaving work on a Friday, he would wish Kane a good weekend, and Kane would respond by asking if he was planning to attend any Katy Perry shows. If Perry was in town for a concert (which was surprisingly often), Kane would spam German's email with links to Ticketmaster seats for the concert. When German drove members of the investigative team to lunch, Kane would search his vehicle for any incriminating Katy Perry or maybe Backstreet

Boys CDs. Even King, who as editor tried to keep herself professionally above the fray in the unit, could not resist— once referencing the cartoonish pop diva when German was discussing his weekend plans in front of the rest of the team. That was so out of character that everyone in earshot nearly fell off their chairs laughing.

There was time for good-natured ribbing, but there also needed to be some hard work coming out of the new investigative team. The unit was a major investment for the newspaper—likely costing seven to eight hundred thousand dollars a year just in salaries and benefits—so it had to produce. It was also touted as the main force in improving the RJ's somewhat lackluster journalistic reputation. Any stories the unit produced would be under a microscope so there had to be impact and results. Many of the team members—other than German—were new to the paper. They had to prove their worth and justify their salaries, which were far above many veteran metro reporters and maybe even some editors.

So after the top editors decided that the LVCVA investigation would lead the redesign, the reporters jumped into action. Kane left the meeting and emailed the LVCVA spokesman an open records request seeking thirteen different document types, including salaries, bonuses, contracts, travel expenses, and gifts.

In about a month, the agency produced more than thirty thousand pages of records. German was overwhelmed, figuring it was impossible to sort through. The team had just added another reporter, Brian Joseph, a diminutive investigator who had worked for newspapers in California and a non-profit. Kane and Joseph showed the technologically unsavvy German how to use a spreadsheet to log various questionable expenses. Dividing the stack of paper records between the three of them, they sat for weeks at a row of three desks logging and calling out what they found.

"Here's a seven-thousand-dollar dinner with three-hundred-dollar steaks," one reporter would uncover.

"Here's an eleven hundred dollars for bottle service," another would chime in.

The investigation bylined Arthur Kane, Brian Joseph, and Jeff German exposed hundreds of thousands in questionable spending at the LVCVA staff. The agency maintained it need to spend tax money on alcohol and other questionable to attract visitors and convention business. But the reporters found considerable questionable spending both on LVCVA employees and the elected officials appointed to the board and charged with watching over it. The corruption and conflicts were clearly spelled out in the thousands of pages of spending records. The story cataloged "$697,000 for alcohol, $85,000 to hire showgirls and hundreds of thousands more for concert tickets, skyboxes, banquets, exotic car rides and jewelry for employees."[148]

The reaction from RJ detractors and the LVCVA was swift, blaming—without proof, again—that Adelson had directed the paper to investigate the government competitor to his Sands Convention Center. At the next LVCVA meeting, the board's Vice Chairman Chuck Bowling, an executive at MGM Resorts International's Mandalay Bay, lashed out at the paper. Behind the scenes, public relations staff tried to connect critics of LVCVA spending with Adelson campaign contributions, and called the recent RJ hires "charlatan carpetbaggers," according to emails German and Kane dug up after the story ran and published to the agency's chagrin.[149]

"The authors went out of their way to ignore certain important facts to try to paint a negative picture of the LVCVA," Bowling said, noting that the agency attracts twelve dollars of business to Las Vegas for every dollar it spends. "Any cursory review of the facts show the LVCVA is by far the most successful destination management organization in the country."

Adelson detractors figured—without knowing German's tips sparked the story—that Adelson was behind it as an attempt to undercut the primary rival to his Sands Convention Center. When he first came to Las Vegas, Moyer had talked to Wright about whether the LVCVA was ripe for an investigation, so Wright assumed Adelson ordered up the story. He conceded that the investigation found significant misspending but couldn't give a convincing justification for why the paper hadn't previously investigated the prominent agency. The RJ staff considered probing the agency before Adelson bought the paper, but Wright contended that reporters were too busy with other stories to pursue the investigation before Adelson's takeover of the paper. Even people long gone from the RJ saw Adelson's hand in the story. Zobell, when he was an RJ editor, ran into Adelson, who complained about a taxpayer-funded agency competing with his convention center. He also was surprised to learn German had come up with the story idea. To increase transparency, every story the paper ran that had to do with Adelson or the Sands Corporation carried a disclaimer: The Review-Journal is owned by the family of Las Vegas Sands Corp. Chairman and CEO Sheldon Adelson. Las Vegas Sands Corp. operates the Sands Expo and Convention Center, which competes with the LVCVA-operated Las Vegas Convention Center. That disclaimer was not enough to mollify critics.[150]

Tweets and comments from former RJ employees questioned the story's motives, but Kane and German knew a story with legs when they uncovered one. And LVCVA employees, who witnessed years of corruption and misspending, started reaching out to the reporters with new outrages. German and Kane collaborated on stories about staff taking valuable items like expensive crystal and iPads from the agency warehouse to give as personal gifts. The warehouse was stocked with the items to give to visiting dignitaries or people planning to bring conventions to the city, but LVCVA officials conceded that there were few checks and balances to keep staff from taking the taxpayer-bought items.[151]

Other stories questioned why security guards, paid by taxpayers to keep convention goers safe, were chauffeuring Ralenkotter—who made as much as eight hundred thousand dollars a year in salary and bonuses—to meetings, events, church, and home. Former mayor Goodman, at the time, had a seventy-two-thousand-dollar yearly contract with the agency that his wife chaired (she recused herself when Goodman's contract came up) to serve as a Vegas ambassador, greeting tourists with an oversized martini and two showgirls. He also was driven around by convention security staff.

Goodman said the story's headline and an editorial—which said good riddance to Goodman's work for the LVCVA—after his seventy-two-thousand-dollar-a-year contract was not renewed made him so mad that he contemplated suing the paper. Goodman maintains the story did not show how necessary his rides were as he needed to be able to get to events quickly. The story also did not focus enough, he thought, on how his work promoted tourism for the city. He had hung up when the paper called to get a comment for the story.

"We are the entertainment capital of the world," Goodman said. "We do have the most fun. This is a place to come look at the mayor. He's a drunk. He's a gambler. He runs around with show girls… It's a worldwide story."

Ralenkotter and the LVCVA gave different explanations for the rides, dubbed by staff as "Rossi Runs," including that Rossi needed help when he was receiving chemotherapy to him needing security at certain events as the face of tourism in Southern Nevada.[152]

The reporters also uncovered emails where Ralenkotter demanded a British Airways executive upgrade Ralenkotter's wife on trips to Europe. At the same time, taxpayers, via the LVCVA, paid for the executive's hotel, meals, and shows.

They even coordinated a comped Grand Canyon helicopter flight when the airline executive visited Sin City with his family.[153]

In the middle of the LVCVA investigation, Las Vegas was stunned by the deadliest mass shooting in US history. On October 1, 2017, Stephen Paddock smashed the window of his comped suite on the thirty-second floor of the Mandalay Bay Resort. He rained down hundreds of high-powered rifle rounds on a country music concert being held across the street. Sixty people were murdered; hundreds more were injured in the rampage. The RJ's investigative team, along with most of the newsroom, dropped whatever they were working on and covered the tragedy. National media flooded the state to cover the shooting. Despite regular mass shootings, the October 1 massacre was unique, both for the amount of carnage and that the killer was a wealthy, elderly man and well-known gambler. Police could never find a motive since Paddock killed himself before Metro officers could break down his hotel door. He also destroyed any digital trail that might shine a light on his reasons for mass murder, and unlike many mass shooters, he did not leave a manifesto or social media ravings.

German instantly started working his sources, producing one of the most significant scoops of the tragedy: Paddock had hoped to blow up airline fuel tanks at McCarran Airport to cause more mayhem and drive concert goers closer to his sniper perch.[154] The attempt failed only because Paddock did not realize only open flame, not a bullet, would ignite the fuel. German also cultivated one of Paddock's brothers, reporting revelations from him about the family.

Unlike previous major mass shootings that nearly guaranteed the local newspaper a Pulitzer nod, print journalism's top award, snubbed the Review-Journal's reporting of the tragedy. The rumor was that the RJ would never get a Pulitzer or even a nomination as long as Adelson's family owned the paper. It seemed to be confirmed every year, even when the paper produced work honored by many other journalism awards, but not the big one. Pulitzer board co-chairman Neil Brown maintains there was never a conspiracy to snub the RJ because of its ownership and that the panels of professional journalists who screen the entries would make that impossible.[155]

As coverage of the mass shooting died down, German and Kane continued their probe of the LVCVA. Eventually, the agency's board learned enough from the newspaper that it ordered an audit. Auditors found that Ralenkotter and other executives stole thousands in taxpayer-purchased Southwest gift cards to fly family and friends on personal trips. Despite the stories questioning Ralenkotter's leadership of the agency, the board gave Ralenkotter a $455,000 retirement package, including a fifteen-thousand-dollars-a-month consulting contract that did not specify what he had to accomplish, and a video tribute. Ralenkotter also received nearly three hundred thousand dollars a year in a government pension for his four decades with the agency. Seven months after the healthy retirement package, police raided the agency, seizing drives and records. In September 2019, Ralenkotter and other executives were charged with felony theft and misconduct by a public official.

District Attorney Steve Wolfson eventually allowed Ralenkotter and others to plead to a misdemeanor charge of violation by a public officer. Ralenkotter quickly had his conviction sealed. He paid a thousand dollar fine and about twenty-four thousand dollars to settle a state ethics commission action. Almost unheard for a prosecutor, Wolfson later defended the deal, listing all the good things the defendant, Ralenkotter, had done for Las Vegas.[156]

Their reporting vindicated by the criminal charges against LVCVA executives, German and Kane looked for other targets. Kane won outstanding journalist in Nevada both in 2020 and 2022 for stories about failure to discipline police, police releasing an impaired driver who killed a family, corruption surrounding a computer system revamp at the Department of Motor Vehicles, and other investigative exposes.

Having decades of experience, German regularly worked on investigations based on court records and sometimes was assigned stories that might not be investigative but needed his experienced touch. In 2019, tired of paying the Las Vegas Sun to produce a product that Review-Journal executives felt was substandard, the newspaper filed a federal lawsuit to disband the joint operating agreement and stop distributing the Sun as part of the RJ. German was asked to write the stories, which were sensitive because the main protagonist was the paper that employed him.[157]

Review-Journal attorneys charged that the Sun was trying to drive away readers from the joint product and to its side businesses by producing a paper mostly of wire copy and stories from other newspapers.

"The Review-Journal argues in court papers in the state case that the Sun breached its responsibilities and fails to abide by a JOA requirement to 'preserve high standards of newspaper quality,'" German wrote. "The newspaper also alleges that the Sun withholds local news content in favor of wire service stories and uses its print edition to drive readers away from the companies' joint print product and to the Sun's website instead.

"Despite the changing times and onslaught of new competition, the Review-Journal has done all that it can to continue producing a high-quality printed paper for the Las Vegas community," German quoted the court filing in a story published August 30, 2019. "The Sun should have cooperated with the Review-Journal and taken all necessary steps to help improve their joint product and meet those challenges."

While not available for German's story, the Sun's attorneys responded with a blistering attack on Adelson in court filings. "Defendant Sheldon Adelson has been a long-time enemy of the First Amendment and the press. For decades, he has filed and prosecuted one frivolous and ultimately unsuccessful defamation case after another. His object has always been clear: chill free speech and silence those that would speak out against him."

The Sun's attorneys charged that Adelson used the JOA to try to damage the Sun. "Adelson has wielded the JOA to place the Sun into economic distress. He virtually eliminated the required profit sharing under the JOA by predatorily adding improper expenses to reduce any share amount to zero," Sun's attorneys wrote. [158]

Despite the Sun's vehemence about upholding journalism, German broke a story saying the Sun owner Brian Greenspun was willing to abandon the JOA for twenty million dollars.

A few months after the family of Las Vegas Sands Corporation Chairman Sheldon Adelson bought the Review-Journal in December 2015, Greenspun offered to give up the Sun and "to make me go away" in return for twenty million, the court papers filed by the RJ's attorneys allege.

The Review-Journal rejected Greenspun's offer, and he later indicated he would accept less money, the court papers say.

"In May 2017, Greenspun proposed ending the JOA in return for $5 million and his own column in the Review-Journal, according to the court filing," German wrote in a January 4, 2021, article. "Greenspun also proposed splitting up the printed media market in Las Vegas, with him staying out of daily publication and the Review-Journal mostly leaving the weekly news and entertainment portion to him.[159]

The Sun had sued the RJ in state court in 2018, complaining about the distribution of profits and promotion of the Sun. That case was stayed as the federal JOA case went forward.

The heated battle between Las Vegas' long-time metro dailies is expected to last years unless the parties can come to an agreement.

***

Top editors also wanted to expand German's media portfolio. They assigned German to host the second season of the RJ's podcast Mobbed Up, which took listeners through Las Vegas' sordid history of organized crime. The Review-Journal had joined with The Mob Museum to produce a series of podcasts recounting the city's organized crime founding and control. It was a good way to promote the museum and a revenue stream for the paper.

Podcasting was far outside German's comfort zone, and he made it clear to Cook and his then-editor Rhonda Prast. German knew the material well, having lived through and written about much of the battle for Las Vegas that was covered in season two of the newspaper's podcast. He just wasn't confident in his broadcast skills.

"You're going to be great at it," Cook, the paper's top editor, told him after giving him the assignment.

"I don't know how to write for audio," German responded. "I'm going to narrate this thing?"

German, after forty years in the business, realized it was an offer he couldn't refuse. "All right, all right," he would say, intoning that I will do it if you say so but I'm not really buying it.

German was paired up with Larry Mir, a tattooed and muscled senior technical director of digital to produce the podcast. Knowing their difference in age but not knowing German well at that point, Mir assumed that German would hate him for his inked arms. He assumed that working with German would be a pain in the ass. Nothing could have been farther from the truth as German took to podcasting like he did to reporting. Mir's main direction was often about

German's tone or delivery, but after a couple of episodes, the veteran reporter had found another form of media where he excelled.

They connected early when Mir brought up the Binion murder case without knowing that German wrote a book about it. German brought him a signed copy of Murder in Sin City. The second season of Mobbed Up focused on many of the stories German covered, including about Judge Claiborne's role in Vegas history. It also told the tale of how entertainer Wayne Newton and talk show host Johnny Carson battled to buy the mob-run Aladdin Hotel.

The biggest hassle for Mir in working with German was his chronic ignorance of technology. The series was taped during the COVID pandemic, so much of interviewing was done through video conferencing. Mir repeatedly had to help German set up Zoom and Google Meets conference calls as the simplest of technology often befuddled the elder journalist. Despite that, the two had a lot of laughs, like when the script required German to swear on the podcast.

"Ross recalls that his effort to get an interview with Guido Penosi in Beverly Hills became a moment of laughter during the trial. Penosi told him, 'Fuck you,'" German would read multiple times because takes were disrupted by laughter that he got to say "fuck" in the podcast.

German told Mir that he was looking forward to the profanity, especially since the podcast included a disclaimer.

"I want to get that one right," he joked.

He talked about his history covering the Mob and even managed to get his story about being punched by Sy Freedman into the podcast.

"I've covered organized crime from the streets to the board rooms of the Strip for more than forty years," Jeff German said in the intro to the episodes. "One night, years ago at a social gathering of politicians and courthouse, movers and shakers at the old Sands Hotel, I was sucker punched by a mob associate," he told the story in "Episode

2" of Mobbed Up's second season. "Unhappy about how he was portrayed in one of my stories, a couple of hours later with four stitches under my lip, I had a war story to tell. The wise guy didn't like seeing in print that he was collecting campaign money for the sheriff and juice money for the Mob at the same time, while on the public payroll, as a justice court warrant officer. What I learned was that writing something bad about the Mob can get you nicked up. What's worse is being in bed with the Mob and crossing it like Jimmy Hoffa. That can cost you your life." [160]

Season one of Mobbed Up had done well. Geoff Schumacher, who was German's editor at the Sun and had taken a job as vice president of exhibits and programs at The Mob Museum, was wary about German hosting the second season.

He knew firsthand about German's reluctance to embrace technology or anything that deviated from his long-practiced print reporting skills. Only when Schumacher started seeing the scripts was he convinced the second season with German would be as good as the first season. As he did with computer research and open records, German embraced the new media and threw himself into the project that posthumously won him a Nevada Press Association award for Podcast of the Year. Listeners agreed, downloading the various episodes of the second season nearly six hundred thousand times all together.

Despite overall praise for the podcast, German was looking to get back to what he knew best.

"I hope I don't have to do this again," he told Mir as they were wrapping up the second season. [161]

***

Around the time German started working on the podcast, COVID had spread across Nevada, the nation, and world. The investigative team and the whole Review-Journal was sent to work from home. German had received a tip right before the world closed about recently retired Clark County Coroner John Fudenberg. Fudenberg had used public money to hire his girlfriend to provide yoga and meditation sessions to employees who were traumatized by responding the October 1 mass shooting, the tipster revealed. German asked Kane if he was interested in pursuing the story, and Kane thought it was worth digging into.

Kane had a history with Fudenberg. As part of an investigation into the deaths of children under protection by the Clark County Department of Children and Family Services, Kane requested child autopsies from Fudenberg's office in 2017. The coroner refused to release them, forcing the newspaper into a nearly four-year legal battle. The state Supreme Court ruled that autopsies are public and repeatedly directed the county to release them. The county continued to ask for a rehearing, which were denied. The county finally released the records on New Year's Eve 2020. County taxpayers had to pay $167,000 of the newspaper's legal expenses after losing the case. With that history, Kane definitely had questions about Fudenberg's transparency and management of the key county office.[162]

Kane and German's multi-part investigation into Fudenberg would expose not only the contract with Fudenberg's girlfriend but other questionable actions. Records showed that upon retirement, Fudenberg appeared to cash out vacation time he took but didn't log into the county's personnel management system. Calendars and other records showed Fudenberg was giving paid speeches— sometimes for five thousand dollars each—on county time despite having an agreement with Deputy County Manager Jeff Wells that any outside work would be on his personal time. During the speeches, Fudenberg touted a master's degree from a Pakistani company that the New York Times had exposed as a diploma mill. State law prohibited using fake credentials, but authorities never dug into the potential violation after the newspaper exposed it.

Kane and German also dug into Fudenberg's failures to address sexual harassment and other employee misconduct in the office at the time he was traveling to give paid speeches. Kane obtained a picture of one of the female staffers flashing her breasts at another employee in the agency's downtown office. That picture said a lot about the culture of an office tasked with the serious business of determining the cause of deaths for homicide, suicide, and accident victims. The story reported for the first time that autopsy delays impacted the office's accreditation. Despite the problems, the county continued to give Fudenberg raises and bonuses.[163]

Wells oversaw the office when he and Fudenberg signed the outside work agreement and when Fudenberg received pay raises and bonuses. Wells also was the final sign off on Fudenberg's lucrative early retirement (one of several hundred employees who took the perk), which totaled nearly one hundred and seventy-five thousand dollars, including cashing out allegedly unused vacation and sick leave, severance, and an early retirement payment.[164] Then-Deputy Manager Kevin Schiller was over the office when Fudenberg was giving speeches on county time but apparently didn't catch those speeches. Schiller maintains he didn't know about the travel and speeches and would have if he had heard about the concerns. [165]

The county maintained the bonuses and other benefits were for Fudenberg's work during the October 1 shooting, and they had stepped in during the accreditation issues to help staff up the department and address harassment. But the litany of problems uncovered by the Review-Journal raised serious questions about the county's oversight of the key office.

Wells maintained that while he approved the bonuses and early retirement, there was a committee of upper managers who reviewed the payments. He wanted to point out that Schiller was over the office when Fudenberg was doing the paid speeches, but he said he wasn't allowed to do that. Wells would also play a key role in German's last investigation.[166]

PHOTOS

Police taped off Jeff German's house the day his body was discovered on the side of the property. Officers are seen standing and discussing the evidence where his body was found. (Clark County Grand Jury evidence)

Police released a photo of the suspect walking around Jeff German's neighborhood before the killing. The image was captured by a security camera on a neighbor's house across the street. (LVMPD)

On Sept. 6, 2022, Police released a photo of the vehicle driven by the suspect, leading to a tip that would identify the suspect and result in an arrest. (LVMPD)

Jeff German and his younger brother, Jay, enjoying beers in front of the Binion's Horseshoe, which would play a key role in Jeff German's career. (Photo Courtesy of Scott Zamost)

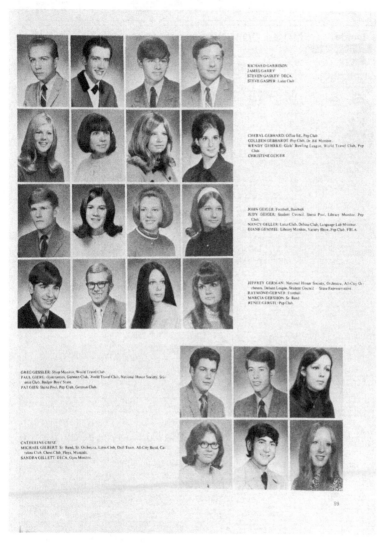

RICHARD GARRISON
JAMES GARRY
STEVEN GASKEY: DECA.
STEVE GASPER: Latin Club

CHERYL GEBHARD: Office Ed., Pep Club
COLLEEN GEBHARDT: Pep Club, Dr. Ed. Monitor
WENDY GEHRKE: Girls' Bowling League, World Travel Club, Pep Club
CHRISTINE GEIGER

JOHN GEIGER: Football, Baseball
JUDY GEIGER: Student Council, Steno Pool, Library Monitor, Pep Club
NANCY GELLER: Latin Club, Debate Club, Language Lab Monitor
DIANE GEMMEL: Library Monitor, Variety Show, Pep Club, FBLA

JEFFREY GERMAN: National Honor Society, Orchestra, All-City Orchestra, Debate League, Student Council, State Representative.
RAYMOND GERNER: Football
MARCIA GERSHON: Sr. Band
RENEE GERSTL: Pep Club

GREG GESSLER: Shop Monitor, World Travel Club
PAUL GIERL: Gymnastics, German Club, World Travel Club, National Honor Society, Science Club, Badger Boys' State.
PAT GIES: Steno Pool, Pep Club, German Club.

CATHERINE GIESE
MICHAEL GILBERT: Sr. Band, Sr. Orchestra, Latin Club, Drill Team, All-City Band, Catena Club, Chess Club, Plays, Musicals.
SANDRA GILLETT: DECA, Gym Monitor.

89

A yearbook photo from Jeff German's senior year at John Marshall High School in Milwaukee.

Monday, October 7, 1985 — MONDAY — LAS VEGAS SUN—B

METRO

LV observes fire prevention week/4B

Mental illness plagued by myths/4B

Inside Story

By Jeffrey M. German

Attorney General Brian McKay is starting to talk more and more like someone who wants to be the state's top lawman another four years.

And he has Richard Wirthlin, President Reagan's top opinion maker, to thank for that.

Wirthlin's latest poll showing that McKay, Rep. Barbara Vucanovich and Jim Santini all would give Rep. Harry Reid a tough race for the U.S. Senate in 1986, has helped push McKay over the hump.

"It's moved me one more step closer to ruling out seeking Paul Laxalt's Senate seat," says McKay.

Although there may be less pressure to keep McKay's name in the running because of the strong showings of Vucanovich and Santini, the attorney general wisely isn't bowing out just yet.

But for the moment, he's feeling a bit more relaxed about staying put.

Rebounding . . . Clark County GOP chief **Ken Sawyer** is sticking to his guns. Sawyer says that, contrary to what's been reported here, he hasn't been apologizing to GOP leaders over his candid remarks about the Wirthlin poll. Sawyer was quoted as saying, "If I came down from Reno, I'd be mad as hell." The implication being the poll was a waste of time. We need more guys like Sawyer who aren't afraid to speak their mind, even if it means biting the hand that feeds them. . . . Metro Narcotics Lt. **Mike Manning** wants to put to rest rumors that a detective under his direction developed a drug habit. "It's not uncommon for allegations like this to arise," says Manning, who's moving on to a new assignment later this month. "There are no drug problems currently existing in Metro's Narcotics Section."

Porno Blues . . . Local pornography stores aren't exactly smiling over the **AIDS** scare. Word on the street is that business at some joints has dropped off as much as 50 percent. Has the deadly virus done in two months what the cops have been struggling to do for years?

Nightclubbing . . . At **Botany's**, friends recently threw an all-night birthday party for **Roy** of **Siegfried & Roy** fame. **Suzanne Somers** was among those on hand for the celebration . . . It was county night at the popular disco Saturday. Commissioner **Manny Cortez**, ex-County Manager **Joe Denny**, County Counsel **James Bartley** and District Judge **Charles Thompson** all made appearances.

The Fall Girl? . . . Is ex-Muni Court Administrator **Marcia Daines** taking the fall for other higher-ups at City Hall? That kind of talk is starting to surface downtown. It seems Daines repeatedly tried to get her superiors to clean up some of the accounting problems at the court, but didn't get much of a response. Then, City Manager **Ashley Hall** asked Daines to resign after the latest embezzlement scandal surfaced. It hardly seems fair.

Mounting Tension . . . If you've seen Taxicab Czar **Don Heim** popping aspirin of late, he's had good reason. One maverick taxi company owner, **Ray Chenoweth**, doesn't like Taxicab Authority's recent decision to raise cab fares 20 cents a drop for health and welfare benefits to drivers. He's challenging it in court. The authority holds a meeting Monday night to discuss the litigation . . . Rumors are circulating that Star Cab Co. mogul **Pete Eliades** is selling out the majority of his interests. Why is Eliades so interested in giving up an apparent gold mine?

No air pollution alerts foreseen this winter

By MARY MANNING
SUN Staff Writer

Michael Naylor isn't a gambler and he doesn't make a bet lightly.

However, after more than seven years as administrator of the Clark County Health District's Air Pollution Control Division, Naylor is willing to wager the Las Vegas Valley won't have an unhealthy day this year during the air pollution season that begins with cooler nights.

"We aren't expecting any unhealthy days this season from air pollution," Naylor said.

The reason is a combination of stricter exhaust emission standards, more freeway miles and better computer-controlled traffic flows.

Autumn and winter days across the Las Vegas Valley leave a blanket of brown haze across the skyline, blurring a formerly clear view of surrounding mountains. Most of the smog comes from nearly 600,000 residents driving their motor vehicles, Naylor said.

Vehicle exhausts spew carbon monoxide, a colorless, odorless gas into the air and particles of carbon from gasoline and diesel fuel exhaust combine to form the cloud.

Naylor noted in a report sent to the U.S. Environmental Protection Agency in June that the air quality has improved in the valley by 35 percent and emissions have dropped by 29 percent.

This year only one day reached very unhealthful levels, and no health alert was called, Naylor said, because strong winds cleared the valley the next day.

In 1983 Southern Nevada counted 31 days as unhealthful, when the air pollution index reached 100 or more on its scale.

It's not the entire valley that suffers from air pollution, either, Naylor said in the report. In fact, with about seven years of close monitoring, the Air Pollution Control Division has identified "hot spots," centering on the intersection of East Charleston Boulevard, Fremont Street and the Boulder Highway (U.S. 95). Primarily, the hot spot there develops from stop-and-go traffic lights.

"We estimate that by 1987, when the East Leg Freeway is opened, sufficient traffic will be diverted from the East Charleston hot spot so that emissions will be below the compliance level," the 1985 report said.

In 1983 the Nevada Environmental Commission approved a motor vehicle emission inspection program.

On Jan. 1, 1986, the exhaust limits are even tougher because the initial program did not reduce carbon monoxide levels to acceptable amounts, Naylor said.

Since only 3 percent of cars failed the pass-fail exhaust test in the past two years, Naylor said tougher standards for cars up to 20 years old will help clear the air faster.

Last year the Air Pollution Control Division also measured ash in the air from wood-burning stoves and fireplaces. As of this year, the soot isn't considered part of the pollution problem, since it accounts for less than 2 percent of all the valley's air pollution, compared to more than 88 percent caused by motor vehicles.

NLRB probing tip-pooling at Laughlin casino

By LISA GODWIN
SUN Staff Writer

The National Labor Relations Board has launched an investigation into a Laughlin casino that fired one of its "21" dealers after he raised objections to the way the Riverside Casino handles its tip-pooling arrangements.

And a source within the Internal Revenue Service, who asked not to be identified, said that, while he could not say whether the IRS is investigating the Riverside per se, the type of tip-pooling the Riverside uses is frowned upon by the agency.

The NLRB is concerned that Richard Morgan, a dealer who was fired last month from the Riverside, may have been prevented from participating in "concerted activities," said Ken Rose, NLRB's resident officer, explaining that the term refers to an employee's efforts to improve working conditions or wages for himself and his fellow employees.

Neither Rose nor Mike Chavez, an NLRB agent investigating the case, could comment on the investigation, other than to say it was active.

Morgan's complaints stem from the way the Riverside, owned by Don Laughlin, founder of the tiny resort town, divides tips earned by its casino dealers. According to Morgan, 39, the floormen, pit bosses, and casino manager share in the tokes, although the standard industry practice is to include only dealers.

One long-time casino manager in Las Vegas called the practice "underhanded, clandestine, and old-timey" and added, "The pit boss and floormen should never get toked — it's just not right."

But the IRS is not concerned with the ethical questions surrounding the practice. The government's concern, rather, is that, "it lends itself to a lot of abuse," the IRS source said.

If management keeps part of the tips itself, it must also pay taxes on that income, the source said, adding that it is difficult to determine if a casino is paying the full amount of taxes.

Richard Segerblom, a labor attorney and director of the state Democratic Party Southern District, suggests that casinos that include their management teams in tip pooling are not paying their fair share in taxes. Casino employees are required to report their tokes to the IRS, he said, but management personnel who share in tips find a way to get around that.

"Management tries to hide the fact that they have control over the tip pooling. They go out of their way to try to hide the fact that they're in control of tips," Segerblom said. "I would urge the guy (Morgan) to go to the Riverside and threaten to go to the IRS if he didn't get his job back."

The reason stated on Morgan's termination slip was "change of personnel" due to a management turnover, but Morgan believes it was because he passed around a letter and petition to be sent to Gov. Richard Bryan protesting the Riverside's tip practices. He was fired a few days after the letter was circulated among Riverside employees.

Don Laughlin, when contacted at his Riverside resort, said, however, that he didn't remember why Morgan was fired but said Morgan was the only dealer he had encountered who objected to including management in the tip pool.

"Here at the Riverside, everyone who works in the casino has always shared in the tips. It creates a lot more harmony in the pit," Laughlin said. "There's no jealousy in the pit or rudeness to customers."

(See TIP-POOLING, Page 8B)

Gail Morrison

Tina Aldridge

Two LV black students gain high honors

By RENELL WYNN
SUN Staff Writer

Each year over 70,000 students request consideration in the National Achievement Program for Outstanding Negro Students.

Las Vegas students Tina Aldridge and Gail Morrison were among 1,500 black students named as semifinalists in the program.

Designed to aid gifted black scholars, the program is operated as part of the National Merit Scholarship which was initiated in 1955.

In its 22nd year, the National Achievement Program identifies and honors black students annually providing a sizable number of scholarships supported by grants from corporations, business organizations, colleges and universities.

Three types of achievement scholarships will be offered in the spring of 1986. The largest block of awards will be the 350 national achievement $2,000 scholarships, for which the finalists compete.

"It is important that programs such as these support young black minds. The participation of black students in these programs is often used as a bridge to opening doors that may not have been open to black students in the past," Aldridge said.

Aldridge is a senior at Bishop Gorman High School and said she has not really been pushed to excel in school. She has been a self-motivator.

She hopes to attend Stanford University as a nuclear physics major in the fall of 1986.

The merit and achievement programs are operated separately and black students may participate in both. However, the qualifying score levels for students who are honored are set independently and differ for the two competitions.

"The whole essence of the program is to aid young blacks. The assistance provided by the program helps talented scholars in their quest for excellence," Morrison said.

Morrison is also a senior. She attends Bonanza High School and likes accounting, which will be her major at UNLV.

"I never really studied a lot, but I was always interested in getting good grades. I guess you could say my interest got me involved with the program," Morrison said.

Winners of the national achievement $2000 scholarship and corporate-sponsored four-year achievement scholarship will be notified in February 1986. Their names will be publicized nationwide in late March. Recipients of college-sponsored four-year achievement scholarships will be notified in April and May. Information about these students will be announced individually in June.

Event opens Tuesday

'Share the Fun' Jaycee Fair theme

By HOWARD BULLOCH
SUN Staff Writer

"Share the Fun" is this year's theme for the Las Vegas Jaycees State Fair that will open Tuesday and continue through Sunday, Oct 13. The fair will be held at Cashman Field Complex.

The opening night begins with a ribbon cutting ceremony at 4 p.m. to kick off a traditional event that all Southern Nevadans have grown to enjoy over 32 years.

This year's Las Vegas Jaycees State Fair may prove to be one of the finest, with over 300 exhibitors from A-1 Vacuum and Sewing to Youth for Understanding. Visitors to the fair will be able to see various exhibits from local merchants which include motorcycles, telephones, jewelry, artwork, automobiles, fireplaces, satellite systems and much more.

The concept of the fair carries with it 2,000 years of history. "The fair has roots which date back to biblical days as a marketplace to support both the culture and commerce of the times," said Kim Myrman, executive director of WFA, a trade association with more than 150 member fairs in 19 states and five Canadian provinces.

Fairs have evolved to quite an extravaganza today with displays of art, athletic competition, drama, livestock displays, games of chance, crafts and cooking, Myrman adds. "Though the exhibits have changed ... the fair industry continues to support excellence by showing off the best the community has to offer."

"Share the Fun" is an especially appropriate theme for the fair this year, especially for those who plan on participating in the various competitions.

The contests include a greased pig chase, a mother and daughter look-a-like, a father and son look-a-like, children's big wheel races, the diaper derby, seniors horseshoe pitching, a pie eating contest, a nail driving contest and a tobacco spitting contest.

And those are just the first night's activities. The lineup is just as impressive every night of the fair.

Appearing at this year's fair will be the San Diego Naval Training Center Band, John Todman's Wonder Show, the Nitro Dance Team, the U.S. Air Force Academy Rock Band and the Jay Ramsey Band.

Events are scheduled each day from 4 p.m. until midnight.

Tax challenge may cost state

CARSON CITY (UPI) — State Transportation Director Al Stone says Nevada counties could lose up to $1.5 million if a Utah trucking firm is successful in challenging a state tax law.

Dave R. Grant Hay Inc., of Odgen, Utah, has filed suit in district court saying out-of-state companies should be able to pro-rate the amount they pay on vehicle privilege tax.

The Hay firm says it does only 12 percent of its business in Nevada but must pay the full cost of the tax.

The suit says Arizona, California, Colorado, Montana, Utah and Washington allow truckers to pro-rate the value of their vehicles for tax purposes.

Jeff German column. He continued to write about the Mob-connected court official who punched him, despite suffering four stitches during the attack.

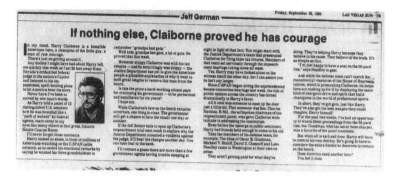

If nothing else, Claiborne proved he has courage

In my mind, Harry Claiborne is a bonafide American hero, a champion of the little guy, a man of raw courage.

There's just no getting around it.

Any doubts I might have had about Harry left me quickly this week as I sat 20 feet away from Nevada's embattled federal judge in the nation's Capitol and listened to his impassioned, spell-binding pleas to let America hear his story.

Never have I've been so moved by one man's words.

As Harry told a panel of 13 distinguished U.S. senators how he was hounded like a "pack of wolves" by federal agents, tears came to my eyes like many others in that great, historic Senate Caucus Room.

I'll never forget those moments.

Harry looked so alone, in front of millions of Americans watching on the C-SPAN cable network, as he ended his emotional remarks by saying he wanted his three grandchildren to remember "grandpa had guts."

Well kids, grandpa has guts, a lot of guts. He proved that this week.

However sloppy Claiborne was with his tax returns — and he admittingly was sloppy — the Justice Department has yet to give the American people a plausible explanation of why it went to such great lengths to remove this man from the bench.

Is this the price a hard-working citizen pays for criticizing his government — to be persecuted and humiliated for six years?

I hope not.

While Claiborne's fate on the bench remains uncertain, one thing is clear. The government will get a chance to face the music one way or another.

If the full Senate fails to oust up Claiborne's impeachment trial next week to explore why the Justice Department mounted a vendetta against the judge, it'll hear the charges another day. You can take that to the bank.

I'll venture a guess there are more than a few government agents having trouble sleeping at night in light of that fact. You might start with the Justice Department's team that prosecuted Claiborne for filing false tax returns. Members of that team sat nervously through the impeachment hearings taking notes all week.

Yes, Harry may have looked alone on the witness stand the other day, but I can assure you he isn't any longer.

Since C-SPAN began airing the unprecedented Senate committee hearings last week, the tide of public opinion across the country has turned dramatically in Harry's favor.

All it took was someone to open up the door just a little bit. That someone was Sen. Charles Mathias, R-Md., the softspoken chairman of the impeachment panel, who gave Claiborne wide latitude in addressing the committee.

Even before the upsurge in public sentiment, Harry had friends bold enough to come to his aid. Take the members of his defense team, for example. The likes of Oscar B. Goodman, Michael V. Stuhff, David Z. Chesnoff and Lake Headley came to Washington at their own expense.

They aren't getting paid for what they're doing. They're helping Harry because they believe in his cause. They believe in the truth. It's as simple as that.

"I'm just happy to have a seat on the 50-yard line," says Headley in jest.

And while the defense team can't match the monumental resources of the House of Representatives, which is prosecuting Claiborne, its members are making up for it by displaying the same kind of energetic drive and spirit that build champions in the world of professional sports.

In short, they've got guts, just like Harry. They've also got the best weapon they could imagine, Harry himself.

For the past two weeks, I've had an opportunity to watch these proceedings from the 50-yard line, too. Goodman, who has never been sharper, was a favorite of the panel members.

But when all is said and done, Harry will have to control his own destiny. He's going to have to convince the entire Senate he deserves to remain on the bench.

Does America need another hero?

You bet it does.

Newspaper clipping of one of Jeff' German's Claiborne stories. He wrote favorable columns about Judge Harry Claiborne, who was close to German's publisher at the Las Vegas Sun. Claiborne would be convicted on tax charges and impeached.

Jeff German's book about the Ted Binion murder trial was a highlight of his career, but the good times would not last.

Jeff German and RJ editors James Wright and Michael Hengel meet with Mongolian judges in 2015. (Photo Courtesy of Mary Ann Price of the Clark County District Court)

Jeff German, far right in light blue shirt, and other members of the investigative and production teams gather with Executive Editor Keith Moyer, in the baseball cap, on March 31, 2017, the Friday before the Las Vegas Convention and Visitors Authority story is scheduled to run. (Photo Courtesy Harrison Keely, then Review-Journal director of digital media)

Jeff German, right with glasses, reviewing documents related to stories about Las Vegas City Councilwoman Michele Fiore with fellow investigative reporter, Arthur Kane, (who is author of this book) in the cafeteria of the Review-Journal building on Feb. 14, 2019. (Photo Courtesy Harrison Keely, then Review-Journal director of digital media)

PUBLIC ADMINISTRATOR - DEM
VOTE FOR 1

Precincts Reporting: of N/A (%)

Candidate	Votes	%/Total
Escobar, Caroline	36,262	33.29%
Reid, Rita Page	37,401	34.33%
Telles, Rob	35,279	32.38%
Total	108,942	

PUBLIC ADMINISTRATOR - REP
VOTE FOR 1

Precincts Reporting: of N/A (%)

Candidate	Votes	%/Total
Brown, Patsy	53,244	50.71%
Casale, Patrick	51,758	49.29%
Total	105,002	

Screen shot of final vote totals in the 2022 primary for Clark County Public Administrator.

Robert Telles and Roberta Lee-Kennett walking near the public administrator's office. Staff took the photo while they were surveilling them in an attempt to prove an inappropriate relationship. (Photo Courtesy of Aleisha Goodwin)

Photo of a vehicle driven by Roberta Lee-Kennett to the outlet mall garage where she was meeting with Robert Telles. The photo was part of surveillance that public administrator employees were conducting on their boss to prove an illicit affair. (Photo Courtesy of Aleisha Goodwin)

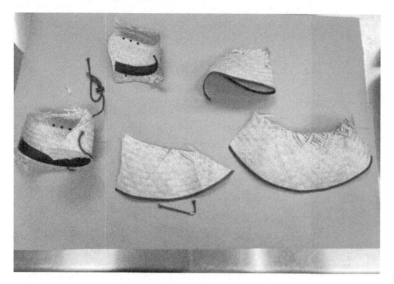

Police found a hat similar to the one the assailant was wearing in Robert Telles garage. (Clark County Grand Jury evidence)

Metro detectives found this partly cut up shoe in Telles' house which they said matched the shoes the assailant was seen wearing during the attack on Jeff German. (Clark County Grand Jury evidence)

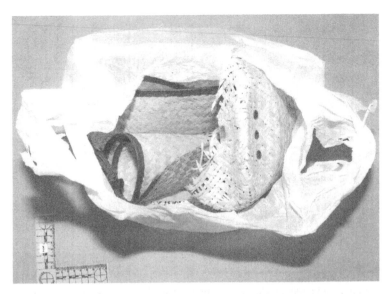

A hat that looked very similar to the one the assailant was wearing was found in a tool box in Robert Telles' garage, police say. (Clark County Grand Jury evidence)

Police photo of the maroon GMC Yukon that investigators say was driven by Jeff German's assailant. The vehicle was parked in front of Robert Telles' house. (Clark County Grand Jury evidence)

Cut up tennis shoe that police said they found Robert Telles' house that matched the shoes the assailant wore during the attack on Jeff German. (Clark County Grand Jury evidence)

Robert Telles mug shot after his arrest in September 2022. (LVMPD)

An invitation for the Las Vegas Review-Journal memorial held in Jeff German's honor.

Jeff German's final resting place at King David Cemetery. (Arthur Kane)

The final desk Jeff German used at the newspaper sits empty in the investigative team area as a memorial to him. Framed stories, dried flowers and his notebooks fill the desk. (Arthur Kane)

A wall in the newsroom is decorated with German's awards, promotional picture for the Mobbed Up season, and a framed photo of the LVCVA story. (Arthur Kane)

CHAPTER SEVEN:
COUNTY CHAOS

Rita Reid was leaving work around 4:30 p.m. on Friday, February 25, 2022,[167] when she noticed her coworker at the Clark County Public Administrator's Office, Roberta Lee-Kennett, driving out in front of her. Instead of turning towards home, Lee-Kennett turned towards an outlet mall near the county offices.

For two years, the office, which handles probate for indigent people who have no relatives or whose relatives don't want to get involved, had been in open warfare. A new public administrator, Robert Telles, was elected in 2019 and quickly alienated long-time employees like first assistant Reid. Telles' critics in the office also were suspicious that Telles, married with children, and Lee-Kennett, also married, were having an inappropriate relationship. Reid and others claimed Lee-Kennett took advantage of her close relationship with Telles to boss and interfere with other employees.

Reid, who had been second in command at the PA office for more than a dozen years, was an attractive sixty-three-year-old with shoulder-length grey hair and a friendly, chatty manner. Her demeanor hid a tough life. Reid had grown up in Henderson, Nevada, with five siblings and loving but religious Catholic parents. Her serene family life changed when she got pregnant as a sophomore at Bishop Gorman High School. Her parents sent her to an unwed-mother's school in San Francisco and basically disowned her. It didn't help that her boyfriend and the father of her son was Black. In 1972, interracial relationships still raised eyebrows.

Without family support, Reid had to work hard through her teens and early twenties. She washed clothes at a hotel laundry, worked at McDonalds, and a university cafeteria. She was holding down multiple jobs to support herself and her son. She also found herself in an abusive relationship that she eventually ended. Returning to Las Vegas, she found work at the area's casinos booking travel for entertainers and high rollers. Some were good experiences but in others, the bosses were abusive or dangerous. She quit one job fearing that her boss carried a gun in a briefcase and would hurt her. Her intuition about the boss was confirmed when the man fatally shot himself after he was caught hustling drugs and sex workers at the property. She eventually secured a job at Las Vegas's top public relations firm, R&R Partners. It was the legendary firm started by Sig Rogich and purchased by Billy Vassiliadis. She also started working on political campaigns at R&R. That led to an opportunity at the Clark County District Attorney's Office after R&R's candidate won the campaign she helped run. After years with the DA's office, Reid moved to the county clerk's office, which at the time, also managed the courts.

In 2007, the judges were going to take over the court clerk functions—splitting the duties between county clerk and court clerk. Reid felt the top judges had not treated the clerk well. The clerk, who had become Reid's mentor, was being treated for cancer at the time of the takeover. Reid decided she couldn't stay in that job and started looking for a new opportunity. She stopped by the public administrator's building where she knew the elected PA from her time working for county prosecutors. The administrator was retiring but the incoming, newly elected administrator, John Cahill, just happened to be in the office. They hit it off and Cahill soon offered her a job as his top deputy.

After his first four-year term, Cahill wanted to retire. He had spent thirty years with the county's juvenile division and had been retired for a decade before deciding to run for the public administrator's office. The PA job allowed Cahill to collect a good salary while drawing his pension because elected officials in Nevada are exempt from the state's prohibition on government employees double-dipping with salary and pension. Cahill, however, decided that he preferred retired life despite the lucrative financial benefits of salary and pension. He urged Reid to run in his place. She didn't want the limelight or the hassle of politics. She had seen it firsthand at R&R, and she liked working behind the scenes. Cahill ran again, unable to find a trustworthy replacement. Each four-year election cycle, Cahill urged Reid to run because he didn't want to retire unless he felt his replacement would run the office properly. It was a small office with fewer than a dozen full-time employees and about twenty part-timers, but Cahill understood its importance to the indigent people and families of the deceased. Each time Cahill broached the topic, Reid refused to run.

At the end of his third term, Cahill again put his name on the 2018 ballot but then found a possible replacement who wanted—and Cahill thought—could do the job. Robert Telles had graduated from UNLV law school a few years earlier. Cahill had put him on the list of contract attorneys who would be paid to handle probate cases for the office. Cahill thought Telles presented himself and the agency well in court. It was also a plus that he spoke Spanish. Many of the relatives whose estates the office handled were not fluent in English.

When Telles agreed to run, Cahill withdrew his name from the ballot, clearing the path for Telles to win the Democratic primary. Clark County had become increasingly Democratic as liberals migrated to Southern Nevada from high-tax states like California. So, securing the Democratic primary in Clark County nearly guaranteed a victory in the general election—especially for a low-profile office like public administrator. When Telles won, Reid and the other employees were excited to have a leader who was a probate attorney and could provide new ideas and a fresh perspective.

Reid was going through a tough time personally right as Telles was taking office. Her husband, William, fell on Christmas Day 2018, hitting his head and winding up in the hospital with a brain bleed. For the first few weeks of Telles' term, Reid would have to leave to be at William's bedside. Her time at work was also proving stressful.

Telles' first meeting with Reid did not go well. She thought they had agreed to meet with the agency's contract CPA, but when Telles found out the accountants were about to enter the meeting, he became angry. He often overacted to what should have been a benign situation. He seemed irrationally to turn to rage like when Reid waived a ten-dollar fee for a family who couldn't afford to pay despite county rules that allowed an indigent waiver.

From Telles' perspective, the office was inefficient, there were unconfirmed rumors of thefts of estate property, and cases were backing up. He felt the legacy employees who were in the office were lazy, preferring to chat the day away instead of working hard to serve the county's clients. When he arrived, he found that Cahill allowed Reid to act as de facto public administrator, and she had implemented a series of policies that didn't make sense and were delaying the resolution of cases. Telles maintains he reformed the office's processes, increasing the closure of cases, but the old-guard workers say he created nothing but tensions and conflict.[168]

One day, a month or so into his term, Telles stormed into Reid's office, slamming his hands loudly on her desk. His approach startled her.

"We're ripping off the bandage," Telles said, not yelling but in a loud voice, "and nobody reports to you anymore. They all report to me, and you have no authority."

He stormed back out of the room.

Reid could only stare in disbelief. She was put in charge of the intake of new cases instead of managing the office functions.

Then, she and coworkers started noticing Telles and Lee-Kennett spending lunches together and giggling behind closed doors. One time, after they thought everyone had gone home, the couple entered a conference room only to find Reid talking to her son on her cell phone in the room. Inexplicably, Lee-Kennett fled as Telles turned beet red. Telles, on several occasions, had angrily accused Reid of spying on him and demanded that she leave the office by five p.m. every day. But he had loaded her with so much work it was impossible to complete without staying late. She believed Telles set the five-p.m. deadline because he wanted to meet privately with Lee-Kennett. Reid was on salary so she received no overtime for staying late so it wasn't a financial decision.

Employees who were concerned about Telles and Lee-Kennett's conduct at work started to notice a pattern: When Lee-Kennett wore a short skirt, she and Telles left through separate exits but their cars headed in the same direction. One time, the employees spotted Lee-Kennett at another parking garage near the office and she saw them. She appeared embarrassed and panicked. On another occasion, several employees were heading to eat lunch at the Cheesecake Factory in the nearby outlet mall. Estate Coordinator Aleisha Goodwin noticed Telles was right behind them. They turned into the parking garage, and Telles turned too. Was he following them? they wondered, but Telles continued down the mall lane to the southern parking garage. Was this where he was now meeting Lee-Kennett?

So on the Friday when Reid spotted Lee-Kennett driving in the opposite direction of her house and towards the outlet mall, she decided to follow. Her heart pounded as she stopped a few lights behind Kennett's SUV. She was feeling foolish.

She kept telling herself to turn away and head home. But she couldn't do it. Lee-Kennett drove past the outlet mall where employees suspected she and Telles were meeting. Reid figured she was just going somewhere after work. But then Lee-Kennett turned down a street that ran along the east side of the outlet mall and turned into the south garage.

Reid continued to follow, fearing she might be spotted but wanted to know if her intuition was accurate. She lost Lee-Kennett's vehicle in the multi-level garage so she started wandering the parking structure warily, hoping to catch sight of her vehicle. Soon, from the stairwell, she saw Lee-Kennett's car in an otherwise vacant area. There was just one more car but she couldn't tell if it was Telles' BMW SUV. She tried to take a few pictures but didn't get anything usable or damning. At least she now knew the rendezvous point. Reid soon told the other women at the office who were concerned about the affair. They regularly started following the couple when the short-skirt signal was in play.[169]

Reid had been with the county a long time but had yet to maximize her retirement. She wanted to file a complaint but was concerned about disruption the office's work. She wanted to know if Telles had the power to fire her.

Reid knew she had to be careful, but she reached out to Deputy County Manager Jeff Wells, who was liaison to the public administrator's office and managed or was liaison to various high-profile departments, including the coroner, public defender, constables, and other agencies. Wells had fifteen departments he was responsible for around that time. About half, like the public administrator, were run by elected officials, limiting his power to collaborating on a budget and using his persuasive powers to address any concerns. Elected officials are governed by the Nevada Commission on Ethics instead of county policies because voters put them into office. The other seven, like the coroner and public defender, are run by appointed officials, which gave him considerably more management oversight as the heads of those agencies reported to him.

Wells had just passed his seventieth birthday. Wiry, smooth, and always in a suit and tie, he was a lawyer and a former politician in Colorado. Reid hoped to get some guidance from Wells but remembers she got the run around. When she finally talked to Wells in the summer of 2020, she was cautious. Her prior interactions with him did not give her a lot of confidence that he would solve the problem.

Wells had overseen departments that were repeatedly revealed in the Las Vegas Review-Journal to have substantial problems. Those problems were often not addressed until news stories ran. He maintains he had limited control over the elected departments and often was not informed of problems unless there was a significant pattern.

Unknown to the public until much later, Wells' son and daughter-in-law were hired at two departments he oversaw: the Clark County Public Defender's office and the Department of Family Services.[170] State law makes it a gross misdemeanor for relatives of elected or appointed officials to be hired to the agencies they oversee. Once the hiring was made public by the newspaper, Wells contended that the law wasn't clear when the county hired his family and the county passed an ordinance to clear it up. That ordinance made sure to grandfather anyone hired before it passed, like Wells' son, Tom.

Jeff Wells worked on the ordinance but maintains that the idea of grandfathering the relatives was another colleague's idea. He also points out that he was not the only top official to have his relatives employed at the county despite the law. The daughter of County Commissioner Steve Sisolak, who would later be elected governor of Nevada for one term, was chairman of the commission when his daughter was hired at the special public defender's office in 2016. Sisolak denied having anything to do with the hiring when it was exposed in the Review-Journal, but the law does not require the official to intervene in the hiring. Nevada Revised Statutes 281.210 bans the hiring of relatives as it's often very difficult to determine whether specific action prompted the hiring or whether subordinates hired a top official's relative to curry favor.[171]

Tom Wells was hired in 2012 by Public Defender Phil Kohn and six years later, RJ reporter Michael Scott Davidson, then covering the county before moving to the investigative team, revealed Kohn was the focus of a sexual harassment investigation. Kohn's employees alleged Wells was protecting Kohn but the internal county investigation found no evidence to substantiate it. The office, however, was moved to another deputy county manager. Years later, after Tom Wells' hiring came to light, Kohn conceded to investigative reporter Arthur Kane that Jeff Wells had introduced Tom to Kohn. Kohn and Wells maintained there was no pressure to hire his son.

Wells said two employees in Kohn's office theorized he was protecting Kohn and told that to investigators but there was no proof. The public defender's office was removed from his supervision because Tom Wells worked in the department. Jeff Wells objected to making the move at the same time there were allegations he was protecting Kohn because it would look like he was. He said County Manager Yolanda King still decided to make the move at that time.[172]

The same year that Kohn was under investigation for sexual harassment, the RJ's Kane revealed that another department head under Wells, Henderson Constable Earl Mitchell, was using county funds to gamble and visit relatives out of state. Kane's stories led to Mitchell's indicted on five felony counts. Prosecutors credited the RJ story for exposing the theft.[173] Mitchell dropped his re-election campaign when he knew the story was about to run. Prosecutors allowed him to plead no contest without admitting wrongdoing to a gross misdemeanor of fraudulent conveyance if he repaid the stolen eighty thousand dollars. He lost his police powers but avoided jail.

Jeff Wells said he believes he was looking into Mitchell's misconduct before the story broke and thought he had approached the police. Police sources told Kane they learned of the misconduct from his story. Wells pointed out he helped police and prosecutors investigate the Mitchell's conduct after it was revealed.[174]

Jeff Wells also oversaw Coroner Fudenberg's office part of the time there was extensive turmoil. Wells points out that he was not over the office when Fudenberg was making speeches on county time. Jeff Wells claims he went to public relations staff asking that they make clear that Kevin Schiller, then deputy county manager and now top manager, oversaw the office during the speeches.

"No, Jeff, they were already throwing you under the bus," he said he was told. "So we're not going to bother to throw anybody else under the bus." Jeff Wells maintains he wanted to discuss many of the issues on several occasions with the Review-Journal, but Schiller, by then promoted to his boss, didn't allow it.

"On one occasion, I went in and said I was going to talk to you and somebody named Kevin basically came storming into my office and kinda, like, if I talked to somebody I might, you know, get canned," Wells told Kane after his retirement.[175]

Schiller contends that he never prohibited Wells from discussing anything pertaining to Wells' actions but there were limits on what could be discussed while there were ongoing human resources investigations.[176]

While some of the time the office was under another county manager, Wells approved bonuses and pay increases for Fudenberg and failed to ensure that Fudenberg kept their agreement that he would take vacation when giving the lucrative speeches.

Having read the stories in the newspaper, Reid was vague when she finally reached Wells. She told him if she gave him all the information, he would be required to do an investigation. She and the office weren't ready for that right now. She told him she feared losing her job and wanted to know what kind of protections she had.

"I've been with the county long-term," she told Wells. "I think I'm a good employee. I think I'm worth protecting."

Wells interrupted her. "Well, Rita, how close are you to retirement?" he asked. She was taken aback, feeling like Wells wasn't interested in mitigating the problems but just wanted her and the conflicts to go away. He asked her if she was interested in any other jobs at the county but there was little available she felt met her qualifications. The conversation just kind of ended.[177]

Jeff Wells remembers it that they were both talking about when they would retire and did not intend the question to make it look like he wanted her to retire.[178]

***

Reid wasn't alone in wanting the county to address Telles' management. There was a group core of about half a dozen employees who had concerns and they clashed with others—many of whom Telles hired. Estate coordinator Aleisha Goodwin had been having problems with Telles not long after he took over. She was bolder than Reid in her camera work during the parking garage rendezvous. The women would follow to photograph and videotape the couple at least half a dozen times. One video showed Telles and Lee-Kennett in the back seat of her SUV. From a distance you could see shadows moving toward and away from each other but little else. When Lee-Kennett exited the vehicle, she had to smooth down her short gray skirt dress.

Goodwin had experience with stakeouts and surveillance. She was also one degree of separation from someone who knew Jeff German. Right out of high school, she worked for her father's private investigation firm. Tom Dillard had been a Metro police detective and a private investigator who helped the Binion family when Ted Binion was found dead. He also was a source for German's daily reporting on the Binion case and the book that followed. Goodwin also worked with another private investigator who knew German. David Groover, the former Metro detective involved in the shooting of Frank Bluestein and who responded to write a police report when German was assaulted by the Mob bagman, employed Goodwin as a runner when she was sixteen. Despite a growing metropolis, Vegas courts and law enforcement were still a smaller community.

She was office manager at her father's private investigations firm for seventeen years and worked as a process server. When Dillard decided to scale back his investigations in 2016, Goodwin started to look for another job. For eighteen months, she worked the thankless and dangerous job of serving people who weren't paying their child support. Once she finished her one-year county work probationary period, she looked for a safer county position, landing at the public administrator's office in September 2017 as an estate coordinator. She had experience looking for assets and finding people as part of the private investigation firm so put those skills to good use in the new job.

Goodwin had been a model employee under John Cahill and was learning quite a bit through the training from Senior Estate Coordinator Noraine Pagdanganan. At first, Goodwin got along with Telles—at least she thought. That was until Telles, Lee-Kennett, and Goodwin went out to visit one of the properties the PA office was managing.

The three started casually talking about how they wound up in Las Vegas, and Goodwin told them about her family history. Her father's side came to Vegas in the 1940s as part of the gambling boom. Her mother's side were Mormon pioneers and some of the first settlers in the area. That day,

Telles' attitude about her changed, she wrote in her 2020 complaint to county human resources.[179]

"He would call the other 2 Estate Coordinators into meetings or talk to them about issues in the office, some that even included me, and did not ever call me in to get my input or let me explain my interpretation of the situation," Goodwin wrote in her complaint.

She asked Pagdanganan about it, and she told Goodwin that Telles makes comments about the "Mormon Mafia" running the county. Telles complained about one of the probate commissioners who rules on estates cases making favorable rulings if the case included fellow Mormons, the complaint said.

"When Rob makes comments to others that are unfounded and untrue about my church and the members, it isn't just hurtful to me, as it is very personal and important to me but, I feel as though I have to defend it and explain to those that he has said those things to that a 'Mormon Mafia' is not real," she wrote. "It is an insult to me and them and there is no reason for such a discussion in a work environment, let alone a government agency."

Lee-Kennett had complained to Goodwin that Telles touched her butt. He had cornered Goodwin in an elevator, creepily telling her she smelled good. Telles was "very touchy" with the office's women until he learned of Goodwin's Mormon heritage, according to Goodwin's county complaint. She said Telles and Lee-Kennett clearly have a "very obvious personal relationship," meet often behind closed doors, lunch together, and would correct her on her work after meetings with Lee-Kennett.

"Lately, it has become unbearable," Goodwin wrote. "I feel very singled out and bullied and harassed, it has become a most hostile work environment."

On August 10, 2020, Telles assigned Goodwin ten cases to review in two hours, which was not nearly enough time. He kept badgering her to finish. The next day, he sat in a cubical reviewing her work, making comments like "Oh my God" and sighing while loudly asking her demeaning questions. Humiliated, she started to cry and had to leave for the day.

Telles continued the condescending and abusive treatment, piling her with excessive work. She felt like crying everyday when she came to work and asked coworkers if they felt the same way. They told her they did, her county complaint detailed.

Goodwin begged county human resources for an intervention and investigation of Telles. The women were at a loss about what to do about their new boss. They complained to HR but were told that Telles was an elected official and there was little county managers could do. Although Reid, Goodwin, and others were county employees and the county had an obligation to protect them, their complaints were amorphous enough that the county refused to act.

Amid the chaos in the office, Telles was facing a more serious issue. In his short time as public administrator, he had clashed with a local real estate company that had been taking over estates with property despite having no connection to the deceased or family. The company would then sell the house—often to the same small group of people—who would then flip the property. Family of the deceased often saw no proceeds from the estate as administration fees would eat up anything remaining equity. The company maintained the houses were underwater so the family never would have seen any money.

The private administration was all made possible by Nevada's lax probate laws that allowed anyone over eighteen and without a felony to petition a judge to administer an estate. Telles convinced lawmakers to pass a bill in the 2020 legislative session requiring that his office be notified when a judge assigns a non-relative to an estate.

He also asked Nevada Attorney General Aaron Ford to look into the practice by the real estate company, which was assigned to hundreds of estates in the past few years. Ford's office refused to intervene so Telles figured no one cared. He approached Las Vegas Realtor Kimberly McMahon, who retired in 2021 as a lieutenant at the Clark County Detention Center, to help him with a scheme that would allow him to profit, sources told Kane. He wanted to let her sell houses if she would kick back some of her commission to him. She refused, and he stopped giving her houses, the sources said. Instead, she went to Metropolitan police who brought the FBI into the investigation, interviewing people in Telles' office and subpoenaing records.

Kane broke a story about the investigation a few months after Jeff German's death. "Telles, whose elected position administers estates and secures the property of dead people while family or executors are located, approved home sales to private individuals he was working with at below-market value," Kane wrote in the November 22, 2022, story. "The buyer then would flip the properties within a few months, splitting the profit with Telles, sources said."[180]

Telles would later confirm that police were surveilling him over bribery allegations during the summer of 2022. He denied accepting bribes and wanted records on the investigation to support claims of police misconduct.[181] By 2023, police concluded that there was no evidence that Telles was attempting to obtain kickbacks from realtors who were selling houses for the probate office or trying to flip houses with co-conspirators for profit. He was doing unusual things for a government official like remodeling houses before letting them be sold, but the conclusion was that he was just trying to create a track record of accomplishments when he ran for higher office. Machiavellian but not illegal. Telles denied any corruption.[182]

By early 2022, and despite the investigation and open revolt in his office, Telles was gearing up for a re-election bid. Realizing the county wouldn't act to stop his conduct, the women opposed to Telles decided the only way to get him out of office was for someone to run against him. They quietly—as to not alert and draw the wrath of their boss—put out feelers to attorneys and others who might want to run for the obscure office. The office paid about one hundred and twenty thousand dollars a year in salary and another roughly fifty thousand a year in retirement contributions and other benefits, so successful attorneys balked.

The women had no luck attracting an alternative candidate so they decided one of them had to run. Reid, with her extensive experience in the office and being closest to retirement, decided to fall on the grenade. She wasn't totally sold and approached her family with the hope they would dissuade her. Her family all disappointed her, saying they were thrilled that she was throwing her hat in the ring. Without an excuse not to run, she waited until the last minute to file her candidacy. One unknown candidate—who Reid says was employed by the company that was clashing with Telles on the private probates—also jumped into the race. Reid felt the woman did not have enough experience or name recognition to unseat Telles. At the last minute, she threw her hat to run in the Democratic primary.

Top county officials did not respond to the complaints and turmoil, but they knew a good political controversy when they saw one.

"I'm not sure if you noticed but Rita Reed who works in the public administrator's office has filed a primary challenge against Robert Telles," Jeff Wells wrote County Manager Yolanda King in March 2022, misspelling Reid's name. "That should make for an interesting workplace over the next three months!!"

King responded: "Yes, I noticed she filed and thought the office environment should be interesting."[183]

After German's death, the Review-Journal obtained the emails through an open records request and published the email exchange between King and Jeff Wells discussing Reid entering the race and what an interesting work environment her campaign would create. For the article about the emails, Reid was quoted as calling the top bosses' emails "dismissive."

"They show a total disregard for the concerns I had voiced," she said after the Review-Journal read her the emails. "I guess I'm not surprised but I'm terribly, terribly disappointed."

The Monday after the story ran, Reid received a call from Jeff Wells asking her about her comments and reminding her that he brought in Mike Murphy to fix the problems. "I'd hate for us to start off on a bad foot," Wells told Reid.

"I'd hate that too," she said. "But it was very dismissive."

"Well, I just hope we don't get off on the wrong foot," Wells repeated. Reid took that as a threat to stay in line and not criticize him to the press.

Jeff Wells said he wouldn't have used the word "bad foot" and was just trying to make sure there were no hard feelings so that they could work together. The email to King was not intended to be dismissive but was just discussing how difficult it would be for the small office when two people working there were running against each other.[184]

The women knew that it would be tough to unseat an incumbent in an office that attracts almost no attention and doesn't garner enough political contributions for an advertising campaign. So Cahill and the women started contacting media about Telles' actions in office. Some told them they would produce a story if the Equal Employment Opportunity Commission found harassment—but not before. The women needed the publicity much sooner than the time it would take the federal government to rule on their grievances.

Cahill sent an email to Steve Sebelius and Jon Ralston telling them they might be interested in the political fight brewing at the public administrator's office.

"Steve, I write you because you recently wrote about odd or interesting Nevada political races," he wrote. "Jon is included because I tell him everything."

The email tells the journalists that Reid filed to run against Telles and that staff called German about the story. The email raises questions about how the county is handling the conflict and taking corrective action, whether there has been another situation where an assistant ran against her boss and that Reid can't disclose personnel problems because of her position.

Jon Ralston at the Nevada Independent begged off, saying his website didn't have the resources to investigate an obscure office like the public administrator.[185]

"My response to him does not reflect what you said and it came after German was already working on the story," Ralston wrote in an email to the author, questioning the relevance of the incident for the book. Usually a competing news organization (the Indy and RJ often compete for stories) would jump on a story if a competitor was digging into it. Sebelius said he didn't remember the details of the email and doesn't believe he talked to German about it.[186]

With no media interested in the campaign or problems in the office, Dillard, who had known Jeff German for decades, approached the veteran investigative reporter to see if he wanted to look into the conflicts. German agreed to meet with the women, but was non-committal, saying he would have to clear the idea with Prast, his editor, and the paper's attorney. [187]

After nosing around, German talked to Prast about the issue in April 2022. She thought he had done his homework and it sounded like a pretty good story.[188] German wasn't sure he could complete the story before the primary, which concerned Reid and other women as negative coverage was their best hope of unseating Telles. If it ran after, there was a chance he could lose the general election, but Republicans no longer do well in Clark County so that was far from a done deal. [189]

On May 9, 2022, Goodwin filed a second complaint against Telles. In it, she complained that Telles moved her out of her cubicle to the reception area where she has no privacy and is continually interrupted by people who think she is a receptionist. He told her it was temporary but she remains in that area while temporary workers are allowed to pick their workspaces. She also complained that Telles took away key duties, micromanages her when she is at her desk, and doesn't provide her opportunities for advancement and overtime. He also excludes her from pertinent work emails and employee lunch parties. She again wrote that she believes Telles' actions are discrimination based on her Mormon faith. She also provided a series of emails that she was not included on and then dropped the bombshell about Lee-Kennett and Telles' inappropriate relationship during and afterwork.

"For the past 2 years, Mrs. Lee-Kennett has used her relationship with Mr. Telles to assume power and privilege in the office," Goodwin wrote, detailing how she and other staff followed them to a parking garage after work where the staff was able to take photos and video of them in the back seats of vehicles. One video shows her getting out and pulling her dress down while another time they sat in the back seat for ninety minutes, shadows showing their heads together, before leaving in their separate vehicles. One date they met was the same date Telles filed his re-election papers and posed for a photo with his wife for social media before going to the garage to meet with Lee-Kennett.[190]

"They are both married with families," Goodwin wrote. "This is unacceptable disgusting behavior for a public servant. Physical contact with a subordinate in a public place and letting that subordinate use the favoritism she is getting from these inappropriate meetings to secure power and privileges above others in the office is affecting most of the staff in an extremely negative manner.

"The county has failed to protect employees from a mentally and emotionally abusive situation," she wrote. She asked that Telles and Lee-Kennett be removed from the office.[191]

German redoubled his efforts on the investigation and less than a month before June 14, 2023, primary, the Review-Journal published a story about conflict in the department.

"The Clark County public administrator's office has been mired in turmoil and internal dissension over the past two years, with allegations of emotional stress, bullying and favoritism leading to secret videotaping of the boss and a co-worker outside the office," German wrote for the May 16, 2023, online story. "A half-dozen current and former employees interviewed by the Review-Journal are alleging the hostile work environment was fueled by the elected administrator of the office, Robert Telles, carrying on an 'inappropriate relationship' with a staffer that has harmed the office's ability to deal with the public in overseeing the estates of those who have died."

Blurry, long-distance video shot by Goodwin was posted with the story, showing the shadows of the two figures with what appeared their heads moving toward each other. Then Lee-Kennett gets out of the car and adjusts her dress. Telles and Lee-Kennett denied having an affair, saying they met in private to discuss the stresses of the office and were in the back seat only to hug and talk face to face.

Telles refused to discuss the allegations later, saying he has said enough and didn't want to damage Lee-Kennett's relationship. He attacked the women who followed him.

"I will say that these folks who have followed me for two years, I don't know how anyone else would feel when you got someone who has the appropriate methods for allegedly proving misconduct in the workplace, does not take advantage of those methods, and instead decide to follow around somebody during their own personal time and evening," he lashed out. "You know, all around and I'm assuming they had to follow me home on numerous occasions. If they supposedly had any wrongful conduct in the office, they had legitimate means for actually addressing those."[192]

The women figured Telles would realize his political career could not survive after the scandalous video was publicized. They expected him to admit to the affair and suspend his campaign, but Telles, instead, went on the attack.

"'I think it's horrible that they recorded this, and they're trying to destroy my life and my marriage, when I'm actually infinitely in love with my wife," Telles told German for his story. "I was just trying to get things off my chest with somebody who understands, and now it's being framed as though I'm cheating on my wife." Telles blamed the controversy on a group of long-time employees who did not like his changes because they had to work hard.

Lee-Kennett is quoted telling German: "I have not had an inappropriate relationship with him. I would not be friends with a man who thinks he's going to have an inappropriate relationship with me."

Jeff Wells continued to downplay the controversy in an email the day the story ran to fellow county managers. He wrote in an email later obtained by the Review-Journal. "I know I can be a cynic when it comes to politics—but isn't it interesting that this article came out just before early voting starts and (Assistant PA) Rita (Reid) is running in the primary against Telles."

Behind the scenes, the county had to act now that the turmoil was made public. A day or two after the story ran, Wells called Mike Murphy. Wells said he didn't know anything about what was happening in the office and was reacting to German's story.

Other than Rita's call, which he characterized as talking about her being removed from her duties and not discussing other problems like abusive behavior or a potential affair, Wells said he did not know anything about turmoil in the office until the story ran. If there is a pattern of problems at a department he oversaw, human resources would notify him but when German's story ran, there were only two formal complaints to HR, so Wells said they hadn't. He hoped Murphy could mitigate the conflict and get the office working properly.[193]

Murphy was a long-time police officer in towns around Clark County, eventually leading the Mesquite Police Department at the county's far northern tip. After that, he took a job with City of Las Vegas' public safety department and eventually was hired by the county. Murphy had served as Clark County coroner for a dozen years before retiring in 2015 and recommending his deputy, John Fudenberg, take over the coroner's job. Murphy spent a few years in Washington, DC, as the forensics director at the National Center for Missing and Exploited Children. When the long-distance commute got old, he returned to Nevada and formed a consulting company with his wife. The county occasionally hired them to clean up problems departments. When Fudenberg took early retirement, Murphy's firm was tapped to run the office until a permanent coroner could be found. If Murphy had been hired to replace Fudenberg even temporarily, he would have had to suspend his government pension. He wasn't willing to do that. So Wells offered to hire his company on contract, which allowed Murphy to collect his pension and a monthly contract payment.

Murphy's job was to bring down tensions and help manage the office, but he found a very dysfunctional and dangerous environment. Since he retired, Murphy was less likely to carry a concealed weapon. Retired police officers are given the privilege to continuing to carry a gun without having to go through the permitting process that non-law enforcement residents must to conceal carry. Soon after starting at the public administrator's office, he started carrying his Glock again. He was worried about the friction and paranoia in the office and not just from Telles. It was just such a volatile atmosphere. With his wife working in the office, Murphy wanted to make sure he had a gun if something happened. He did not want to be caught emptyhanded.

Goodwin was thrilled to have Murphy in the office. She had witnessed one interaction between Murphy and Telles before he was hired to help mitigate problems in the public administrator's office. When Murphy was acting coroner—after Fudenberg retired—Telles and some of his staff had a meeting with Murphy. Telles was proudly sporting a fancy top coat with his collar up. Goodwin described Telles as "peacocking" with the coat on. It was his favorite coat.

Murphy, not always the best at filtering his reactions, sarcastically exclaimed: "Wow, nice coat."

Telles clearly did not take it well because staff never saw him wearing the favorite coat again. The interaction showed Goodwin that Murphy wouldn't roll over for Telles. She knew after the comment that she liked Murphy, and Wells had made a good choice to have him keep calm in the office.

While Wells assured Murphy that Telles approved of Murphy coming into the office, Murphy's interactions with Telles were often terse and unsatisfying. He spent days putting together a memo of how to assign staff and run the office. Telles agreed with the suggestions but never implemented them. Telles would shoot off nasty emails, but when Murphy would try to discuss the problem, Telles would say it is handled.[194]

***

Telles wasn't the first public administrator to face negative media coverage. These low-level offices that few administrators or reporters pay attention to are often a hive of corruption. Decades before Telles took over, a public administrator was convicted of fraud in the 1970s for overcharging estates for storage, and in 1983, an estate manager and investigator were charged with stealing from dead people.[195]

Telles lashed out at German and the story, hoping to rally his supporters before the election. "While many of you have contacted me with support, I know that some may believe the allegations made in the article by the local rightwing paper. You may believe that I betrayed your trust. You may believe I am not the man that I have always portrayed myself to be. Some of you may not know all the good work that I have done for Las Vegas. I hope by the end of this page you will see what I know to be true. The article was false.

"The article was intentionally gut-wrenching. It was so ugly that you almost had to believe it was true. I can understand why you might have, with the writer's skill at pushing buttons. Also, the timing of the article was very convenient for my opponent, Rita Reid."

After the story ran, Telles called Patrick McDonnell, German's former editor at the Sun who had become an attorney. McDonnell had known Telles when they were both at UNLV law school and reconnected over lunches after they both passed the bar exam. A law firm where McDonnell worked had their attorneys meet with other attorneys in case they had work to refer to the firm. Telles knew McDonnell previously worked at newspapers and wanted to know if he could file a defamation or libel lawsuit against German and the Review-Journal. McDonnell assured him it would be a waste of time and money. Libel law is pretty clear that there is a high bar for a public official to sue a newspaper as the aggrieved politician would have to prove actual malice. It was very doubtful Telles could even prove that anything in German's story wasn't true. He recommended writing a letter to the editor with the hope they will publish his views on the story.

The night of the June 14 primary, as polls closed, German called political consultant Lisa Mayo. Mayo and German had a long-time source relationship as she would call with tips or information her clients wanted out in the public.

"What are you hearing?" German asked Mayo. "Do you think my story will make a difference?"

"He's done," Mayo responded.[196]

Mayo political intuition was correct. Telles came in third out of three Democratic candidates though it took a while to get the final results. On June 22, 2022, German published a story saying Telles was conceding the race.

In the meantime, Telles lashed out and mocked German, who was continuing to investigate Telles. On his Twitter account (now called X), Telles mocked German's reporting with sarcastic tweets:

> Wife hears rustling in the trash. Her: 'Honey, is there a wild animal in the trash?' Me: 'No, dear. Looks like it's @JGermanRJ going through our trash for his 4th story on me. Oh shoot. I left a pizza box and sushi containers in the trash. In the next article, I'm going to have mob and yakuza ties[197]

Behind the scenes, Telles was also complaining to Wells about Murphy interfering with the work of the office and siding with the employees who were rebelling against his management. "The office is a little black box where it is easy for the public administrator and staff to abuse the office," Telles wrote Wells. "This includes the potential for ineptitude, theft and kickbacks from vendors."

On June 24, 2022, Telles wrote Wells again:

> I am frankly shocked at the way (Murphy) has acted so far. If his contract states he is to back up the people from the article no matter what he sees in the office, he is doing his job well. I would appreciate it if you could have a talk

with Mike about not immediately buying every
little thing they say.

Telles writes Wells that his antagonists are trying to get
him to resign now, but he won't do it. "The last thing I need
is another article from Jeff German about my resigning and
how it supposedly justified their claims. I'm sure they will
persist in these silly little games because that is what they
really want, another article."

German, the bulldog he was his entire career, continued
to file open records requests about the office despite his
articles already resulting in Telles losing his re-election
bid. German had learned that the public administrator's
office used an internal messaging system and wanted to see
if Telles and Lee-Kennett discussed anything on there that
might be newsworthy. The emails he received pertained
almost exclusively to county business but would Telles and
Lee-Kennett let their guard down in the internal messaging
system?

On September 1, 2022, the Thursday before Labor Day, a
county attorney sent Lee-Kennett and Telles emails notifying
them that the county would be releasing information to
German in response to his records request. The documents
were scheduled for release September 6, the Tuesday after
Labor Day. At 7:30 a.m., on Friday, September 2, Lee-
Kennett emailed Telles about the records release notification
from the county attorney. He responded that he would
review it.[198]

CHAPTER EIGHT: RETRIBUTION

Jeff German had taken a few days off leading up to the 2022 Labor Day weekend to work on his fantasy football team. Since starting at the Review-Journal more than a decade ago, German maintained a ritual in the days before Labor Day. Each year, the league held its draft day every Labor Day sharply at ten a.m. To continue his unprecedented record of victories, German had to be prepared. He also hadn't taken much vacation time that year, and he would lose any he didn't use by December 31. Private business, unlike governments, did not allow staff to accrue huge banks of paid time off to cash out for a big payday at the end of their careers.

That morning, casually dressed in black shorts, a light blue t-shirt, and tennis shoes, German drove to Roberto's Taco Shop to pick up some lunch. It was a quick run about half a mile away. Then he returned with lunch to work on the task at hand.

Right before eleven a.m., a short man in a broad straw hat and reflective shirt drove into the neighborhood in a GMC Yukon Denali, parking just outside the cul-de-sac where Jeff lived. He walked around the neighborhood for about twenty minutes. At 11:18, he walked into the gate on the west side of German's house. It was not locked. Five minutes later, German opened his garage door and walked towards his back gate. The assailant jumped out and attacked German as soon as he opened the gate.[199]

The assailant stabbed German in the neck, slashing a three and quarter-inch incision that cut his larynx and carotid artery. He fell back into a bush on the side of his property. The attacker continued to stab German in the left side of his neck twice and another stab on the right side. The assailant then stabbed German three times in the torso. German tried to protect himself, suffering superficial defensive wounds to both his forearms and hands. At some point during the attack, German was able to scrape the assailant's skin with his right hand.[200]

The assailant walked quickly to the Yukon. But then he stopped. Was his victim dead? He drove the Yukon back to German's house, parking in front of his driveway. He walked briskly to where German's body had fallen. Looking, he saw that German was dead. There would be no eyewitness to the brutal stabbing other than a neighbor's security camera. Satisfied, the assailant walked back to his truck and drove out of German's neighborhood.[201]

German died very quickly but lay behind a bush at the side of his house overnight. That Friday night, his neighbor from across the street, with whom German would often talk sports or about a story he was writing for the paper, saw German's garage door was open. They had lived across from each other for twenty-six years. German didn't leave his garage open, so the neighbor texted German, figuring he might have left it open accidentally and went out of town. German did not respond. As it started to get dark, the neighbor walked across the street, and closed German's garage door. He did not see German laying by the side of the garage. The next day, the neighbor went back over and saw German laying in a pool of dried blood. German's body was face up, eyes open, with right arm straight over his head and his left curled close to his body. Dried blood soaked the top of his shirt and covered the lower part of German's face almost like a mask. The neighbor, appalled at his friend's condition, quickly called police.[202]

Police arrived at the bloody scene, removing German's iPhone, keys, and wallet from his pockets. Inside, they found a neat house with no signs of break-in or burglary. German's Honda was parked in the garage. Police dusted the house and car for fingerprints and seized four Apple computers and a hard drive from German's house. Those devices and German's phone would be a major point of contention between police and the Review-Journal in the coming months, leading to an expensive legal fight and delaying the trial.

***

On September 3, 2022, Rita Reid and her husband were relaxing in their Henderson home when William came across a disturbing article.

"Oh my gosh, Jeff German was killed," he told Rita.

Rita refused to believe it, figuring it was some gossip post off Facebook or some other fake news. She grabbed the phone, scrolling down the article that the Review-Journal posted about German's murder. She still deluded herself into thinking that the newspaper had made a mistake. She just couldn't believe German was killed. When she calmed and realized German was dead, her first thought went to Telles. But she quickly put that out of her mind. It couldn't be.[203]

The news of German's death brought a lot of concerns and questions throughout the Las Vegas Valley. John Cahill fished out the handgun he'd stopped carrying after leaving his job as a juvenile officer and put it in his pocket.[204] Murphy and his wife saw the news and started debating who might have killed German. The burglary theory that police put out didn't sit well with Murphy because burglars usually avoid confrontation. Murphy's wife thought it was Telles, but Murphy dissuaded her from jumping to conclusions. It just didn't make sense. Telles was a bully but Murphy didn't think he had the balls to brutally stab someone to death.[205]

At the Review-Journal, all the staff was also wondering what had happened. Who had killed their friend and colleague? Most of the staff followed Reid and Murphy's path—considering it might be Telles but then quickly putting that out of their minds. It was just too crazy to think a politician—an attorney with no serious criminal record, a family, and a practice he could return to—would resort to murder over a story that had already been published. Sure, the story had got him booted out of office. German, however, never uncovered anything that could get him indicted. Why risk life in prison for a story that might have damaged his political career and raised questions with his wife but didn't otherwise seriously impact his life? After the late-night Saturday news conference, police were close-lipped about the case. Sunday passed with no news.

On Labor Day, police released images of the assailant dressed in the straw hat and reflective long-sleeve shirt. Behind the scenes, police had been searching for a GMC Denali and had found one that matched and was registered to Mary Ismael, Robert Telles' wife. She lived at 9624 Spanish Steps Lane in Las Vegas. Once the assailant's photo was released, police started receiving anonymous tips that German had written stories about Public Administrator Robert Telles, and that Telles was upset by the coverage. Police found the articles and realized that Telles was married to Ismael. They both lived at the same address where the Yukon was registered.

Police obtained phone data that showed at the time of the murder, Telles' phone was at his house. The phone only received incoming calls and texts that morning. No phone calls or texts were made from the device until after the slaying. That made police think Telles had left the phone at home if he killed German. Police had also obtained other video showing that the Yukon left Telles' neighborhood around 9:12 a.m. and returned to his neighborhood at 11:51 a.m. That window gave plenty of time to kill German.[206]

Police were also still following the possibility that Jeff German was murdered after surprising a burglar. That same day, police served a search warrant on Google to get GPS, cell phone, and Wi-Fi data on eight businesses that were robbed by people dressed like German's assailant. Police had very distant video of the attack but it was difficult to see what happened beyond German walking to his gate and an assailant jumping on him.[207]

The next day, despite connecting Telles to the Yukon, police released a photo of the Yukon Denali that German's killer was driving. They also released video of the suspect walking down German's street. It is unclear why the police released the photo of the truck since it could have tipped Telles that police were closing in on him. He could have fled or destroyed any evidence in his possession.

Upon seeing the Yukon, employees at the public administrator's office recognized that Telles occasionally drove the truck when his BMW was being serviced. The office brought the information to Murphy, who at first disputed it, saying Telles had a BMW and his wife drove a Telsa. But they had a photo of the couple in front of the truck so Murphy texted police. The FBI joined in the case, requesting search warrants of cell phone traffic the day of the murder. Special Agent Zach Franklin filed the search warrant affidavit on September 6, 2022.[208]

***

Assistant City Editor David Ferrara, who worked courts with German before German joined the investigative team and Ferrara was promoted to editor, had been telling anyone who would listen that he thought Telles was connected to the killing. He closely reviewed the video police released of the suspect walking in German's neighborhood. Then he compared that with the video of Telles walking with German for the original May story on the public administrator office that German had produced with photographer Kevin Cannon. To him, the suspect and Telles looked about the same height. He looked at the picture of the suspect and thought he could determine that he wasn't very tall. He barely was the height of the sedan he walked past in the police-released photo.

Most of RJ staff dismissed it as a conspiracy theory. Either way, there wasn't much use in speculating because the newspaper couldn't use the information for a story unless police identified Telles as a suspect. That would clearly be defamatory.

Ferrara didn't give up. Ferrara looked up Telles' home address, learning he didn't live far from German. He theorized that a county official could easily get ahold of a reflective shirt like the suspect was wearing. A county official also had access to databases that could pinpoint German's home address. He felt they were tantalizing facts.[209]

Ferrara ran into the RJ's top editor, Glenn Cook, at the gym and pulled out his laptop to show Cook the similarities between Telles and the assailant photo and video that police were releasing. They talked about it for forty-five minutes but, again, there was little that they could do until police publicly identified a suspect.

Ferrara then ran into Kane in the RJ newsroom, explaining his theory of the murder.

"It would be a hell of a story!" Ferrara exclaimed.

Kane was hearing different things from his police sources. None of them thought it had to do with German's work, or at least that's what they were saying. Kane would need to see more than circumstance and supposition to convince him that a politician killed a journalist. He needed facts, dismissing Ferrara by offering to bet a hundred bucks that Telles wouldn't be implicated in German's death. Ferrara instantly agreed to the bet.

The Tuesday after Labor Day, Telles showed up at the public administrator's office for a couple of hours. Murphy asked him if he had a minute to talk about an issue, and

Telles responded with a blunt "no." He left soon after and it was the last time he would be seen at the county office.

At the RJ, soon after police released a photo of the Yukon, former reporters texted Ferrara a screenshot from Facebook of Telles and his family standing in front of a similar SUV. Google maps also had a photo of a maroon SUV in Telles' driveway.

Ferrara showed it to City Editor Carri Geer Thevenot. She got chills. For the first time, she thought maybe Ferrara was onto something.[210] Ferrara sent the Facebook photo to a Metro source he knew and called the officer, who was not involved in the investigation.

"Holy shit," the officer said when he looked at the SUV.

Ferrara marshalled his staff, sending court reporter Katelyn Newberg and police reporter Brett Clarkson to Telles' neighborhood. Review-Journal video anchor and producer James Schaeffer had an app that tracked Metro's police helicopter. It was flying circles around Telles' neighborhood. Driving around Telles' neighborhood, Clarkson and Newberg saw Telles in his driveway. She told Clarkson to get in the back of her SUV, filled with firewood from a camping trip, so he could look out the back. Editors told them to stay far enough as not to interfere with any investigation. They drove to a school parking lot a block from Telles' house and sat.

Metro detectives were in fact in the neighborhood keeping an eye on Telles. Police and reporters both saw Telles exit his house and start to wash the GMC despite the 109-degree heat. David Wilson relieved the two reporters as evening descended, but he left around midnight when it looked like nothing would happen. Early the next morning, reporters returned to find the Telles' house roped off with yellow police tape. Police were executing a search warrant.

Police had stopped Telles early during a traffic stop and taken him into custody. By coincidence, Metro detectives investigating corruption allegations against Telles had planned to surveil him the day of German's murder. At the last minute, the plan was changed to conduct the surveillance a day earlier. The officers following him noticed he appeared agitated and not his usual put-together self. They could not have known what police later believed he was planning the following day, but there was something different. They learned later that the county had notified him of the release of Microsoft messaging records between him and Lee-Kennett. The change in surveillance schedule would likely have not saved German's life because detectives could not follow Telles into the tight cul-de-sac where German lived without him spotting the tail. However, it would have made identifying a suspect almost instantaneous. There were signs that Telles knew that detectives were investigating him at the time of German's slaying. He had been searching counter-surveillance tactics on his phone and had installed cameras outside his house and for the bottom of the GMC, likely to make sure no tracking devices were placed on his vehicle.

If Telles is convicted of German's murder, it will have been a spontaneous and brazen act especially if he believed detectives were tracking him. There is no evidence that he had staked out or even visited German's neighborhood before the morning of German's stabbing. He clearly was upset by the records that the county was about to release because he called county officials after German's death, arguing that there was no longer any reason to make those records public.[211]

After the traffic stop, detectives produced search warrants signed that day and took Telles' DNA and his clothes. In a run-of-the-mill case, police and prosecutors would have just arrested the suspect as they had enough probable cause after searching his house. But District Attorney Steve Wolfson got involved in the decision because German's death was such a high-profile case. He wanted to wait to arrest Telles until the DNA evidence was a match. That would take a few hours so Telles was released and later caused significant risks to himself and first responders. Telles returned home in Tyvek-style HAZMAT coveralls while police lab techs analyzed the DNA. Around six p.m., police returned to Telles' house to arrest him. The DNA under German's fingernails matched Telles. This time, Telles refused to come out.[212]

Telles was holed up in his bathtub trying to commit suicide. He had created a noose from some clothes and tried to hang himself. When that didn't work, he slashed his wrists. Rumors were the cutting was a superficial attempt, but a source showed Kane a photo with the bottom of Telles' tub filled with blood. He told police he couldn't put his family through a trial but eventually asked that they come in and get him. It was too dangerous. Police didn't know what weapons he had or what he was planning in his distraught state. They sent in a drone to check Telles' condition.

Osvaldo "Ozzie" Fumo, a prominent defense attorney and Nevada state assemblyman at the time, knew Telles when he was at UNLV law school and through the Democratic party functions. Police called Fumo, who was in the middle of a trial and preparing for the next day in court. Police told Fumo that Telles said Fumo was his attorney. He was not but he rushed down to the standoff to see if he could help solve it peacefully. It was a forty-five-minute trip so right before Fumo arrived, police were able to get Telles to exit his house.[213]

Police cleared reporters and camera people out of the area before bringing Telles out, but always resourceful Review-Journal photographer Kevin Cannon had befriended a neighbor who let him shoot photos from his property. Cannon had been with German that spring when he interviewed Telles at the public administrator's office for the original investigation so he had been with the story from the beginning. The exclusive photos show Telles being brought out on a gurney and loaded into an ambulance. Telles was given medical treatment and booked into the Clark County Detention Center.

Inside Telles' Spanish-style home, police found a tennis shoe similar as the ones the assailant was wearing in the surveillance video. Under a leather reclining couch there was also a plastic bag with what appeared to be cut up chunks of the second shoe. In the garage, police found a grocery bag stashed in a toolbox. Inside was a wide-brimmed straw hat with the same vent holes as the hat worn by the assailant. It had also been cut up. Police also seized a shoulder bag that looks similar to the one in the video from German's neighborhood.[214]

***

In the public administrator's office, Murphy was scrambling to make sure the staff was safe. Coordinating with County Manager Yolanda King, he sent all the staff to work from home for the rest of the week. If they didn't hear from him before Monday, they were expected to return to work. The locks were changed. Key cards were deactivated. He told staff individually that if their card didn't work to go to the front desk and wait for a supervisor who would tell them whether it was a glitch or they were not supposed to be there. Murphy and administrators could not rule out a larger conspiracy.

In the weeks after his arrest, Metropolitan Police and even the FBI would file a series of search warrants for Telles' social media, phone, and messaging, and even a Fitbit he bought in 2022. The warrants to Meta, Facebook, Twitter, telephone companies, and for the county, and his home would look for a motive and any information linking Telles to the crime. After his medical condition was stabilized, Telles was held in the Clark County Detention Center.

On October 20, 2022, Robert Telles was indicted on one count of murdering a person over the age of sixty. A judge refused to set a bond to allow him to leave jail while awaiting trial. Usually, the time between an indictment and a trial is a quiet time in a criminal case. Telles, however, continued to make regular news during various pretrial motions and hearings. The case would also raise historic First Amendment issues, such as whether a reporter—or his news organization—could protect confidential sources even after a reporter's death.

***

The murder of a journalist for doing his or her job is unfortunately a common occurrence in many countries. The Committee to Protect Journalists lists more than 2,200 who have died around the world since 1992. About one thousand of those deaths were classified as murders as opposed to journalists killed covering wars or during other dangerous assignments. Of the murdered journalists as of the end of 2023, Iraq had the greatest number with one hundred and twelve, followed by the Philippines with ninety-four, and Mexico with sixty-one.

In the United States, a journalist killed in the line of duty is exceedingly rare. Seventeen journalists, including German, are listed as being killed while on the job. Nine of those were classified as a murder. Five of those US killings happened during a mass shooting by a disgruntled reader in 2018 at the Capitol Gazette. Most of the rest of the seventeen (murdered and dangerous assignments) were killed by criminals, a disgruntled coworker or died in the World Trade Center during the September 11 terrorist attacks and subsequent anthrax mailings. Of the journalists murdered in the past three decades, the United States is tied for eighteenth with two other countries.[215]

You would have to go back to more than seventy years to find a journalist in the United States who was killed by a disgruntled government official. In 1949, Texas radio journalist Bill Mason was shot by a deputy sheriff, Sam Smithwick, after he aired a broadcast critical of Smithwick.

Mason had told listeners that he was being threatened after he had criticized prostitution at a dancehall on property owned by Smithwick. Smithwick was convicted of the murder and hanged himself in prison in 1952.[216]

Despite being fairly immune to the dangers reporters faced in dictatorships and lawless countries, US journalists have often publicized their peril and hazards of their work. But again, major media organizations often colored the narrative with their political beliefs instead of examining the facts.

The 2016 campaign of President Donald Trump sparked a large outcry from national reporters that his rhetoric was endangering them. Trump's speeches were often idiotic and over the top as he threw out red meat for his supporters. He talked regularly about fake news and reporters being the enemy of the people. Those speeches might prompt angry looks and insults thrown at the reporters covering events. There were a few reports of actual violence—a phone knocked out of a reporter's hand a rally; a BBC cameraman shoved by a guy wearing a MAGA hat. Attacks and harassment of media were also reported during the January 6, 2021, riot that attempted to overturn President Joe Biden's election. But none of it matched the outcry by reporters.

Along with rhetoric, Trump attempted to misuse his office by applying pressure to media organizations he didn't feel were favorable. Trump reportedly tried to block the merger between Time Warner and AT&T because of his hatred of CNN, which is a division of Time Warner.[217] He also expressed concern to Rupert Murdoch when he was selling his Hollywood holdings to Disney until he learned that Murdoch was to continue to own Fox News, which provided favorable coverage to Trump.[218]

But if Las Vegas police and prosecutors are correct, when someone actually resorted to murder to silence a journalist, it was ironically a liberal Democrat. Telles tried to distract from his misdeeds in office that German exposed by saying those stories were "allegations made in the article by the local rightwing paper."

German, who leaned liberal himself, would privately rail against every Trump outrage and could not be calmed by discussions of attacks on the media by prior administrations. What he and others couldn't see is that it was the institution of government is often inherently against transparency and accountability was, therefore, often, the true enemy of the people.

There was also little coverage of action by Democratic leaders against news organizations—maybe that was because they did not engage in the same heated rhetoric as Trump. Often it is easier for national media to discuss words and speeches instead of digging for the real truth.

The Obama administration engaged in some of the most aggressive tactics to silence the press. But there was never the same outcry in the national media that Trump's "fake news" or "enemy of the people" received. Whether that was because of liberal bias or establishment bias or just plain laziness, coverage of Trump's anti-press actions was ubiquitous.

Obama's actions—which some may say were more insidious—were covered but never received the kind of exposure that Trump did.

In 2018, the Associated Press, arguably the least partisan and most factual major national journalism organization, called out Obama for his attempts to silence the free press. "Trump may use extraordinary rhetoric to undermine trust in the press, but Obama arguably went farther—using extraordinary actions to block the flow of information to the public," the September 11, 2018, AP Fact Check said. "The Obama administration used the 1917 Espionage Act with unprecedented vigor, prosecuting more people under that law for leaking sensitive information to the public than all previous administrations combined. Obama's Justice Department dug into confidential communications between news organizations and their sources as part of that effort. In 2013, the Obama administration obtained the records of 20 Associated Press office phone lines and reporters' home and cell phones, seizing them without notice, as part of an investigation into the disclosure of information about a foiled al-Qaida terrorist plot.

"AP was not the target of the investigation. But it called the seizure a 'massive and unprecedented intrusion' into its news-gathering activities, betraying information about its operations 'that the government has no conceivable right to know.'

"Obama's Justice Department also secretly dogged Fox News journalist James Rosen, getting his phone records, tracking his arrivals and departures at the State Department through his security-badge use, obtaining a search warrant to see his personal emails and naming him as a possible criminal conspirator in the investigation of a news leak."[219]

That assessment happened before the Trump administration made an unprecedented move against press freedoms. Trump's Justice Department indicted Julian Assange, founder of Wikileaks, in 2019 on espionage allegations. Obama's Justice Department investigated the leaks to his website that exposed civilian deaths in Iraq, embarrassing diplomatic cables, and Democratic National Committee favoring Hillary Clinton over Bernie Sanders in the 2016 campaign.[220] Obama decided against prosecution.[221]

Top Trump officials, including CIA Director Mike Pompeo, went even further, discussing kidnapping and even killing Assange, according to a Yahoo! News investigation. The CIA viewed Wikileaks as a non-state intelligence service and claimed Assange conspired with hackers to steal government secrets. But it is very difficult to argue that he was not a journalist as the website regularly revealed government misconduct and potential war crimes that most news organizations would have eagerly exposed if they had been provided the records and video leaked to Assange's website. Surprisingly (or maybe not) the elite national media was far more outraged by Trump's rhetoric than allegations of a contemplated assassination.[222]

German's murder punctuated an increasingly hostile atmosphere for reporters from the government and the general public. The animosity was clearly building for years but few thought it would get to the point where a US government official was charged with murdering a US reporter because of what he wrote.

CHAPTER NINE:
POLITICAL DYNASTY

Robert Richard Telles was born four days before Halloween in 1976 in Biloxi, Mississippi. Telles' father, Raymond Rutherford Telles, was in the air force so the family moved often. After one enlistment, Raymond Rutherford decided to return to the border town of El Paso, Texas, where he was born and his family had established a political dynasty. The Telles clan rose from poverty and obscurity to lead the border town into a diverse modern time. Some of the family's politicians, however, also attracted law enforcement scrutiny. None of their alleged crimes would be as significant as the one Robert Richard Telles was arrested for and charged with in 2022.[223]

Robert's great uncle, Raymond L. Telles, was elected the first Mexican American mayor of a major US city in 1957. After two terms as El Paso's mayor, President John F. Kennedy appointed him ambassador to Costa Rica in 1961. His daughter would be appointed to the same position more than half a century later.[224] Raymond L. Telles found success with presidents of both parties. President Nixon appointed him to work at the Equal Employment Opportunity Commission.[225]

But in 1977, he pleaded guilty to aiding and abetting an illegal alien to enter the country and violating the minimum wage law—both misdemeanors—after being indicted on felony violations of immigration and labor laws. Raymond Telles and his wife had been charged with bringing a Costa

Rican woman to the United States under false pretenses to work for his family and failing to pay her the minimum wage. Prosecutors dropped the charges against his wife.[226]

The ambassador's brother, Richard was a county commissioner and president of the board of trustees for the El Paso Independent School District. Richard's son and the father of the suspect in German's murder, Raymond Rutherford Telles continued the family's political dynasty after his stint in the air force. But he also found himself in prosecutor's sights. He twice won the election for the El Paso city council seat. He was defeated in an attempt to follow his namesake uncle into the mayor's job. His political career ended in corruption. He was part of a large group charged with conspiracy to bribe local officials, pleading guilty to fraud in 2008. He was sentenced to probation.[227]

His son, Robert Telles, the suspect in Jeff German's slaying, graduated from Cathedral High School, a private Catholic school, in 1995. He was looking for a direction in his life. Robert Telles was estranged from his father after he divorced his mother, Rosalinda. Robert Telles moved to Colorado, working in IT and living in the upscale suburb of Greenwood Village.

But money was tight. He met his first wife, Tonia Burton (née Melendrez) while working at Super Kmart in a seasonal job over the holidays. He was a cashier and she worked in returns. They started as friends but found each other attractive and started dating.

They then both started working for an apartment complex, managing units and screening potential tenants. The owners sold the building and both were laid off so they moved to California because Burton's family was there. Telles was adamant he didn't want to return to El Paso. Burton and Telles married in Las Vegas in 2002—less than a year after meeting at the Kmart.[228] Around 2004, the couple moved to the Las Vegas, and Telles took a job repairing air conditioners in homes and businesses, a key industry in a town that often saw summer temperatures top 115 degrees.[229]

Telles was a staunch Democrat, hating guns, though mental issues made it difficult for Burton to imagine her Telles stabbing anyone. He had an obsessive-compulsive disorder that drove him to make sure his hands were always clean. He couldn't even eat an orange since it would squirt juice all over his fingers. During their relationship, Burton noticed that Telles always thought of himself as the smartest person in the room. It was a characterization many people who knew him would give whether they liked or hated him. He also always believed he was right, no matter the evidence disputing it.

In his free time, Robert Telles liked to play video games, but favored a flight simulator in contrast with the more popular shoot-'em-up games. Telles started drinking relatively late in life, taking up the habit when he was twenty-two. He quickly got in trouble with booze. Telles would later label himself an alcoholic, but Burton only saw him drink socially when the couple was together. When he drank around her, he liked to sing karaoke. He also kept up his fit appearance, which helped his wandering eye for the ladies, who were attracted to him despite his diminutive stature. He was seeing other women during his marriage, Burton contends, and she couldn't ignore that. But Robert Telles' career aspirations are what eventually ended the relationship.

Telles was completing an undergraduate degree in business administration online and planned to attend law school. She didn't know it at the time, but Telles was also thinking of getting into politics, as that was the family's legacy. He loved the public eye, but Burton shunned the spotlight. She could not imagine exposing her life to public scrutiny.

Their daughter was born on February 9, 2008. That July, Telles filed for divorce.[230] Their different visions for the future eventually ended the marriage, though the couple remained friendly.[231] On November 13, 2010, Telles remarried. He and his second wife, Mary Ann Ramirez Ismael, also took their vows in Clark County. She had a son from a previous relationship, and the couple soon had a child together.[232]

With three children to support, Robert Telles took a job at College of Southern Nevada, supervising a team of repair people who fixed air conditioning units around the campuses. He also enrolled at William S. Boyd School of Law at the University of Nevada-Las Vegas at night.[233]

In law school, Telles first dipped his toe into politics but found more controversy than success. He ran for president of the student bar and was elected in 2012. Many of his fellow students found him charismatic, affectionately calling him "Mr. Clean" in a reference to his shaved head. There, however, were already signs of the control freak that would appear later in his career. At first, it was minor things. Instead of reaching a consensus on a remodel of the locker room, Telles dictated what he wanted to happen. The same occurred with planning for the school's welcome back party.

Carlos Morales was the second-year class representative to the student bar and noticed that Telles didn't like to compromise. That was not necessarily unusual or a bad trait for a future lawyer. For a politician, however, it could prove problematic. Around the time he met Telles, Morales was serving as president of the Phi Alpha Delta fraternity. The fraternity planned a "rager" party for the beginning of the 2012-13 school year. Two kegs, a ton of hard liquor, and cigars for as many as one hundred and fifty guests who would pass through the frat house that August night.

It was getting dark and about fifty to seventy-five people were already partying. Morales was talking to a group of people when a student flagged him, pointing over to Telles. Morales scanned the room and saw Telles standing between two female students. One was wearing short jean shorts—

Daisy Dukes, in popular vernacular—and Telles had his hand on her inner thigh. From her face, Morales could tell the student was not welcoming Telles' advances. She looked terrified.

Morales he quickly wove his way through the crowd. He towered over the five-foot-seven-inch Telles. Morales placed both his hands on Telles' shoulders and flipped him around, drawing him away from the woman. Morales laid into him, telling him how inappropriate he was behaving, especially with his leadership position of student bar president. Telles seemed so wasted that Morales' lecture didn't seem to register. Later that night, Telles was going to drive away, but the other fraternity members took his keys away. He wandered around the neighborhood and even to downtown several miles away. Finally, around four a.m., he came back to the party, crying and begging for his keys so he could go home.

The following Monday between classes, Morales ran into the woman Telles had groped. She was mortified to be identified as the victim in the incident. She didn't want to file a complaint, fearing Telles might damage her career after she graduated. So Morales thought that was the end of the incident. The incident was boorish but by no means a crime, he thought.

A drunken frat party and minor groping incident is hardly unusual and probably would not be noteworthy, except what happened next. Several people at the party witnessed the incident. At the September 5, 2012, bar board of governors meeting, several women brought up that Telles' behavior was unbecoming of a leader. Instead of apologizing, Telles pushed back with legal maneuvering worthy of a felony case. He sent letters to the board directing them to retain all documents and threatening to sue the board for defamation.

Morales' wife was already an attorney and she told him how serious Telles' actions were. Morales was pissed. He had just had a young daughter, and Telles was endangering the financial livelihood of his new family over a mistake of his own making. Telles also started trying to aggressively ferret out the identity of the woman he groped, being too drunk the night of the party to remember who he had accosted. He called and texted people who might know, demanding they reveal the woman's identity. He went to people's houses to bully the information out of fellow students. Fortunately, he never found her.[234]

There was talk of impeachment but the students determined the organization's bylaws didn't allow that. They suggested Telles resign, but he refused. The board then organized a vote of confidence. Telles loss that vote and he was removed as president in November 2012. Despite his removal, he continued to come to the meetings, which was awkward for everyone else. Telles didn't seem to care.

Despite the controversy, he was making solid contacts in law school. Ozzie Fumo would help his partner, Thomas F. Pitaro, teach classes and noticed the up-and-coming attorney. With Telles' glad-handing and wide grin, Fumo figured he would soon see Telles' shiny head on the ubiquitous "ambulance chaser" billboards around town that solicited victims of car accidents or falls at Strip hotels for personal injury lawsuits. That was the kind of attorney Fumo expected Telles would be, based on his personality. Fumo also found Telles was easy to talk to and, at the time, took criticism well. Telles graduated in 2014 and passed the bar the in January 2015.[235]

He soon opened his own firm, Accolade Law, focusing on probate and family matters but occasionally taking on minor criminal cases like DUIs. He never had a felony criminal case and only represented people in three civil cases that went to trial.[236] His inappropriate behavior with women didn't stop at the law firm. A paralegal he hired complained of his constant sexual harassment. Her attorney sent a letter demanding Telles stop the unwanted hugging, kissing, and grabbing of her private parts, like her butt.[237]

An Accolade client, Brandy Hall, had a similar story of sexual misconduct as well as Telles' failure to properly perform his attorney duties. Hall worked as a director at a local funeral home and referred clients to Telles for probate work when their relatives died. Telles started asking her to lunch. He sent her a Christmas tree one year and a five-hundred-dollar fruit basket, prompting teasing from her coworkers that Telles had a crush on her. He also started sending her late-night pictures of his penis and a video of him masturbating. With a bawdy sense of humor, Hall would show coworkers the inappropriate visuals as a laugh and just delete the offensive advances. She was surprised that he would send the photo because what it showed was far from impressive, she thought. She also knew she could also handle herself. When Telles put his arm around her waist and tried to pull her in for a kiss, she stopped it with a strong arm to his chest. By that time, Telles had announced he was running for public administrator but didn't seem concerned his behavior would be revealed.

Hall was going through a divorce, and Telles offered to represent her for free. Short on money and not put off by his crude advances, she agreed, figuring she could handle his nonsense to save money. It was a mistake. In a custody hearing, Telles showed up unprepared and failed to object when the judge was about to approve joint custody with Hall's estranged husband. She lost sole custody. Distraught and nauseous, Hall fled to the bathroom as Telles followed.

She found another attorney, who was LDS like her, to help regain full custody. She shared the history of Telles' misconduct with him. But neither Hall nor any of the other people who had negative run-ins with Telles filed complaints with the State Bar of Nevada or went to the media when Telles ran for public administrator. Morales figured the public administrator's office was so obscure that it wasn't worth contacting the media. No one would care. Morales promised himself if Telles ran for a more prominent office, he would let people know the type of person they were electing.

With the backing of the outgoing public administrator, Telles ran unopposed for the Democratic nomination. In overwhelmingly blue Clark County, he easily won the county position. He beat Republican Thomas L. Fougere 53-41, even with an independent third-party candidate, who garnered about five percent of the vote.[238]

Telles still didn't stop drinking when he was elected to public office.[239] On the evening of February 29, 2020, about a year after his election, Telles got drunk at the Bellagio Casino and started arguing with his wife. While the couple drove home, he grabbed her by the neck and hit her arm, police detailed in a report. The argument continued at the house.

He yelled, "Kill me!" while his wife and their two children hid in a room, police documented. She finally called 911, and Telles grabbed her in a bear hug and wouldn't let go until his children pried their mother from his arms. When police arrived, he refused to cooperate, flexing his arms across his body so officers couldn't handcuff him, and collapsing into a chair. He refused to get up when police ordered him to cooperate.

As officers finally led Telles out of his house, he tried to talk—slur, really—his way out of an arrest, hoping his government office might get him a pass.

"You guys just want to take me down because I am a public official," he wailed in angst. "I did not touch anybody. I didn't hurt anybody."

He repeated that over and over as seen on the police body camera.

An arresting officer warned him to comply: "Don't do anything more stupid than you've already done, please."

Telles continued to resist, complaining his civil rights were being violated. "Who the hell did I hit?" he complained. "Can anybody tell me who I hit?"

"It may have something to do with how drunk you are," the officer told him.

"I've been way drunker than this, chief," Telles replied.

"I'm sure your supervisors will love to see this body cam when they see it," the arresting officer admonished.

Telles then name-dropped someone he said worked at the detention center, stating that she would vouch for him.

"The way the domestic battery law is written, it doesn't matter who vouches for you," the officer patiently explained.

"I am not a batterer," Telles replied. "I love my family. I love my wife. You guys want to take me down, that's all it is."[240]

He was charged with domestic battery and resisting police in the early morning of March 1. A year later, a plea agreement allowed Telles to have the domestic violence charge dismissed after he paid a $418 fine and agreed to classes on stress management and coping with relationships.[241]

As is Metro policy, police notified top county officials of the arrest, but officials did not let any of the people in Telles' office know about the violence. People in his office who were complaining about Telles only found out about the domestic violence arrest after he was arrested for German's murder. They were appalled that the county didn't warn them of his arrest.

As public administrator, Telles took actions that were surprising for a licensed attorney. In one 2019 incident, he tried rescinded a job offer because the woman regularly served on a federal grand jury, according to a lawsuit she filed. Brandy Carman had given notice at the county's aviation department after he offered her a job that paid nearly seventeen thousand dollars more per year. She cried when Telles told her she needed to get out of the jury duty if she wanted the estate coordinator's position in his office, the lawsuit and a Review-Journal story reported.

"Don't you cry to me," she is quoted in the story recounting what Telles told her. "I don't know who you think you are, and I don't know who you think I am, but I'm not here to give you sympathy."

She complained to the county but human resources officials maintained they had no control over Telles because he was an elected official. County recruitment manager Becky Dutro acknowledged that what Telles was doing was "illegal" and that a lawsuit might make him realize that.[242]

"Maybe that's what needs to happen to get his attention," Dutro is alleged to have told Carman, according to the lawsuit. "He wants to continue down this path, even though we have advised him what he's doing is wrong and illegal." The county and Telles denied violating the law but settled the lawsuit for thirty-five thousand dollars in 2021.[243]

Telles also tried to rescind another job offer when he found out the applicant was pregnant. Deputy County Manager Jeff Wells intervened, and Telles made the job offer. But the woman wisely decided to find work elsewhere after the controversy. Anyone with basic knowledge of the law and employment policies would know that it was illegal to discriminate based on pregnancy.[244]

In the public administrator's office, two sides quickly formed after Telles' election. Old-time employees complained about his actions. They believed his policy changes were destroying the office and impacting families who just lost relatives. Another contingent sided with Telles, agreeing with him that the women who opposed him just wanted to remain in control.

Some contend he improved conditions at the public administrator's office. In 2021, Telles hired Nichole Lofton as an estate coordinator. She found him to be a supportive and effective boss. Lofton, who dubbed the old-school staff as the "mean girls," contended he did nothing wrong and the legacy employees just didn't like his management style. Lofton, who had real estate experience before joining the county to learn more about Nevada's sometimes crazy housing market, said he trained her when the "mean girls" would not.

Telles tried to build cohesion in the office by supporting another employee's idea of a birthday club. She claims the women opposed to Telles refused to attend the celebrations. She does concede that the video of Telles in the back seat with Lee-Kennett was inappropriate, even if there was no sexual activity. They were both married and he was Lee-Kennett's boss. She said she is suing the county and has filed an EEOC complaint, saying she was mistreated and harassed at work but not by Telles.

After the German's death, Lofton was moved to the county's law library where she is charged with making sure the homeless don't get out of line and handing out books. It is not a job she likes or that in line with her skills and experience. She plans to stay only until her lawsuit is settled.[245]

Telles maintains he was alcoholic during the episodes at UNLV and during the domestic. He stopped drinking right after his domestic violence arrest. He tried to drink socially many times, but a few drinks would quickly turn into a blackout so he stopped cold turkey. He admitted he didn't know if he made sexually inappropriate advances when he was drunk but denied any impropriety when he was sober.

Telles maintained that he improved the county's processes and doubled the number of cases closed in the department despite the turmoil. He railed against Jeff German because he said he provided the Review-Journal reporter plenty of documentation about his successes and disputing claims by what he called the disgruntled employees. He said German failed to investigate his claims. German, instead, just took what his opponents said since there were five or six of them and ran with the story. Telles maintains if the problems had been substantiated, the union representing the workers would have acted way before the allegations got into the press.

"The claims made by those other folks were inflammatory," he told Kane in December 2023 over jail-video conference. "I'm a little bit irritated."

He continued to maintain he had nothing to do with German's murder despite the overwhelming evidence police released. He said he was framed in a complex conspiracy. The chances of the DNA found under German's fingernails being anyone but Telles was estimated by Metro's evidence staffer to be 4.46 octillion to one. That's a four with twenty-seven zeros.[246] Vegas is a town that likes long odds but those numbers dwarf the world's population of eight billion.

Additionally, a hat, shoes, and bag similar to what the assailant was seen wearing on the neighbor's surveillance video the day of the murder were all found in at Telles' house. Finally, a vehicle similar to one registered to his wife was seen leaving his neighborhood and parked near German's house. That same vehicle was driven by the killer to check on the German's body after the stabbing and then driven back to Telles' neighborhood in the timeframe of the murder. His alibi to RJ court reporter Katelyn Newberg was that he was at home when German was stabbed—not exactly a bulletproof alibi.

In the interview with Kane on December 5, 2023, at the Clark County Detention Center, Telles had all the answers, showing he still liked to think that he was the smartest person in the room. When asked directly, he denied any narcissistic tendencies, saying he had only really wanted to help people.

He maintained that a real estate company that he was in conflict with over independent administration of probate cases killed German to frame him, planting evidence in his house. He regularly told the same story in court and to journalists who interviewed him. More surprisingly, and for the first time, he told Kane that somehow the people who framed him obtained his DNA and planted it on German's body—maybe even police were involved.

"Whether the killer did it or whether someone at Metro did it, we'll see," he said when asked how his DNA got under German's fingernails. "I don't know that the video doesn't show the planting either."(247)

Telles said that police are engaged in wrongdoing that prevents him from proving his innocence. Kane, incredulous, challenged Telles.

"It's quite a conspiracy—" Kane said. "They basically had killed the guy who got rid of you out of public office at least, right? So why would they go after him? If they were willing to kill someone, they could kill you or something like that? I don't understand what the theory of the of—the of setup would be then?"

Telles said killing him would not make the police investigation of the real estate company disappear. "If someone were to kill me, would that actually stop the investigation into (the realty company) or would it accelerate them?" he responded. "I thought about that myself. Why wouldn't they kill me instead?"

The murder was intended to undercut his credibility, he contended. "If they killed me instead, I believe it would have just accelerated the investigation," he continued. "And framing me for the murder puts things in a position where now I look like I'm the one who has no credibility so everything goes by the wayside."

Kane continued to press, asking whether the average person on the street would believe that a real estate company would kill a person and plant a bunch of evidence to set him up.

"If it sounds farfetched, I don't know what to say. It's the truth," Telles contended. "I'll do everything in my power to make sure people know that I'm innocent."

CHAPTER TEN: THE PAPER & THE COURTS

The day of Robert Telles' arrest, Review-Journal's chief legal officer was mentally preparing for the potential of a big, precedent-setting legal battle. If it happened, the fight would set the rules for press freedom and source confidentially for Nevada and possibly the whole country. Ben Lipman hoped it didn't happen, but he knew he had to be prepared if it did.

Lipman had moved from St. Louis, Missouri, in 2019 to become in-house counsel for Nevada's largest news organization, The Las Vegas Review-Journal, and smaller papers in the chain. Throughout his life, he had close ties to the newspaper industry, though he never worked as a professional journalist. His work in the law was arguably more important for government transparency and accountability.

Lipman's father, David, ran the St. Louis Post Dispatch for more than a decade. Ben Lipman graduated from Washington University law school in 1991 and became an attorney working media law and corporate cases. His media work helped newspapers fight for records, defend defamation cases, and reviewed stories to prevent libel lawsuits in the first place. As the financial health of newspapers declined, it was rare to have a full-time media attorney on staff. But it was invaluable for the reporters to be able to pick up the phone or stop by Lipman's office without the fear of incurring hundreds or thousands of dollars in legal bills. German and the investigative team relied heavily on Lipman, who was fifty-six at the time of German's slaying, to argue with governments that illegally denied records and to regularly sue them when they failed to comply with state law.

Once German was murdered, Lipman assumed that police had seized his cell phone and computer, which was probably full of four decades of confidential sources. He later learned that German had four computers and a hard drive at his house that police also grabbed. Those also were very likely to contain privileged, news-gathering information. Unlike Nevada's toothless open records laws, the Silver State has one of the country's strongest reporter shield laws, giving journalists nearly blanket privilege to withhold the identity of a confidential source from police, judges, and prosecutors. The reporter's shield law, however, was usually exercised by a journalist who was very much alive. German had used it in his younger years to protect his sources, including when he broke the story of the wiretap in the Bluestein case. After his death, however, he no longer could keep his promises to protect his sources. That would fall to his newspaper, Lipman, and a team of pricey outside powerhouse attorneys.

After Telles' arrest, Lipman called the Clark County District Attorney's Office to feel out their position on German's devices. Prosecutors acknowledged the shield law would protect news gathering materials. They were not planning to allow police to search the devices for evidence that may either convict or exonerate Telles until the paper and the courts agreed on what was protected by the state's shield law.

Complicating matters was that Lipman and his wife were leaving on a bucket-list vacation to Africa in two weeks. They planned to go on safari to see lions, elephants, and giraffes in their natural habitat. The couple had no children, but they loved animals. When their dog died, they adopted an elderly neglected pit-bull mix from a Vegas rescue who no one else wanted so she could live her final years in comfort.

Lipman's initial conversations with prosecutors gave him comfort that there was time to make sure German and the newspaper's First Amendment rights were protected. Prosecutors would also contend German's First Amendment rights conflicted with Telles' Sixth Amendment rights to know the charges and evidence against him. On September 16, 2022, Metro counsel Matthew Christian, who was also leaving on vacation, would send Lipman an email confirming judicial approval would be needed to search the devices. He failed to notify Lipman that Detective Derek Jappe, who had been investigating Telles on corruption charges, had already looked at German's phone right after he was killed to obtain leads on a suspect. Jappe had done a preliminary search just to determine whether German had any communications with a potential suspect in the slaying. That comfort would disappear the day before Lipman was scheduled to fly to Africa.[248]

***

Down the hall from Lipman's wood-paneled office, past a series of high-school-like lockers, the newsroom was gearing up for one of the biggest stories in Las Vegas history. Already, news organizations from around the country and the world were contacting RJ reporters and editors for interviews about Jeff German and the government official arrested in his bloody slaying.

Court and police reporters dug into every aspect of the criminal case while the paper's investigative team dug into Telles' background and the county's culpability in allowing his abusive management to continue until German wrote about the problems at the public administrator's office. The team also vowed to finish any stories German was reporting and writing before he died—the paper couldn't allow his stories to die with him.

The Review-Journal's court reporter, Katelyn Newberg, was scrambling to cover what would likely be the highest-profile criminal case in Las Vegas in decades. Newberg, in her mid-twenties with long auburn hair, liked to read and write. She was attracted to journalism after taking an introductory reporting class as an elective at the University of Florida at Gainesville. She had interned twice at the Review-Journal before the paper offered her a police reporter job. She quickly impressed editors enough for them to promote her to one of the most prominent beats in the newsroom. Las Vegas courts were a mammoth beat with one journalist covering state, federal, and civil matters for the state's top newspaper.

That was in contrast to the days when Review-Journal editors complained that they only had three courts reporters—German, Geer Thevenot, and Ferrara—to cover the beat. Now, Newberg covered it all. She often wrote two or three stories each day. The Telles trial, however, would be a stand-out case, not just because her colleague was the victim but also because of the unique circumstances of an elected official accused of murdering a journalist. Her editors all the way to the top would closely follow each of her stories. She also felt internal pressure to cover the case as well as German would have done when he was a star court reporter for the RJ and Sun.

The attitude of prosecutors was also different than other cases she covered. Prosecutors often would comment during a routine trial or at least give guidance on background. In the Telles case, they directed all questions to District Attorney Steve Wolfson. It didn't make it easier that the Review-Journal was in court, trying to protect German's electronic devices against police and county attorneys prosecuting the case. Law enforcement believed the newspaper had no place to intervene and made it as difficult as possible for the paper to do so. Newberg's final challenge in the case was intense competition from media in Nevada and all over the world. With media nationwide contracting, Newberg was often the only reporter covering a run-of-the-mill case. In the Telles trial, that would not be the case.

In court, prosecutors said the motive for German's murder was the series of stories he wrote about Telles. German's reporting "ruined his political career, likely his marriage," said Chief Deputy District Attorney Richard Scow during a hearing in the case.[249]

Telles' willingness to talk to the media was another unusual aspect of the case. Newberg would interview him at least three times in the months following his arrest. In court, he would ask the media to contact him on specific matters. Most defendants, abiding by their attorney's wishes, wisely shunned the press. Each time Newberg talked to Telles over the videophone link at the detention center across from the courthouse, Telles would proclaim his innocence. He also claimed to the media and in court that he was framed for the murder by private probate administrators who were mad that Telles was interfering with them profiting by selling of deceased property whose families couldn't or wouldn't be found. It was a grand conspiracy to not only kill German but to frame Telles by planting the killer's clothes at his house and somehow obtaining and planting his DNA under German's fingernails. Few people other than Telles could fathom it was true, but he repeatedly pushed his defense theory.

Newberg was struck by how reasonable Telles sounded while trying to explain what was clearly a farfetched scenario. He would try to connect with Newberg by repeatedly using her first name. Like many people who met Telles, she was struck by the impression that Telles thought he was the smartest guy in the room. He thought he knew best and was going to walk away a free man after exposing all the evidence and law enforcement misconduct he claimed was part of the case. It was difficult to determine whether he was just trying to get someone to believe his theory of the case or whether he truly believed he was innocent of German's murder.[250]

The newspaper's investigative team dropped all the other stories they were writing and dug into Telles' background. Reporters attempted to obtain the records that German was seeking before his death, but the county was now refusing to release them in violation of state open records laws. The district attorney claimed a privacy exemption that does not exist in state law.

A week after the murder arrest, Kane and Erickson learned about Telles' March 2020 arrest on domestic battery and resisting arrest. Their story questioned whether Telles should have reported the arrest to the Nevada bar. Attorneys who face criminal convictions—even suspended sentences or reduced changes—have to reveal those cases for the bar to review and determine whether the crime will impact their law license. Staff at the organization that regulates attorneys said it was a close call, but Telles' plea agreement was structured in a way that would likely have allowed him to avoid disclosure. Telles' attorney, Ross Goodman, who is the son of former mayor and Mob attorney Oscar Goodman, did his job well.

"It looks like Mr. (Ross) Goodman got him a pretty good deal without a conviction," State Bar of Nevada Counsel Daniel Hooge told Kane. "He probably did that intentionally as to not trigger the reporting requirements."[251]

Erickson obtained the body camera video, showing Telles tried to use his position to get out of the trip to jail. It didn't work. But he did get lucky when the case ended up in Las Vegas city court that handles mostly DUIs and domestics and that no reporter in the city regularly covers. The domestic arrest didn't come to light until after Telles was arrested for German's murder.

After the Review-Journal posted the police body camera video of the arrest, Telles agreed to an interview with Newberg. He refused to discuss his homicide case but told her he had a drinking problem. He stopped drinking after the domestic arrest.

"It was just me blacking out and, again, not being in control of what was going on," he said. "Like any other person, I've certainly made mistakes, and I've just really tried to do my best to live my life doing good for others, and I'm hoping that, again, with everything that's rolling around in the media these days, that people really see that."[252]

***

The fight Lipman was hoping the paper could avoid came to a head just as he was packing for his safari. On the afternoon of September 21, 2022, D.A. Wolfson called him. Wolfson explained that law enforcement had decided to renege on their agreement not to search the devices. His prosecutors planned to ask the judge immediately to review the phone, hard drive, and four computers. Their explanation for the change was that the defense wanted to see if anything on German's devices pointed to another suspect in the case. Lipman scrambled, roping in Boulder, Colorado-based attorney Ashley Kissinger from Ballard Spahr LLP who had been hired to help with the case. She specialized in First Amendment matters and had more expertise in this kind of case than anyone locally.

Wolfson left Kissinger a voicemail saying his prosecutors scheduled a meeting with the judge the next day. Prosecutors wanted to get a quick decision from the judge in chambers, which Kissinger vehemently opposed because she felt the judge would not be able to get all the information required to make the appropriate decision. It also wasn't in open court, so not exactly transparent. Lipman left on vacation early the next morning but was on the phone at each layover and basically every day he could get cell or internet coverage in Africa.

On September 22, 2022, the newspaper sent a letter to police and prosecutors, demanding that they abide by the Nevada reporter shield law and national privacy laws that protected journalists. Kissinger, who didn't practice in Nevada but worked in often-more-gentile Colorado, was surprised by the arrogance and dismissive attitude of Vegas Valley police and prosecutors. They spared no expense of taxpayers' money to try to convince the court to let them look at German's devices. Emails and calls went unanswered, which Kissinger couldn't remember happening in her quarter century as a practicing attorney. She was shocked by the lack of professionalism. Lipman, who had fought at least a half-dozen records lawsuits against Metro since coming to Vegas—and won nearly all of them for the paper—wasn't surprised by law enforcement's attitude. But he also lamented the waste of newspaper and taxpayers' resources in the fight he believes could have been settled amicably if police and prosecutors were just willing to compromise.

The fight over German's devices would last for more than a year. Police came up with what they thought was a compromise. They were willing to have officials—top Metro brass—other than the detectives investigating the case search the devices. From the paper's perspective, that was probably worse than having the detectives do it. The top brass would be just the people to retaliate against officers or deputy prosecutors who were German's sources. Instead, Kissinger came up a protocol the paper thought was a good compromise. The Court would appoint independent special masters—a retired judge and former prosecutor—to go through the devices and determine what was protected by the reporter privilege and what was evidence in the case.

Police and prosecutors balked. They filed motions saying the paper had no standing in the case since the seized devices belong to German and not the Review-Journal. They contended that the newspaper should not even be able to weigh in on what happened.

Top Vegas criminal defense attorney David Chesnoff joined the RJ team to provide advice on evidence in criminal cases. He suggested former district attorney David Roger, who knew German well through the Binion case, as one of the special masters to search the devices. Chesnoff was a big name in criminal defense, both in Vegas and around the country. After leaving a big firm in Houston, Chesnoff moved to Las Vegas to work with another top criminal defense attorney. Chesnoff's first big case was the high-profile defense for Judge Claiborne that German closely covered. Chesnoff's work on that case so impressed Oscar Goodman that he asked the young attorney to be a partner in his law firm. That led to a storied career where Chesnoff, long grey hair swept back to his collar, represented a stable of naughty rock stars, actors, and famous poker players. His client roster included Mötley Crüe front man Vince Neil, A-List actor Leonardo DiCaprio, boxer Mike Tyson, rap record mogul Suge Knight, television personality Martha Stewart, and star poker players Phil Ivey and Johnny Chan. He didn't work cheap. Though without the star roster, Kissinger's hourly rate when the German device case started was five hundred and seventy-five dollars. It later increased to seven hundred and eighty dollars. Inflation was rampant. The paper would spend more than one million dollars on the fight, the attorneys would testify in court.[253]

**

The RJ investigative team also was pushing hard to finish stories German was working on before his death. Reporter Briana Erickson scrambled to publish a German story about the leader of the Oath Keepers anti-government group and his upcoming trial. Stewart Rhodes, a former Las Vegas resident, participated in the Bundy standoff with Bureau of Land Management in 2014. German was interested in that case as he covered the subsequent Bundy trial. After the

January 6, 2021, riot at the US Capitol, Rhodes was charged with seditious conspiracy and other crimes as part of a group of Trump supporters who tried to overturn the election of President Joe Biden. Rhodes was scheduled to go to trial in the case in the last week of September 2022, and German's profile had to run before that. Erickson was able to get the story, with German's co-byline, posted on September 23, 2023.[254] Rhodes was convicted after the trial and received eighteen years in prison.[255]

Two days later, Kane published a story questioning why Deputy County Manager Jeff Wells oversaw or was liaison to four county departments, including Telles' public administrator's office, that had serious misconduct allegations. Many of those allegations appear to only be addressed after the newspaper wrote about them. Wells and elected county commissioners fled out of a back exit, tipped by their highly paid spokesman, when Kane attended a public meeting to get comment. The county officials refused to talk, citing the criminal investigation. They also declined to release the records German had been requesting before he died—despite promising to release them right after Labor Day.[256]

The day after Kane's story ran, the Review-Journal went to court, asking a judge to block police and prosecutors from searching German's electronics and offering the compromise to set up a special master to identify evidence in the case while keeping journalistic sources private.[257] More than forty news organizations—including The Washington Post, Los Angeles Times, and Associated Press—urged the judge to not allow police to the search German's devices.[258]

The same day as the case over the sources was heard, a lawsuit German had been tracking closely was filed. Before his death, German had written extensively about the tawdry tale of two Las Vegas city councilwomen getting into a brawl after a council committee meeting. Victoria Seaman and Michele Fiore had been close friends on the city council before having a falling out in January 2021. Seaman charged that Fiore attacked her after the meeting, grabbing her finger, breaking it, and slamming her to the ground.

The city had a video of the fight that German worked hard to obtain. At first, the city demanded $63,680 to review footage from the city's one hundred and fifty cameras that were operating the day of the fight. The paper refused for obvious reasons. City officials knew exactly where the fight happened but refused to abide by the state law that required agencies to help records requesters narrow down their requests.

When German finally learned of the exact location, the video had been destroyed. The city's policy was to keep video for sixty days. It was clear city officials used every underhanded tactic to violate open records laws and make sure the fight video was never released to the taxpaying public.[259]

German had been following Fiore's colorful career for years. As a state lawmaker, Fiore came to some prominence and notoriety in 2016 for supporting the Bundy family in the Bunkerville standoff with federal agents over grazing rights. It was the same standoff that attracted Stewart Rhodes. Fiore was quoted in interviews as saying citizens have a right to shoot back in self-defense against federal agents if law enforcement was pointing guns at them. A gun rights activist, she sent out Christmas cards with her whole family— even the youngest members—touting semi-automatic weapons. Despite that radical resume, she was elected to the Las Vegas City Council from the city's northwest side and her colleagues named her Mayor Pro Temp. She, however, had to give up that position in 2020 after making racially insensitive comments about affirmative action. If "my white ass is more qualified than somebody's Black ass," Fiore said, her "white ass" should get the job.

In 2019, German recruited Kane to help dig into Fiore's campaign finances and checkered history of IRS liens. He and Kane wrote a series of stories showing Fiore failed to report the tax liens and rental income on her state financial disclosures. She also spent hundreds of thousands in campaign money to fill up her gas tank, eat at restaurants, travel, hire relatives, and pay her own political consulting business.[260] Additionally, as part of their LVCVA investigation, Kane and German wrote about how much Fiore and other politicians appointed to the agency's board spent on luxury travel.[261] She was definitely a frequent flier at taxpayer expense, despite her small-government rhetoric.

German and Kane met the week before his death to discuss some new questionable spending that German had dug up in Fiore's campaign reports. At the same time, German was writing about a lawsuit Seaman planned to file against the city because officials' actions after Fiore allegedly attacked her. The paper's policy prevented publishing a story on lawsuits until the case was actually filed, but German had most of the story written and ready to go for the day it was. Going off German's draft, Kane added a few sentences from an interview with Seaman and court records, contacted the city and Mayor Carolyn Goodman, who declined comment, and published the double-byline story. It would be Kane's last story with German.[262]

Four days later, Kane exclusively obtained an internal review the city commissioned about its handling of the Seaman/Fiore fight. The report by an outside law firm determined that both Fiore and Seaman violated city policy by attacking each other. It also detailed questionable actions by city staff in deleting the video they knew was potentially evidence of a crime—or at least required to be released under state open records laws.

"The 61-page report by an outside law firm also described details of the staff's viewing and eventual overwriting of a key surveillance video of the altercation that the report stated posed a 'substantial risk of damage to the political images and reputations' of the two women and 'the part each played in the physical altercation,'" Kane wrote for the September 30, 2022, story. "Las Vegas City Attorney Bryan Scott spoke to both women in March 2021 to tell them the video was about to be overwritten, and neither wanted a copy, the report said. But Scott told the Review-Journal in September the city had 'no records responsive' to the newspaper's request despite three previous requests on file." Scott didn't respond to Kane's requests for comment for the story and retired in August 2023 after three years as the city's top lawyer.

On October 5, Telles was removed as public administrator at a court hearing so the county no longer had to pay him while he awaited trial behind bars. Two days later, Erickson published a story about the First Amendment implications of the newspaper's fight to protect German's sources.[263]

Around the same time, a judge granted a temporary injunction against law enforcement searching German's devices.[264] Metro quickly appealed the ruling. The paper would later learn—after a judge required the search warrants to be released—that Metro had already searched German's phone, despite telling the paper it hadn't. An outraged newspaper asked for sanctions, but District Judge Michelle Leavitt refused to hold Metro responsible for its misdeeds.[265]

In the meantime, the Nevada Supreme Court suspended Telles' law license, saying he transferred nearly two hundred thousand dollars out of an account he maintained for client money. The courts did not know what happened to the cash. The bar later determined that while Telles was late in disbursing the money and shouldn't have represented clients after he was elected to public office, none of it was missing. It really didn't matter because if Telles was convicted of German's murder he would lose this law license permanently, officials said.[266]

On November 16, Kane published a story revealing the police investigation into Telles' house-flipping scheme. There were accusations that Telles also solicited kickbacks from real estate agents who wanted to sell the houses overseen by the public administrator. That investigation ended in 2023. A source told Kane that while police believed that Telles was trying to get the kickbacks and stopped giving houses to an agent who refused, there was not enough evidence to proceed with a criminal case. Telles told Kane that he never participated in any illegal bribery or fraudulent schemes. The investigation in the bribery case, however, would play prominently into Telles' defense strategy.[267]

About a week after Kane's bribery investigation story ran, Erickson published a long, detailed narrative about all the problems in Telles' history. It exposed the groping at UNLV and allegations of sexual harassment, sending explicit pictures to a woman he represented in a divorce, rescinding job offers for illegal reasons, and bullying fellow students and subordinates. The story painted a picture of a corrupt and flawed politician whose misdeeds had flown below the radar—until German got on the case—because the office he sought was so low profile.[268]

***

The courts initially assigned Robert Telles two public defenders. Taxpayers paid Edward Kane (no relation to reporter Arthur Kane) nearly three hundred thousand dollars in pay and benefits the year Telles was charged with German's murder, Transparentnevada.com pay data showed. His colleague, David Lopez-Negrete, made more than two hundred thousand dollars that year.[269] In applying for the public defender, Telles noted significant assets, including a Las Vegas house with a mortgage and rental properties. But he somehow claimed he was indigent.

Public defenders are reserved only for clients with no resources to pay an attorney. One of Arthur Kane's sources told him Telles should not have received taxpayer-funded counsel. Kane dug into the story, finding the rental properties in Little Rock, Arkansas, and attempting to use public records to determine the equity in those properties and Telles' Las Vegas house.

The Arkansas houses were in an LLC that didn't have Telles' name on it. Those properties had at least two hundred thousand dollars in equity, so clearly Telles was not indigent. The police had also been looking for the houses but couldn't find them. Kane received a call from a top police official the day the story ran, asking how the hell he tracked the houses down.[270] Kane was able to find the rental houses only after asking the Hot Springs tax collector for any property tax bills sent to Telles' Las Vegas address. A week after the story ran, Telles fired his public defenders and proceeded to go through several attorneys before making a decision that legal experts thought was a mistake.[271]

The Friday after his arrest, defense attorney Ozzie Fumo visited Telles in jail. Telles was in the unit for prisoners on suicide watch after slashing his wrists when police tried to arrest him. Telles asked Fumo to represent him, but Fumo demurred because he was closer to German than he was to Telles. Fumo recommended Vegas attorney Ryan Helmick.[272]

Telles hired Helmick at the end of October though he maintains Helmick agreed to do the high-profile case pro bono, or for free. Helmick has repeatedly refused to discuss the financial terms of the arrangement. Then less than three months later, Helmick received court notification that Telles was again switching attorneys. Telles hired Las Vegas criminal defense attorney Damien Sheets.[273] Telles never talked to Helmick before filing the change of counsel and never told him why he made the switch.[274]

Telles, while thinking was Helmick a great guy, decided he didn't think Helmick had the necessary experience and his caseload would have made it difficult for him Helmick to prove Telles' innocence. Telles was also pushing for the trial to happen as soon as possible. Figuring he would be acquitted, Telles didn't want to stay in jail longer than he absolutely had to. [275]

In February 2023, Telles change attorneys again. Sheets told the court that he and Telles had a communication breakdown.[276] Telles and Sheets started off on the wrong foot, according to Telles. Telles wanted Sheets to prioritize filing motions to challenge police conduct in the case and maybe get the search warrants invalidated. That might allow Telles to exclude the damning evidence found at his house or maybe even the DNA found under German's fingernails. Without those items, prosecutors didn't have much of a case. Telles maintained that Sheets initially agreed to file the motion but once he took over the case, he changed his mind. Sheets also wanted to push the trial out ten months, which Telles didn't want to do.

In the end, Telles felt Sheets was just trying extract as much money as possible, "bleeding him dry," he told Kane.[277] Telles had mortgaged his house and sold the properties in Arkansas, paying off the second mortgage and then planning to use the rest of the money for an attorney. He didn't have that much money and the disagreements with Sheets required a change.[278] Telles had decided to represent himself despite having almost no criminal defense experience and only representing clients in a handful of civil trials.

Only Telles thought that was a good idea. When he told District Judge Michelle Leavitt he wanted to represent himself, Leavitt advised him that was a bad idea and quizzed him on his knowledge of the criminal courts for about thirty minutes. Helmick used an old attorney saying when asked about Telles' decision: "A client who represents himself has a fool for a lawyer," adding Telles' decision is "dangerous and unwise." [279]

Adding to his woes, Telles was also having trouble getting along with Judge Leavitt. The scorched-earth tactics he employed in his Boyd law school controversy and at the public administrator's office didn't fly in her courtroom. In March 2023, Telles filed a motion to disqualify the judge, saying that he did not feel Leavitt was treating him fairly. He charged that she was badgering him and violating his constitutional rights.

Leavitt pushed back at the hearing. "And you understand that once you decide on self-representation that you don't get to change your mind in the middle of the proceedings and then request an attorney?" she told him. "I think I've made it pretty clear that we're not playing games here."

Telles responded with a motion to disqualify Leavitt, saying that the judge had no right to prevent him from exercising his constitutional rights of having counsel if he could raise money and hire one in the future. He was probably right about that. He eventually found an attorney, Gary A. Modafferi, to provide advice on criminal procedure as he defended himself.[280]

Telles' complaint with Leavitt stretched beyond the attorney issues. When Telles asked for better housing at the Clark County Detention Center and more access to legal research, Leavitt told him she wasn't going to tell the sheriff how to run the jail. They also repeatedly argued about procedural issues in open court.

"Judge Leavitt's opinion of Defendant and his self-representation displays a deep-seated antagonism that will make fair judgment in future hearings impossible," Telles wrote in his first motion to remove Leavitt.[281] But even getting that motion filed as contentious.

"I have here a motion for Your Honor's recusal that I would like to have heard before any other orders," Telles told the judge.

The hearing was scheduled to appoint a standby counsel to advise Telles on criminal procedures. A bailiff took Telles' motion, but Leavitt was clearly not happy with Telles. "If you want to file a motion to disqualify, that's not the way you do it," she said in court. "You'll be required to follow the rules."[282]

At the end of March, District Judge Jerry Wiese declined to remove Leavitt, finding her rulings complied with what most of the criminal court judges would have done in similar cases.[283] In late 2023, Telles would again try to disqualify Leavitt, delaying a key part of the case revolving around German's electronics.

***

Two days after dumping Sheets, Telles started telling local media that he had been framed in German's murder. He claimed he was helping to investigate estate fraud while public administrator and that people who didn't like that planted the evidence police seized. He filed motions claiming that the officers investigating him for the house flipping before his murder arrest had provided information to homicide detectives before detectives obtained the warrants to search his house and his person. He also questioned why body camera video of a traffic stop where he was arrested was no longer available. Police said it was filed as traffic stop and not with the homicide case so those files were erased. Telles also wanted detailed information about when the warrants were signed, saying police conducted the searches illegally and before they had a judge's authorization.

He accused prosecutors of covering up for the misdeeds of the detectives investigating him during a May 10, 2023, hearing that was supposed to be about German's privileged devices.

"The cover-up is more—it's really just more evidence of their misconduct in this case and it's frightening really that the D.A. and LVMPD are so boldly violating my constitutional rights when the citizens of Clark County are watching," Telles said.

He talked about the Metro investigation he sparked of the real estate company and how Detective Derek Jappe started pursing a bribery investigation against him instead of going after the realty company. He said, without explanation, that Jappe should have known someone was going to murder German.

"It's a huge coincidence if Detective Jappe was not aware that someone intended to murder Mr. German and frame me for it," he said in court. He then alleged that Jappe and detectives working on the murder case conspired to obtain evidence either without warrants or with faulty search warrants and then refused to provide the evidence of their misconduct.

"I need to convey the seriousness of what is going on here," Telles told the judge. "Not only are we now talking about police misconduct, we're talking about prosecutorial misconduct and obstruction of justice."

At the hearing, Chief Deputy District Attorney Christopher Hamner had enough of Telles' allegations. "Listen, it's a riveting speech, but it is chock full of total inaccuracies about the law of the State of Nevada," he told the Court. "Clearly, Mr. Telles has no understanding about how discovery is turned over in a case."

Prosecutors said Telles should file a motion to suppress the search warrants if he believes they were faulty, but Telles said he can't do that until he obtains evidence, which he claimed law enforcement was withholding.

Hamner wasn't convinced. "He spins out things like conspiracies and working and subterfuge and all of these kind of fancy words to make it sound as if there's some sort of obstruction going in play," he said in court. "We're not trying to obstruct anything. We are bound by discovery statutes."

Later in that same hearing, the hearing got around to what it was intended to discuss: whether German's devices could be protected from a police search. Metro attorneys clashed with the Review-Journal and the paper had an unexpected ally.

Metro Assistant General Counsel Matthew Christian insisted that the Review-Journal shouldn't even be allowed to argue about German's devices. "The reporter's privilege was, is, and always will be personal," he told Leavitt. "It's not the RJ's devices. It's not their property."

Leavitt seemed to disagree. "Well, it can't be that the privilege just dies with the reporter," she said. "I mean, that just isn't logical."

"Well, maybe it's the family's privilege," Christian offered. "Maybe they—but the RJ didn't inherit it… They've intervened and they're interfering with an investigation when they have no standing to do so. Maybe the family has standing. It's their property. But the RJ does not have standing."

Kissinger said Christian was completely incorrect in his assertions. "It actually arises from public policy, the public policy in protecting a free press, a free press's ability to uncover corruption and wrongdoing and provide information on matters of public concern to the public," she told Leavitt. "And it's—it is shown to be so strong by the fact that this state has entered one of the strongest such privileges in the country, it's an absolute privilege. So I want it to be clear that the Review-Journal's position is that no party in the courtroom can overcome this privilege, not Mr. Telles, not the State under any circumstances. So we have an absolute privilege."

The hearing highlighted the strange bedfellows the case was creating. Telles sided with the Review-Journal and refuted that police were searching the devices to protect his constitutional rights.

"Originally, they claimed that they needed to respect my constitutional rights and that my constitutional rights trump the constitutional rights of the LVRJ and that was the basis for the argument that they be allowed to go from end to end on all of Mr. German's electronic devices," Telles argued in court. "Again, it is clear that LVMPD has a bad faith purpose for-for trying to get into these devices."

Nearly every hearing the case during 2023, Telles complained about police and prosecutors withholding evidence that will clear him.

"In fact, you know, frankly, you know, the way that this process has been working so far; I mean, when we're talking about taking three months for me to get to this point in obtaining this evidence, it's pretty, it doesn't look great," Telles said during a July 6, 2023, hearing where he was trying to get additional evidence. "So I'm looking for all the emails between the judge, D.A. Weckerly, and Detective Gatus for that day and all the drafts of the document, all the other materials because of this search warrant was done in a way where there was-there were a lot of misrepresentations done in the search warrant, many."

***

One story that German's colleagues decided not to finish was a business piece about the FBI investigating a Ponzi scheme. As most government accountability reporters, the investigative team didn't have the expertise for a business story. The story also wasn't particularly investigative. With only two reporters left on the team, Kane and Erickson focused on investigative pieces. The Review-Journal's business section—with half a dozen staffers putting out a daily section—likely didn't have the resources to do the story justice.

Despite its business focus, German was planning an in-depth story, talking to victims of the scheme. It was a court-based story he liked to do, jumping on high-profile cases to add some depth and context. The scheme garnered significant press both because the suspects allegedly targeted Mormons for hundreds of million dollars and because one of the suspects shot it out with FBI agents when they showed up to arrest him at his $1.6-million mansion on the city's northwest side. Days after German's slaying, editors at the Washington Post had offered to help out if needed. The Review-Journal's editors decided that was a good story for the venerate DC paper to complete.

The Washington Post sent reporter Lizzie Johnson to Vegas to research and write the story that the Post and Review-Journal then jointly published. Johnson, in a beautifully written, detailed story, painted a compelling picture of victims fooled into squandering their life savings. She detailed the scheme that made the organizers as much as five hundred million dollars to fund a lavish lifestyle. The story included a private jet, multi-million-dollar properties in Nevada, California, and elsewhere, and a forty-nine-year-old attorney who pulled a gun on FBI agents before they shot him.[284]

Despite arguably being one of the least impactful of German's final stories—at least for residents of Southern Nevada—Johnson's story garnered the most accolades, demonstrating that for the East Coast media, the only important journalism are stories that originate from elite newspapers in New York and Washington, DC. Johnson was honored with the President's Award from the National Press Club, and the Reporters Committee for Freedom gave her the Press Catalyst Award. The RCFP also invited Review-Journal photojournalist Rachel Aston, who contributed her usual top-notch visuals to Johnson's story, and Executive Editor Glenn Cook to the ceremony. But the focus was clearly on the member of the national media's exclusive club. The work the RJ staff did covering the criminal case, finishing German's stories, digging into Telles and county corruption did not receive any national recognition.[285]

***

Review-Journal reporters continued to dig into the county's corruption. A source who read Kane's story on failures by the county told him about another scandal surrounding Jeff Wells. He was placed on leave late in 2022—not for his handling of departments under his watch but intervening in county discipline against his son. Jeff Wells oversaw the public defender when his son, Tom Wells, was hired. Nevada state law prohibits the relatives of elected officials and top bureaucrats from being hired at agencies where their relatives work. Despite that, Tom Wells was hired first as an investigator in 2012 during the mortgage crisis at the county public defender's office. A few years later, he graduated from law school and was rehired as an attorney in the public defender's office. His wife, Nicole, was hired the following year at the County Department of Children and Family Services. Children and Family Services also reported directly to Jeff Wells at the time. Wells maintained he had nothing to do with the hires.

When allegations broke about sexual harassment by Chief Public Defender Phil Kohn, who had hired Tom Wells, two employees told investigators that they thought Wells was protecting Kohn. Kohn was accused of telling off-color jokes and talking to colleagues with his leg up and his crotch in their faces. He retired soon after the investigation.

The county determined Wells was not protecting Kohn, but County Manager Yolanda King moved the public defender to another manager. Jeff Wells said that was because his son worked for Kohn. His son had worked at the agency for years without any action. He was concerned removing his son from supervising the agency at the same time as the sexual harassment investigation made it look like he was protecting Kohn. He said he was not personal friends with Kohn and did nothing to intervene in the sexual harassment investigation.[286]

For the news story on the hiring of Tom Wells, Kohn told Kane that Jeff Wells introduced him to his son before the hiring, but he felt no pressure to hire the younger Wells.

"I know the optics," Kohn told Kane in a phone interview for the March 9, 2023, article. "At the time (Tom Wells) was as qualified as anyone who came through."

Tom Wells was a bank vice president and previously a licensed mortgage broker. He wanted to move from Colorado to Nevada, and the public defender's office was looking for investigators to defend cases of mortgage fraud that prosecutors brought after the 2008 real estate crash.

Tom Wells' hiring so concerned then-county manager Donald Burnette that he made sure there was no undue pressure from Jeff Wells.

"I was asking if it was his decision and wanted to confirm he wasn't influenced in making that decision," Burnette told Kane for the story. "The other message that came from me is, 'Treat Tom like every other employee, and if something came up to warrant some sort of action, let me know.'"

Instead of following state law and prohibiting the hiring of Jeff Wells' family members, the county passed its own ordinance that mirrored the state prohibition on hiring the family of top officials. Officials justified the need for a county ordinance by claiming it was unclear whether the state law applied to department heads when they weren't the appointing authority. But county officials slipped in one key difference to the state law: anyone hired in violation of the state law, including Tom and Nicole Wells, got to keep their jobs. Wells worked on the ordinance but said he did not push the grandfathering clause.

Years after he was hired, Tom Wells did something that got him in trouble. The county never would reveal what it was, but Kane learned that Jeff Wells tried to intervene in his son's discipline, earning him a paid suspension. An internal investigation that Kane obtained through open records laws showed that Wells approached the county attorney to discuss the investigation and tried to get his son transferred to the district attorney's office. Jeff Wells contended that the DA already offered his son a job, but records from the office show Tom Wells declined an interview in February 2023 so there could have been no offer.[287]

In a follow-up email exchange with Jeff Wells, he conceded that there wasn't a formal offer but an expression of interest and offer of an interview. "He was offered an interview in early February, but prior to the interview date, he was called again by an attorney in the criminal division and was told that a senior attorney in D.A. administration would prefer that he wait until his case was resolved before he sought a transfer," Jeff Wells wrote. "Out of respect for that request, he declined the interview." After the county, Tom Wells joined a private firm to do civil litigation, Jeff Wells wrote.

***

Jeff Wells, an attorney, moved to Las Vegas in 2006 from Colorado after serving for a dozen years as senate majority leader in the Colorado General Assembly. Colorado Governor Bill Owens tapped Wells to run the Colorado Department of Labor and Employment and Department of Personnel & Administration. As Owens' final term was coming to an end, Wells had offers to lobby but didn't see himself in that role. Wells had connections to the Las Vegas main industry, creating a table game that ended up at Harrah's Casino and other gaming houses.

Jeff Wells was having lunch with a Clark County attorney who had previously worked at the Colorado capitol, and she suggested he apply at county. He was offered a job as Clark County's director of administrative services. Jeff Wells thought he could have stayed on the cabinet of the new Colorado governor, but Colorado legislative staff learned of the Clark County job offer. It was leaked to The Denver

Post. So he took the Las Vegas job and was later promoted to assistant county manager—a position later renamed deputy county manager.

He believes Kane's coverage of problems in departments he oversaw was not proper. "To take 16 years of pretty damn good work for the county and try to take three or four little isolated incidents and say therefore I must have been the world's worst manager out there all this time, in my mind, is remarkably unfair," he told Kane in December 2023.[288]

County Manager Kevin Schiller told Kane that he was concerned about Jeff Wells' actions in his son's discipline case. Wells had already been planning to retire. In April 2023, Wells, then seventy-four, left with a lucrative exit package worth about two hundred and fifty thousand dollars, including more than eighty-two thousand for salary and benefits while on administrative leave, and nearly one hundred and seventy thousand for accrued sick and vacation leave that he did not use. The taxpayers also picked up more than thirty-five thousand dollars in attorney fees to investigate the misconduct allegations against Tom and Jeff Wells.

Wells, for his part, maintains he did not intend to use his position to influence his son's discipline investigation though in retrospect he understand that there was at least an appearance of impropriety. He said he called Lisa Logsdon, the head of the county's civil division and county counsel, telling her he wanted to talk about his son's discipline. If she thought it was inappropriate, he maintains, she should have declined or said she wanted to think about it. Instead, she scheduled a meeting an hour later. At the meeting with Logsdon, Jeff Wells said Tom had an offer to work at the district attorney's office—another department he was liaison to as deputy manager. He proposed that they could just move Tom there and avoid a drawn-out disciplinary process.[289]

***

As the new year started, the Review-Journal continued to fight to protect Jeff German's sources. In January 2023, Leavitt sided with police and prosecutors, saying they can search the devices. The Review-Journal asked the state Supreme Court to decide the issue. Telles also filed a subpoena to get information from German's devices. On March 24, the Review-Journal filed a motion to block it.

"Several of the subpoenas appear to endanger the privileges and protections for newsgathering materials that led this Court and the Nevada Supreme Court to enter injunctions protecting those materials," the motion to quash his subpoenas said.[290]

Telles also went after officers investigating the murder, filing complaints with the LVMPD Citizens Review Board. The CRB handles citizen complaints of excessive force and misconduct by officers. Telles alleged violations of policies and misconduct interacting with the public. But the agency threw out Telles' complaint at the end of July 2023.[291]

A month after the newspaper's lawyers moved to block Telles' subpoenas of German's devices, newspaper staff received an email from Telles' mother, saying he no longer wants to see German's devices. In April 2023, Telles said in open court that he is siding with the newspaper and doesn't want to reveal any confidential information in the devices police seized.

"I believe that with the materials I'm seeking, I can vindicate my constitutional rights while also avoiding a confrontation with the constitutional rights of the Las Vegas Review-Journal," Telles said. "So implicit and explicitly in my motion is the intent to not request anything that came from Mr. German's devices whatsoever at this point."

He also reiterated his decision to Newberg. "I understand that you all have your own First Amendment rights that you want to protect, and I respect that," Telles told a Review-Journal reporter. "I can't tell you that I pledge to decline those materials if they give them to me. All I can say is that

I'm hoping that we don't even have to get to that point, frankly."[292]

Telles' decision undercut the prosecution's main argument that they were trying to protect Telles' rights. Lipman and Kissinger were hopeful that would end the battle but that would not be the case. Police and prosecutors continued to fight to see what was in German's electronic devices. The standoff sent the case to the state Supreme Court. In October 2023, the newspaper won a historic victory to protect the press.

The Supreme Court ruled that the paper had standing and that the privilege survived Jeff German's death.

"Permitting the search to proceed would therefore allow 'the government's fox [to be] left in charge of the appellants' henhouse," the justices wrote with no dissenting opinion.

The Court sent the case back to Leavitt to implement the ruling. The Court did agree with Leavitt about not imposing sanctions on Metro for searching the devices when they promised not to. The standard for sanctions is very high, requiring a manifest abuse of discretion. The Court also left a crack open that in the future there might be some situation when the shield law could be breached by a defendant's rights. That was disappointing for Review-Journal attorneys but overall, it was a historic victory.[293]

Police and prosecutors saw the devices battle from a different perspective, charging that the Review-Journal attorneys were the ones who caused the delays, failed to compromise, and forced law enforcement to waste taxpayer money.

The "LVRJ took a scorched-earth approach that included unnecessary court filings, unwarranted accusations of sanctionable conduct, and unreasonably complex and unworkable proposed search protocols," a thirteen-page statement to the author charged. "A vast majority of legal arguments presented by LVRJ have been rejected. The one and only issue upon which the LVRJ prevailed was whether anyone beyond Mr. German himself could assert the reporter's privilege in information contained on electronic devices owned solely and exclusively by Mr. German."

Nowhere in the statement did police and prosecutors address the key issue of the case: Protecting German's confidential sources and making sure police and prosecutorial supervisors do not retaliate against people who provided German and his news organizations confidential information. They didn't respond when questioned about that and repeatedly declined an interview.

Police did win the battle of avoiding sanctions for searching German's phone without permission and then taking a long time to come clean. And the court's ruling notes that the reporter shield privilege has to be balanced with a defendant's right to a fair trial, which could be a substantial issue if the newspaper and police get into a conflict over specific items German's devices being included in the Telles murder trial.

"We have already recognized that the privilege under the news shield law statute is not absolute 'when a defendant's countervailing constitutional rights are at issue, in which [case] the news shield statute might have to yield so that justice may be served,'" justices wrote.

But to say the Review-Journal only prevailed on their right to defend German's shield privilege would not be a fair reading of the opinion. Prosecutors in filings and in their statement contended that Glenn Cook's email to Sheriff Lombardo right after Jeff German's murder about the stories he was working on waived any journalistic privilege to protect his sources. "[W]e conclude that the waiver of the privilege as to that information does not otherwise affect our decision," the opinion said. The Court also instituted the Review-Journal's special-master search protocol and reverse the lower court's decision to lift the preliminary injunction that prohibited law enforcement from searching the devices.

Along with their statement on the legal fight, police and prosecutors also warns that failure to turn over all the evidence to Telles could result in his eventual freedom even if he is convicted of killing German.

"It is the State's responsibility to ensure that all the exculpatory material is provided to Mr. Telles," the statement said. "The failure to do this will undoubtedly result in Mr. Telles receiving a new trial should he be convicted of the murder of Mr. German... If subsequent reversal of a conviction occurs, the responsibility for such action will rest squarely on the shoulders of the LVRJ."

Maybe top prosecutor Chris Lalli, who had tried the defendants in the Binion case after the Supreme Court overturned that conviction but failed to convict on murder, was flashing back to his earlier failure. Either way, the newspaper's lawyers contend that the First Amendment implications of the case outweigh any possible future rulings in the criminal trial.

***

The same month of the RJ's victory in the Supreme Court, Telles was still fighting to get evidence from police that he said would exonerate him of German's murder.

In an October 31, 2023, hearing, Telles again alleged misconduct by police. "Detective (Justine) Gatus engaged in a course of conduct, really misconduct, throughout the entire investigation," he said. "I want to demonstrate by her other misconduct that she intentionally lied, and she intentionally omitted facts in the search warrant."

Deputy District Attorney Pam Weckerly protested. "Mr. Telles is representing himself," she said. "These kinds of comments are inappropriate. He needs to file a motion, and we need to have a hearing. He's not allowed to make statements like this without sworn testimony, without evidence."

And law enforcement's loss in the Supreme Court over German's devices prompted police and prosecutors to switch tactics. Instead of a special master, police offered that the journalists at the Review-Journal look at what was on German's devices and determine what they believed was privileged and not evidence in the case. The newspaper would produce a log of what it believed was privileged and then police and prosecutors could challenge items if they believed they were key for the prosecution. Review-Journal attorneys pointed out that if law enforcement had agreed to that protocol from the start of the case, all the time, effort, and expense would not have happened.

The new law enforcement proposal shocked the judge.

"You guys are kidding, right?" Leavitt asked Metro attorney Matthew Christian.

"Nope," he answered.

"Anything that moves it along and you all agree on, I'm for," she said.

"Well, the concern is that we're not moving along," Christian said.[294]

The fight has cost taxpayers more than seventy-five thousand dollars for outside counsel, according to billings obtained under state open records laws. Neither police nor prosecutors could say how much of staff time and compensation was spent on the fight that Review-Journal attorneys contend could have been settled from day one by agreeing to let the RJ review the devices and determine what was privileged.[295]

The order was submitted to Leavitt right before the Christmas holidays 2023, but there was another inevitable twist. Telles again filed a motion to disqualify Leavitt, which wouldn't be heard until January 11, 2024, so Leavitt had to wait to approve the order.

In court on January 16, 2024, Telles made an explicit allegation that he had been telling reporters in jailhouse interviews. He claimed that Las Vegas-based Compass

Realty & Management framed him for German's murder. When he was public administrator, Telles clashed with Compass, charging their staff members were taking over the administration of probate cases and profiting by selling dead people's houses while leaving heirs with nothing. He had urged the Nevada attorney general, county prosecutors, and state real estate regulators to investigate, but they either declined or didn't find any violations of state law.[296]

"I believe that Compass Realty framed me for Mr. German's murder," Telles said during a hearing to have Leavitt removed from the case. He presented no evidence to support the allegations.

Compass officials were naturally shocked by the allegation, releasing a statement to the Review-Journal that said Telles is just trying to avoid accountability for his felonious actions. "Mr. Telles is a desperate man who has been charged with violently murdering a beloved local journalist. It appears he will do and say anything to escape answering for this charge," the statement said. "For Mr. Telles to accuse Compass Realty & Management of anything is unconscionable and irresponsible, and Compass Realty & Management is evaluating its legal options."[297]

About a week later, Chief District Judge Jerry Wiese rejected Telles' second request to have Leavitt replaced on his case, saying that the defendant had produced no evidence of the judge's bias.

"To the extent that Mr. Telles disagrees with Judge Leavitt's decisions and rulings, he can appeal them," Wiese wrote in rejecting Telles' request. "However, filing successive Motions to Disqualify is not the proper process."

Soon after Wiese's ruling, Leavitt signed the motion to allow the Review-Journal staff to review German's devices for any privileged journalistic information. By the time Wiese again refused to remove Leavitt, Telles found yet another attorney to represent him.[298]

Robert Draskovich fell into the law by accident. He was working construction and planning to go to grad school in Chicago when he was arrested by a traffic officer for arguing with him. He represented himself in the case and was acquitted, leading the judge to commend him for being so articulate. Draskovich changed course and went to law school.

It was clearly the right move. He has been named one of the top criminal defense attorneys in the country and took more than one hundred cases to jury trial in his quarter century of successfully representing clients who ranged from CEOs of companies to Hells Angeles motorcycle gang members. He is one of the few attorneys, who are not public defenders, certified to handle Nevada death penalty cases.

Draskovich knew German because the reporter had covered some of his high-profile clients. In 2015, Draskovich had secured a twenty-seven-month sentence for family court Judge Steven Jones when prosecutors wanted him to spend more than twice as long in federal prison. Jones was accused of using his office to assure investors in a fraudulent investment scheme run by his former brother-in-law. He pled guilty to one count of conspiracy to commit wire fraud. German had covered the case along with other Review-Journal court reporters.[299] In 2017, Draskovich secured an acquittal for a Bellagio Casino club host charged with kidnapping and sexual assault for allegedly drugging and raping women.[300]

Draskovich is reluctant to talk about his prior clients though he touts dozens of acquittals and hung juries in tough criminal cases. That is because his otherwise impeccable reputation was marred by a 2021 bar association reprimand for violating the confidentially of a client with whom he had a dispute over billing, communication, and other issues.[301]

He is not sure how Telles found him and his early contacts with his client gave him the sense that it will be a tough and contentious case both against the prosecutor and with client. He plans to go to trial without delay as long as the German devices issue is settled.[(302)]

***

The trial date was reset for March 18, 2024. But it is unknown how long it will take Review-Journal staff to review Jeff German's devices and whether law enforcement will dispute any of the items the newspaper believes are privileged. If so, that could mean another court battle that could again go to the Nevada Supreme Court. Without that settled, it is a mistake to bet when Telles will get his day in court.

Telles remains in the Clark County Detention Center, housed in a wing designed to protect high-profile inmates. It's not unheard of for inmates to attack someone who has been the focus of significant media attention, and Telles arguably had the most media coverage of anyone currently in the county jail. He spends his days preparing for trial, getting one hour a day to exercise—usually alone.

His wife, kids, and mother visit regularly. His father visited about a month after his arrest. His investigator, Richard Franky, and occasional media also stop by to talk. Only one person who labeled themselves a friend visited him in the log release in response to an open records request.

Telles lamented but understood that most people wouldn't stand by him after the charges against him. "When you get caught up in a public nightmare, people don't want to get involved," he told Kane during an interview on December 5, 2023, for the book. "You know, that's just a fact."

He also acted like he fully expects to be exonerated and walk out of the jail after the trial, which he says can't come quickly enough. As the hour-long timer on the jailhouse interview started to run out, Kane asked Telles if there was anything he wanted to say that they hadn't covered. He, surprisingly, wanted to relitigate German's original story and the accusations of the women who complained about his leadership.

"I do hope that you do get to investigate further," he said on the other end of the videocall right before the screen went black. "Even what happened at the public administrator's office with respect to these alleged claims that I was, you know, a tyrant. Because I think you'll see that if you pull up objective data, if you did a FOIA request for, for case management details, you'll see that the place is really running very, very well."

***

After Jeff German was killed, he was repeatedly honored by his friends, colleagues, and national news organizations. The Nevada Press Association inducted him into the Nevada Newspaper Hall of Fame three weeks after his death. He also won an award for best podcast for the Mobbed Up season he wrote and narrated. The Investigative Reporters and Editors announced a fifty-thousand-dollar scholarship in his name and awarded him the Don Bolles Medal, named after the Arizona Republic investigative reporter killed by a car bomb while he was investigating underworld figures. Bolles' death was the birth of the nation's top investigative association, and Prast, Erickson, and Kane traveled to Orlando, Florida, for the annual convention to give the keynote speech at IRE's award luncheon. In January, the National Press Club put up German's picture in its lobby. Even the city officials that Jeff German pursued honored him. Governor Steve Sisolak proclaimed September 24, 2022, Jeff German day, and the Las Vegas City Council proclaimed January 4, 2023, in honor of German.

The Review-Journal also hosted an upscale memorial service at The Smith Center a month after his slaying. Reporters, editors, photographers, friends, and attorneys packed Myron's venue there to recount stories about

German, have a few drinks, and laugh. Prast, as German's boss, was supposed to speak but was overcome by emotion and prompted an unprepared Kane to go up and represent the investigative team. It was far from the best speech of the night.

Jeff German's last desk in the Review-Journal newsroom remains empty and serves as a memorial to him. There is also a wall in the newsroom with his photo and all the awards he garnered after his death. It is completely indisputable that German would have been thrilled by the attention and accolades.

German's brother and sisters decided not to attend the award ceremonies or Review-Journal memorial. They had a small funeral attended by family and close friends. His Review-Journal friends and colleagues were not invited.

Jeff German is buried at King David Cemetery. Dry flowers and unlevel ground surround a small tombstone that was recently placed at the head of the grave. It has a reporter's notebook etched into it and an inscription of "BELOVED SON, BROTHER AND UNCLE. ALWAYS IN OUR HEARTS." It ends with –30– which was traditionally used by journalists to signify the end of a news story.

EPILOGUE

Since Jeff was killed, I have been asked repeatedly by friends, fellow reporters, and in interviews whether I feared for my life when continuing his reporting, writing this book, or just doing daily investigative journalism. Reporters usually aren't philosophical, but the answer requires perspective. For me, Jeff's death really exposes the randomness of life and death.

For years, Jeff covered some of the most dangerous psychopaths in the world. People who would order a hit with the same amount of emotion that they would order a sandwich. Yet he escaped reporting on the Vegas Mob for years mostly unscathed. The worst was a few stitches after a sucker punch.

If police and prosecutors are right, Jeff met the end at the hands of a two-bit political nobody who killed him either as an act of macho revenge or to prevent further revelations about his misconduct and potentially keep an affair from getting out. Either motive is ridiculous. It wasn't Jeff who was pushing forward the story about Telles' misconduct. Jeff was just doing his job, collecting and confirming information and documentation from sources and writing about allegations of government misconduct. For Telles to say Jeff didn't investigate the issue is just a failure to understand reporting. Even if the office ran better under Telles, there were still serious allegations of misconduct and an affair with a subordinate that taxpayers needed to know before the next election. Jeff was providing that service to the public.

Press freedom is the basis of our democracy and political system, specifically because exposing government misconduct is the best way to punish and prevent future malfeasance. The press was gifted the First Amendment and tagged as the Fourth Estate specifically because it was an independent investigator of government corruption, malfeasance, and waste. The founding fathers made the First Amendment first for a reason. No other mechanism exists when corrupt officials protect each other and law enforcement looks the other way.

If Telles didn't want something revealed, he probably should not have taken those actions in the first place. If he killed Jeff, he should have given a moment's thought to the fact that getting rid of Jeff would not stop the stories. It only increased scrutiny and exposure of Telles' life and actions. In my interview with him, he claimed the reason the realty firm that he accused of killing Jeff and framing him did not kill him was it would have supercharged the investigation. Killing Jeff, if that's what Telles did, resulted in far greater media coverage than if Telles had been killed.

It would be surprising if Telles, who is clearly intelligent, if flawed, didn't think that Jeff's colleagues would not just take up his work but would do so with more vigor and tenacity than even the notoriously dogged German could have mustered. The newspaper and its staff had to make it clear that killing a journalist would not stop his work. That was important both because it could protect other journalists from violence and that it was exactly what a newsroom would be expected and would want to do to honor a fallen colleague and his work.

***

Jeff's death mostly brought an end to the tired, unsupported narrative that Adelson pulled the strings in coverage at the paper. Jeff would have been happy to see that go into the dustbin of history. In the six years I worked with him, we both bristled at the negative, often unfair or poorly researched attacks on the Review-Journal's ownership. The national media and Nevada detractors saw nearly every story we did as having Adelson's prompting or stamp of approval. In reality, Jeff and I never met or talked to the billionaire or his family. We were never told Adelson wants this story or wants to kill this other one. By the time I had arrived at the RJ, the family had pretty much backed out of any editorial decisions, allowing Keith Moyer and Glenn Cook to set editorial policy as they saw fit. I wrote some hard-hitting stories about politicians the Adelsons supported with significant campaign contributions. None of those stories were modified beyond the usual editing process. They were not softened and all appeared prominently on the front page. As far as I know, we never received any backlash for what we wrote except Publisher Moon's failed attempt to fire me at Lombardo's urging. I only learned of that years after Moon was gone, and my understanding is it had nothing to do with the Adelsons. Moon just wanted to placate a powerful person instead of standing up for hard-hitting journalism. Or at least that is what it seems happened since he didn't return my calls or messages to talk about that incident or his own firing.

For the first time since Adelson's purchase, German's death wasn't colored by the Adelson narrative that nearly everyone at the paper had tired of and knew wasn't true. The major media organizations from around the country and world flooded into Las Vegas to tell the story of Jeff's death. CNN, Fox News, The New York Times, and other top national publications sought interviews and wrote stories about the murder of a reporter allegedly by a politician who wanted to stop an investigation. CBS did a morning-show segment. Its magazine 48 Hours spent a week pulling together an hour-long episode.

Honors and accolades for Jeff and the work the newspaper did after his death poured in even from people who were previously critical of the newspaper and its ownership. NPR media writer David Folkenflik, who wrote repeated stories about the impact of the ownership, praised the paper to me when I interviewed him.

"There is a terrible price to pay for accountability journalism," Folkenflik told me in a second of two interviews before Christmas 2023. "It should be honored and acknowledged. And, I would hope, certainly, that nobody's looking at (criticizing it) because of the nature of the ownership of the paper because there's nothing brought to my attention about the coverage that leads me to believe it was anything but inspired by the best traditions in American journalism."

I was able to connect with Folkenflik only because we had appeared on a local NPR station together to talk about difficulties getting open records (the RJ had started a feature exposing agencies that don't abide by the state records laws and transparency). My repeated attempts to get to him through NPR's public relations people were going nowhere, and unlike the RJ reporter's contact info, NPR phone numbers are not readily available.

During the local KNPR discussion, Folkenflik did make a statement that irked people at the newspaper. "Jeff's colleagues at the Review-Journal, even under the ownership of its relatively recent owners are continuing to dive deep in difficult and uncomfortable areas, honoring the work he did in (the) life he led," he said. I guess old habits die hard.

Despite blanket coverage of the purchase, Folkenflik also didn't write anything about Jeff's killing, which was a surprise considering it was a national story. "I encouraged us to reach out to people locally," he explained to me when I asked. "There's some times where people who have been doing the reporting—like I think we had on some of your editors and I think we had on some folks from KNPR." He said the timing was not right for him to dig into the piece. "You know, between budget cuts and the pandemic, I just have not done very much traveling. And so, I just haven't done it, but I think it's, I think it's a good story."

Rick Edmond, a media business analyst at Poynter Institute, closely followed the Adelson takeover and the resulting questions of bias and journalistic malpractice. "The Adelson family have said we're kind of keeping hands off in terms of the journalism with the possible exception of the editorials," he told me, adding that appears to be the case.

Poynter is a respected non-profit that provides "fact-checking, media literacy, and journalism ethics training" for journalists and the public. But its president, Neil Brown, who also co-chairs the Pulitzer Prizes, was involved in one of the most hurtful episodes to Jeff's friends and colleagues.

During the 2023 video announcing the prior year's Pulitzer Prizes, Brown gave an impassioned speech about the dangers faced by journalists.

"Journalists pay a substantial price for holding the powerful to account," he said on the streamed message. "Too often they are harassed and threatened and even violently attacked and held hostage."

But instead of noting Jeff's murder, Brown only named Wall Street Journal reporter Evan Gershkovich, who was jailed in Russia. One could feel the outrage in the newsroom building as German's name was nowhere in the ceremony clearly designed to honor journalists who were victims of violent retaliation for their work.

Moyer, not one to back down from a fight even with the most prestigious journalism awards, called Pulitzer administrator Marjorie Miller to inquire about the failure to mention German. She told him it was an oversight and her people should have flagged her. Moyer told her the paper submitted an awards entry for the work RJ reporters had done in covering German's murder, completing his unfinished stories, digging into Telles' background, and other allegations of corruption and misconduct that had not yet been uncovered. So it should have been fresh in her mind. He felt that Miller was just clueless about the whole situation and didn't get any indication that she realized how thoughtless it was to leave German's name out of the ceremony. Moyer felt that instead of awarding Pulitzers for the best work, the prizes were now controlled by elite East Coast media staff who still discriminate against the Review-Journal over the Adelson purchase controversy.

During the actual Pulitzer ceremony in October 2023, Miller addressed the oversight, naming Jeff after reiterating the facts of Gershkovich's imprisonment.

"Second, we condemn the slaying last year of Jeff German, an investigative reporter for the Las Vegas Review-Journal, who was stabbed to death outside his home," she said, looking uncomfortable. "A public official who German was investigating at the time of his death is facing trial for murder." She did not respond to the emails and calls I left asking for an interview for this book.

Brown told me the Wall Street Journal had reached out to ask the Pulitzer's express concern about Gershkovich's imprisonment. RJ editors had not reached out. It was a story for days in all the East Coast media.

"You know, to be honest with you, that was just an oversight," he told me. "The Journal folks contacted Marjorie Miller, the Pulitzer board, and wanting to sort of speak up for him... So we wanted to sort of make a statement there because he was obviously remains... unlawfully detained."

But Brown backed Miller when I asked whether she was lying to Moyer or really didn't know about a reporter slain in what police say was retaliation for his work a few months before the announcement.

"What Marjorie reads or knows is up to Marjorie," he said, seeming frustrated at the questioning. "She's doing an excellent job... I mean, I just don't like, I don't know, that's not really what Jeff's case is about. Really. I mean that. So it's up to you, man, but I'm just telling you straight up, like, I don't know what she means or not. She's a very talented, very accomplished journalist."

Poynter did honor Jeff German with a video of his colleagues discussing his sacrifice at a gala in November 2023.

Arguably the worst attack on Jeff's legacy came from the editor of the news organization run by his old nemesis, Jon Ralston.

Less than month after Jeff's death, the editor of the Nevada Independent, Elizabeth Crum-Thompson, sent out a newsletter questioning German's journalism skills and accomplishments.

"Is it just me or does anyone else think the lionizing of reporter Jeff German (has) been a bit much?" Thompson wrote. "Yes, people generally hesitate to speak ill of the dead. On the flip side, dying doesn't make you an insta-hero—and by all candid accounts, Jeff definitely wasn't one. I'm of the opinion that we should tell the truth about people, dead or alive, for better or worse. I'm silly like that."

Questioning German's reporting skills had been a regular habit for Thompson's boss, Jon Ralston, as the two threw literary punches at each other for decades. Ralston did not answer my inquiries about whether he knew or put Thompson up to her statement in the newsletter. Thompson also did not respond to requests for comment.

Ralston and his organization received national attention as critics of the Review-Journal during and after the Adelson purchase and was quoted in negative coverage about the RJ. Now that his organization was under scrutiny for an unforced error, he lashed out in the emotional way that German often documented in his Sun columns.

I emailed him this question on September 25, 2023: "I found some stuff you wrote in the Ralston Report about Jeff. German 'is not known as one of Nevada's most insightful or competent journalists,'" Ralston wrote in one newsletter, noting in another that German was "spoon-fed" information. "This seems to echo Liz's controversial letter sent to Indy staff after German's death about German not being much of a reporter. Did you have any involvement in writing or asking Liz to write that letter? What was your reaction to what she wrote?"

His response was less than revealing.

> Hi, Art,
>
> I do appreciate you reaching out, but I think you have everything you need.
>
> You clearly have decided to take at face value what Jeff wrote and are relying on people with axes to grind. It's your book, and I wish you the best with it.
>
> JR

Thompson's staff condemned her:

> We are saddened and embarrassed by the words. ... Words matter, and we know the comments were trivializing to other media members grieving the death of a colleague, friend and mentor. As a staff, we want to apologize for the hurt it caused.

This forced Thompson to issue a sort of an apology.

> I did not foresee that members of our newsroom would feel embarrassed or think my opinion on the matter could be a problem for our brand and/or was in conflict with our mission.

Ralston tried to spin the controversy away on Twitter (X):

This is an unfortunate situation. … Having said that, @elizthompsn is a tremendous leader of @TheNVIndy newsroom. She is a good, caring person who made a mistake. … We support her but we also understand why people are upset. Onward!

Comparing Thompson and German's journalistic resumes reveals she does not have much to back up her being "silly that way." Instead of forty years of hard-hitting reporting that resulted in indictments, removal of officials, and changes in state law, Thompson's resume before the Indy was mostly punditry.

Thompson's "television work includes hosting Nevada Week in Review on Vegas PBS for most of 2014, co-hosting the daily political talk show The Agenda on KSNV News 3 from 2012-2013 and working as the political analyst for KTNV News 13 from 2009-2011. E's been published in the Wall Street Journal and National Review Online and has provided political analysis and commentary for CNN, MSNBC, Fox News and numerous Nevada television and radio stations," her bio on the Indy website says. "She is the founder and former publisher (and still sits on the executive board) of the Nevada News Bureau, a nonprofit that serves as the parent company of The Nevada Independent. The Bureau's primary initiative, a news website covering state government and politics, first went live in late 2009 as a media project of Citizen Outreach. E's Nevada media stint started in 2008 when she launched an indie political blog covering Nevada and national politics. The following year, she won the Sam Adams Alliance's Best New Political Blogger Award. In 2010, she co-founded RFC, an internet radio station featuring political talk plus classic rock, and also served as the Nevada correspondent for National Review Online's Battle '10 election blog.

"She is also the founder of E Thompson Media, a small consulting firm specializing in copywriting, media management, custom digital content, marketing and public relations."

Since I started in journalism, I went out of my way to write about politicians and officials who refused comment. I stole the tactic from the Chicago Sun-Time's Fran Spielman, who often led stories with the public officials who wouldn't talk to her. I think it says something when people beg off, say "no comment," avoid calls, or try to use tactics to manage the interview.

While dozens of Jeff's former friends and colleagues gave generously of their time, one of the biggest surprises was journalists and others who refused to talk or even answer repeated attempts to contact them about Jeff's life and their interactions with him. I thought this was a story all journalists would want to help tell because it hits about as close to home as possible.

I understood Jeff's sisters' and brother's refusal to participate in the project. They have not spoken on the record to any media about Jeff's death and declined even to learn what I had uncovered in my research. I can only imagine the pain and loss they felt after Jeff's murder. But I was concerned that they also actively dissuaded people from talking, which only served to prevent me from including more voices of people who loved and respected Jeff.

I do not know if the family's reluctance was prompted by prosecutors and police urging them to decline comment or some sort of hostility against the RJ, myself, or rivalry with the Sun. Sun editorial cartoonist Mike Smith is married to Jeff's oldest sister, Julie. After Jeff's death, Mike and Julie allowed me and Prast to collect Jeff's notes and work product from his house, but they have steadfastly refused all other interactions with local and national media. The book would have benefited from their participation. I can only hope that Jeff's life and work is represented fairly and completely. It was never my intention to provoke any more suffering, but like Jeff often did with his journalism, I felt his story had to be told.

The police, prosecutors, and many government officials Jeff and I covered also refused to be interviewed. I understand their concerns about tainting the case, but the story may be less complete without their input. The spokeswoman for Governor Joe Lombardo, who was sheriff when Jeff was killed, did not return repeated calls and emails seeking an interview with the state's top elected official. Taxpayers pay Elizabeth Ray to field just such inquires and if she can't be bothered, then maybe it is an easy budget cut.

The journalists who refused to comment were the biggest surprise. I foolishly thought that all of the journalists and former reporters and editors would jump at participating in a project that tells the story of a journalist apparently murdered for no reason other than doing his job. Whenever a police officer is shot, all the other cops band together to find the killer and make sure it is well known that killing an officer will not be tolerated. I assumed that would be doubly true for the death of a journalist whose job should not subject him to the same dangers that police officers regularly face.

My disappointment stemmed not from personal insult but the fear that the book may not be as complete and compelling as it would be with their memories in it. No matter what kind of interactions—positive, negative, or otherwise—people had with Jeff over the years, I figured all journalists would want to help tell the story of a murdered colleague, if only as an effort to prevent future such attacks and protect themselves. I was sadly wrong about that.

My biggest surprise came when former RJ Assistant Managing Editor Rhonda Prast, who was Jeff's and my supervisor for about two years, refused to be interviewed for the book. She was taking every opportunity to speak about her work with Jeff and her role in the coverage after the murder. When I called her to ask her to meet for an interview, she demanded that she edit the book, saying she was the person who knew the most about the story. I declined for a number of reasons. The publisher was providing one of their editors, and I felt that her editing of my RJ articles when she was my boss often did not produce the best version of the story.

Clearly upset, she demanded: "What's in it for me?"

People I was told were Jeff's friends, like long-time Vegas TV reporter George Knapp, did not return several messages left on their cell phones. I have no idea why. Joan Ann Morrison, who covered courts at the RJ when Jeff was doing the same at the Sun, emailed, declining an interview. I also have no idea why since she was always emailing support for stories Jeff and I were writing at the paper.

Mitch Fox, president of the Nevada Broadcasters Association, declined to talk, emailing he had few interactions with Jeff and Jeff regularly turned down offers when Fox hosted Nevada Week in Review. He answered a few emails but was less than helpful.

Howard Stutz, who vocally opposed the Adelson takeover of the RJ, would not talk about his work with Jeff or the tumultuous time when the RJ was being sold to the casino mogul. "I just wanted to let you know I'm really not interested in being interviewed," he emailed. In fact, all of the people who investigated the Adelson purchase for some reason did not respond to requests for interviews except Jim Wright, the editor at the paper deeply involved in the story. He provided good insights and anecdotes from the time. I couldn't find a good number for Jennifer Robison so I left messages at PG&E where she was a public relations person and asked Wright to reach out to her. Wright messaged back, saying she is declining: "Jennifer received my message but is choosing not to participate out of respect for the wishes of Jeff's family." James DeHaven did not respond to calls and emails at numbers I found for him and at places I believed he worked.

Former top Sun Editor Michael J. Kelley did not return my repeated calls to talk. I think I left him half a dozen messages because he was key to Jeff's early career at the Sun. Kelley lives in Kansas so a personal visit to attempt to get him to talk was not possible. Brian Greenspun, whose father first hired Jeff and who continues his father's "Where I Stand" column in the Sun, did not respond to repeated calls and emails. His PR person also would not explain the reasons for his refusal to comment. I reached an editor at the paper and he said Greenspun wants to abide by the family's wishes. I understand the RJ and Sun are in a legal dispute over the joint operating agreement, but I would have happily accepted a no comment on that issue to get his recollections on the early days of Jeff at the Sun.

Former RJ features writer Art Nadler, who I was told was one of Jeff's closest friends, did not respond to repeated calls.

Columnist John L. Smith, who wrote extensively about Jeff's murder for various outlets, also begged off an interview, writing: "On a long project deadline. Not sure what I could add that I haven't written. Good luck." I responded with, "Is that declining to comment?" He now works for Ralston's Indy and got angry when I persisted. "As for not jumping at you're [sic] pushy attempts to grab a quote from me, did you ever think the problem might be you?" he wrote in a Twitter (X) direct message exchange. I've been a journalist for thirty years, and persistence and being pushy is usually thought of as a virtue in this business, not a problem. I would have liked to have him discuss his legal battles with Adelson and Wynn.

My attempts to get Smith's boss, Jon Ralston, to interview for the book were some of the most frustrating and shocking exchanges. When I first reached out to him, he tried to blow me off.

"Jeff and I never worked together per se," he emailed, wishing me luck on the book. "When I was at the Sun, I was never really AT the Sun. I never—or rarely—came into the newsroom. So we interacted very, very little. I couldn't be of much help."

When I persisted and uncovered more and more evidence of his and Jeff's long-running feud that I felt was a compelling subplot in the story, he said he's happy to fill out or respond to individual anecdotes, but said: "I'm just not that interested in trying to recall what may now be faulty memories."

As my questions got tougher, Ralston started using tactics usually adopted by politicians to avoid questions they don't want to answer. Maybe Ralston has been covering politics for too long.

He refused to have a phone or in-person interview, only answering questions by email. Most journalists abhor the tactics as it hinders getting at the truth of the matter. I rarely agree to written questions, but I needed his input so I decided to engage in an email exchange. I was right that it did little to illuminate the issues.

Other politician-like tactics included repeatedly questioning the relevance of inquiries, claiming he was being bullied, and attacking me and impugning my motives. He especially bristled when I asked him about comments about his personality or professional motives that people who knew him described during interviews.

"I was told by multiple sources (see how this works) not to trust you and even when you showed ignorance of the subject matter, I answered your questions. You asked not one question with substance—just hearsay, speculation and innuendo.

> Here's what I am not willing to do: Indulge you in character assassination of me to make your subject look better. If you think it is journalism to assert 'people are saying bad stuff about you,

what do you say?' that tells me a lot. The book
is about Jeff, not me.

It has now become clear to me why the family
is opposed to this book.

JR[303]

While journalists have to deal with such tactics from
people they are writing about, to invoke Jeff's family
was so patently inappropriate and appalling, considering
the mutual hatred they felt for each other that I was left
uncharacteristically speechless.

***

Some people have questioned my motivation for writing
this book, insinuating that I plan to profit from the death of
a colleague. Unlike Jeff's book, where he received a sizable
advance and sold the movie rights, the work on this book
was solely on my personal time. Any reporting expenses
were paid out of my pocket. I will only make money if
the book sells. It will have to sell very, very well for me to
make more than the minimum wage, considering the hours
invested in reporting and writing the story.

So then why take on the project just as I accepted a
promotion to Investigations Editor at the Review-Journal?
First, like Jeff and his book on the Binion trial, I feel
that writing a serious non-fiction book is the pinnacle of
journalism. Journalists are said to write the first draft of
history in their daily articles. A book is much closer to the
final draft. I have wanted to write a book since I started in
this business and have suffered a few false starts. I trust this
one will turn out better.

Second, one thing that has irked me about the news
business and working as a staff writer is the lack of
entrepreneurial spirit of the job. You can work your butt off

and dig up great stories, landing on the front page regularly. But that is rarely rewarded monetarily. Especially as revenues declined, there are rarely bonuses, pay increases, or advancements that top performers see in other fields. Stock options or any other ways to participate in the success of the enterprise are unheard of in this business. The schlub in the cubicle next to you who does the bare minimum not to get fired often gets treated not that much differently in newsrooms as the stars. I will honestly say the RJ is better than most at rewarding high performers and getting rid of dead weight. The paper doesn't have a union to protect people who aren't pulling their weight like other places I worked. But I have been looking for a project that will succeed solely based on its merits and hopefully find a wide national audience. This book is that project.

Finally, and most importantly, this story has to be told. I feel that my close work with Jeff and my reporting after his slaying makes me the perfect person to tell it. The killing of a journalist for doing his job is an appalling assault on democracy and press freedoms, so everyone should have access to the story in a detailed, comprehensive, and easy-to-follow narrative. I hope I have done that with this book. I also hope that Jeff would have been proud of it even when it exposes some of his foibles. Also, the book ventures to give readers an inside view of the news business, life in newsrooms, and the crazy, Wild West place that is Las Vegas. Most visitors have little understanding of this mecca in the desert beyond the Strip or Downtown casinos. People think the corporate takeover of casinos has softened the city's edges. That may be true, but this place started with so much edge that it will be a long time, if ever, before it's a dull place. There is some irony and sadness in writing this book. While it was only in jest because we never thought it would happen, Jeff and I promised to tell the other's story if something like this happened. With this book, I have tried my hardest to keep that promise.

ACKNOWLEDGEMENTS

Many authors wait until the end to thank family, but I have to give credit to my wife first and foremost. Without her, all my life's successes and joys would not be possible. Denise Marie Thomasson is the most intelligent, driven, beautiful, and accomplished person I know. After thirty years together, we still have conversations that are as engrossing and revelatory as with anyone else I know. And I have some pretty interesting and funny friends and colleagues. She has supported every crazy idea I had and steered me away from some that would have in retrospect been disastrous. I can't think of a better partner in life and do not know what my life would have been like if without our chance meeting in 1991 at a rock club in Minneapolis. I love you always.

My agent Sandra Bond worked tirelessly to sell this book even when most of the major publishing houses passed. She was dedicated to the project even with the likelihood that it may generate little or no commission. Steve Jackson, Michael Cordova, and Stephanie Johnson Lawson at WildBlue Press were enthusiastic about the story. The fact Steve and I shared a history of living and working in journalism in Denver for many years helped start us off on the right foot.

I have to thank my friend and former colleague, KMGH chief investigative reporter Tony Kovaleski, for general support in my career and the introductions that led to this book getting a publisher, including to former Denver television investigative reporter Paula Woodward, who connected me with Sandra.

The staff and management at the Las Vegas Review-Journal were supportive from the beginning and took time out of their busy schedules to provide recollections, documents, and perspectives on Jeff German, his life, and his horrific death. Publisher Keith Moyer has easily been the best boss I ever had in thirty years in this business. I found he is always willing to do the right thing no matter what the personal consequences. Executive Editor Glenn Cook bent over backwards to provide me an insight into his interactions early in the murder investigation and his long history working with Jeff. It took a quarter of a century, but I finally have a boss who is as dedicated and driven to ferret out government waste, corruption, and malfeasance no matter the consequences. Managing Editor Anastasia Hendrix and Assistant Managing Editor Carri Geer Thevenot were supportive as I balanced the duties of my new position with researching and writing the book. RJ attorney Ben Lipman was always helpful and reviewed the chapter on the legal fight over Jeff's devices for accuracy and completeness as I know just enough law to be dangerous. My reporters on the investigative unit—Briana Erickson, Mary Hynes, and Eli Segall—supported the work and were a great sounding board for things I was learning and ideas I had to present the book. Assistant City Editor David Ferrara knew Jeff for years, covering courts, and provided key insights to both his life and the murder. Ferrara was one of the only people at the paper who believed Robert Telles may have murdered Jeff. I'm a hundred bucks poorer for doubting his instincts but the book is that much richer for his drive to get at the answers about what happened to Jeff.

This book could not have been done without the reporting from the Metro staff. The whole newsroom deserves praise and accolades for handling one of the toughest stories—one that involved a friend and colleague—with the type of professionalism that one could only hope for in such a difficult situation. I apologize if anyone is inadvertently left out but the cops and courts team of Brett Clarkson, Katelyn Newberg, and David Wilson spearheaded the breaking news coverage of the investigation, making sure we were not scooped. Their stories helped me understand and report the issues that I wasn't a part of covering after Jeff's death. Briana Erickson, at the time a colleague and now one of my reporters, pulled together a phenomenal profile of Telles that gave me a road map for much of his problematic history. She also took time to review the chapter on Telles for accuracy.

One of the best writers I ever worked at a newspaper, Jason Bracelin, reviewed a draft of this book, providing insights that greatly helped the narrative. He's also a great partner for drinking and hitting metal shows, and a rare newspaper music critic who actually likes good music (or at least music I think is good).

The people who took time out of their lives to talk to me about Jeff are too numerous to name. Many are cited in the book but a few couldn't be named because they needed to remain anonymous. I thank them all and hope I told their stories as fairly and accurately as possible. Scott Zamost and Harrison Keely provided key photos for the book.

UNLV librarian Priscilla Finley went out her way to help me navigate the less-than-user-friendly archives of the Las Vegas Sun. She went above and beyond looking up articles for me on ancient microfiche. Jennifer, whose last name I never learned, from the Milwaukee Public Library, dug up articles Jeff wrote for the Milwaukee newspaper as well as biographical notices and yearbook information that helped me find sources and fill out parts of his early life before he moved to Las Vegas.

Finally, I have to thank Maynard James Kane even though he can't read. That is because he's a dog. Whenever I had a key passage or difficult chapter to complete, he would invariably come to my office to demand dinner, a quick pet, or a walk. I love him very much despite his often bad behavior and dismissive attitude.

ENDNOTES

1   Account of Glenn Cook's notification of Jeff German's death based on a long interview and follow ups with Cook.

2   Interview with Keith Moyer

3   Interview with Rabbi Gil-Ezer Lerer

4   Jeff German column on Max German's 75th birthday published in the *Sun* on May 16, 1993

5   June German obit in the Las Vegas.

6   Recht did not respond to repeated messages left at what was believed to be his phone number.

7   Jeff German column on Max German's 75th birthday published in the *Sun* on May 16, 1993

8   Yearbook pages and Sherkow's newspaper ad and interviews.

9   Interview with Sharon Maiman-Rosenberg

10   Jeff German column on Max German's 75th birthday published in the *Sun* on May 16, 1993

11   Interview with Sharon Maiman-Rosenberg

12   Jim Romenesko interview

13   Carol Vogel interview; Chris Chrystal did not respond to repeated voicemails left by the author on her phone.

14   Interview with Scott Zamost, recording of Jeff German telling story, various stories recounting it and Eater article about hangouts of Spilotro: https://vegas.eater.com/2013/1/31/6487437/6-places-frequented-by-tony-the-ant-spilotro

15   Interview with Mark Schaffer, producer of POV for the Las Vegas Sun in the 1980s who heard the story from German and Smith.

16   https://en.wikipedia.org/wiki/Michael_Milken

17   https://en.wikipedia.org/wiki/The_Mirage#cite_note-MirageReal-31

18   https://lasvegassun.com/news/2002/nov/29/ex-metro-cop-blasko-dies/#:~:text=On%20Sept.,%2Dthe%2DWall%20Gang.%22

19   Yablonsky interviewed by George Knapp for *Remembering Joe Yablonsky: A look back at the man who pummeled Las Vegas' Mob* documentary.

20   https://www.reviewjournal.com/local/local-las-vegas/joseph-yablonsky-former-las-vegas-fbi-chief-dies-at-90-1670551/

21   https://en.wikipedia.org/wiki/Harry_E._Claiborne and news articles and Binion Biography "Blood Aces" by Doug J. Swanson.

22   Author's email exchange with current SPJ leadership.

23   George Knapp for Remembering Joe Yablonsky: A look back at the man who pummeled Las Vegas' Mob documentary; https://www.reviewjournal.com/local/local-las-vegas/joseph-yablonsky-former-las-vegas-fbi-chief-dies-at-90-1670551/; https://thenevadaindependent.com/article/joe-yablonsky-las-vegas-should-remember-the-man-it-prefers-to-forget

24   https://en.wikipedia.org/wiki/Sig_Rogich and Rogich interview

25   Rogich interview

26   Rogich interview and Wikipedia background.

27   http://ganglandwire.com/tony-spilotro-2/ and Groover interview.

28   https://johngrant.wordpress.com/2008/08/02/the-death-of-frank-bluestein/

29   Interview with Bob Miller

30   *Las Vegas Sun* article (no byline) on Aug. 26, 1981 titled "Cops Probe Sun On Wiretap Leak."

31   https://johngrant.wordpress.com/2008/08/02/the-death-of-frank-bluestein/ and Groover interview by author; articles by German and others in the *Sun* during the 1981 controversy. Many of the details are impossible to confirm because both The Battle for Las Vegas – The Law vs. the Mob author Dennis Griffin, and Metro Intel Commander Kent Clifford have since died.

32   Interview with David Groover

33   https://thenevadaindependent.com/article/learning-to-appreciate-news-reporter-jeff-german-a-remembrance

34   UPI story from Reno April 28, 1988; Phone interview with Brian McKay and interview with Bob Miller. McKay said he doesn't remember making those comments but conceded that if there was a television interview he must have said those things. McKay grew to

respect German's tenacity as a journalist, telling the author in 2023 that: "He was a tiger. If he got ahold of something he wouldn't let it go."

35   Mary Manning and Sig Rogich interviews – Other reporters who were in Carson that session dispute it happened because they had not heard of it until the author asked about the incident.

36   Text exchange with former state Sen. Sue Lowden who was victorious in the 1992 campaign.

37   Interview with Marilyn Gubler

38   Author's email exchange with SPJ

39   Interviews with friends like Steve Sebelius, George McCabe and others

40   George McCabe interview

41   Interview with Doug McMurdo who worked for the RJ as court reporter competing with German.

42   Goodman interview

43   Interviews with Tom Dillard and other sources who requested anonymity. Ralston email exchange: Aug. 22, 2023: "It never happened. Sarah never dated Jeff. Or if she did, I never knew about it!" Follow-up email same day: "Oh they may have gone out I honestly don't recall. Been 30-plus years. Couldn't have been more than a time or two if it happened. Maybe I am more senile than I thought! I don't think he harped on that. But maybe so."

44   Highlights from Ralston Report cited in *New Times* article May 5, 1994. The author attempted through a number of sources, including the TV station, to obtain the video of the clash but was unable to find a copy as archives were not maintained and the station moved offices, leaving much of the archival material behind.

45   German misspells the SNL character Roseanne Roseannadanna in the column.

46   Ralston declined an interview but answered questions in emails, including one about the nicknames where he wrote: "I came up with neither of those nicknames (as I did not come up with one for Jeff you mentioned) and have only heard of one of them. Molly is a friend of mine, and we had dinner here last year, and Patrick is a donor to The Indy. It's simply not true. Of course you can imagine it's disturbing to hear these falsities -- plenty about me to criticize that's true!"

47   Coolican emails Sept. 28, 2023 when asked about Ralston's propensity to use nick names: "i think i heard him use Jeffy. nicknames

were in his repertoire… I heard the Molly one. I hadn't heard the one about me, but apparently it's true."

48   Author's exchange of emails with Ralston who declined to do an interview, writing he was "not that interested in trying to recall what may now be faulty memories."

49   German Column 9/28/1996

50   Ralston emails with author.

51   https://en.wikipedia.org/wiki/John_Ensign_ scandal#:~:text=Ensign%20resigned%20from%20the%20 Senate,of%20potential%20violation%20of%20laws & https:// lasvegassun.com/news/2009/jul/08/transcript-jon-ralstons-interview-doug-hampton/

52   Email exchange with Fox as he also declined an interview. He wrote: "As I recall Jeff was miffed that he wasn't selected to be on the reporter panel, which resulted in the column. I didn't mind the barbs as it generated some buzz for the debate."

53   Ralston Reports 2/6/22 and 1/26/20

54   Wisconsin Marriage Index provided by the Milwaukee Library

55   Interview with Mary Manning and https://www.latimes.com/ archives/la-xpm-1995-11-11-mn-1928-story.html

56   Interview with Billy Vassiliadis and Bob Miller

57   Cathy Scott interview

58   Hotel executive Binion told his life may be in danger Las Vegas Sun story on Thursday, Feb. 6, 1997 by Jeff German

59   Subpoenas served in hearing targeting casino executive Ted Binion Las Vegas Sun story on Tuesday, March 12, 1996 by Jeff German.

60   https://www.nbcnews.com/id/wbna9927522 & https://knpr.org/ show/knprs-state-of-nevada/2013-05-21/being-oscar-goodman-former-mayor-of-las-vegas-aired-2013 & https://lasvegassun.com/news/2009/ jan/22/senators-ideas-impose-tax-brothels-make-prostituti/ & https:// www.nytimes.com/1999/05/02/us/a-colorful-lawyer-is-running-for-mayor.html

61   Goodman interview

62   Interview with Ron Flud

63   Retired Coroner Ron Flud interview.

64   https://www.latimes.com/archives/la-xpm-1988-07-18-mn-4466-story.html

65   Richard Wright interview

66   Binion Biography "Blood Aces" by Doug J. Swanson and news stories

67   Wayne Petersen interview

68   https://lasvegassun.com/news/2004/oct/28/lawyer-recounts-why-he-cut-murphy-out-of-will/

69   Roger and Baden interviews

70   Glen Meek interview

71   Doug McMurdo interview.

72   Roger interview. PERS Data shows retirement first collected 1/4/12 and in 2019 the amount was $12,306 a month or about $147,000 a year.

73   Bonaventure interview

74   Dr. Michael Baden interview

75   Michael Cristalli and Michael Baden interviews

76   Michael Cristalli interview

77   David Roger interview. Lalli declined to comment about the Binion trial.

78   Michael Cristalli interview

79   Will Kemp interview

80   Will Kemp and George McCabe interviews

81   Reporter's journey from story to screen: TV movie on Ted Binion's death ends long, frustrating, but

ultimately satisfying process for *Sun*'s by Jeff German Nov. 7 2008

82   Sig Rogich interview and news stories

83   https://en.wikipedia.org/wiki/Jim_Gibbons_ (American_ politician)

84   Campbell did not respond to repeated requests for comment.

85   "Between 2005 and 2015, the Annual Profits Payments to the Sun had been as much as $12 million per year, and never less than $1.3 million per year," according to a federal lawsuit filed by the Sun: Case No. 2:19-cv-01667.

86   Sam Skolnik and J. Patrick Coolican interviews

87   Interviews with Drex Heikes and a half dozen reporters and editors then at the Sun.

88   Interviews with Heikes, Sam Skolnik and J. Patrick Coolican and news stories.

89   https://en.wikipedia.org/wiki/Operation_G-Sting

90   Secretive lab, UNLV part ways: Security institute to refocus on academics story in the *Las Vegas Sun* Sept. 28, 2007 by German, Jeff

91   Kane worked at the Denver Post when the papers were entering the JOA and covered the closing in 2009 as a producer at KMGH-TV.

92   Interview with John Temple

93   John Temple interview

94   Mary Manning interview.

95   Tom Dillard interview

96   Clark County recorder records

97   George McCabe, Doug McMurdo interviews and interviews with other reporters at the Sun and RJ as well as public records from the Clark County Recorder's office.

98   Carol Vogel interview

99   Author's discussions with German prior to his death.

100   Sig Rogich interview & Sherm Frederick in an interview said he doesn't remember Sig calling him but would have welcomed the input.

101   https://lasvegassun.com/blogs/ralstons-flash/2009/aug/31/rj-publisher-responds-nonexistent-threat-senator-t// & https://www.politico.com/blogs/on-congress/2009/08/reid-wants-*Review-Journal*-out-of-business-020992

102   https://www.youtube.com/watch?v=m7zmp-pfgj0

103   Doug McMurdo interview

104   Fertado died in 2014 and Nadler did not return repeated calls for comment.

105   https://en.wikipedia.org/wiki/A.D._Hopkins and A.D. Hopkins interview.

106   Charles Zobell interviews

107   Interview with Glenn Cook who has been on the RJ Fantasy Football team for years and Ferrara interview.

108 Interview with James Wright

109 https://abcnews.go.com/Business/attorneys-nevada-homeowners-association-scandal-dead/story?id=16013470 & https://www.reviewjournal.com/crime/courts/death-of-attorney-targeted-in-hoa-case-ruled-suicide/

110 https://www.reviewjournal.com/news/ex-cop-linked-to-hoa-probe-clearly-carried-burden-before-apparent-suicide/

111 https://www.reviewjournal.com/crime/courts/federal-prosecutors-under-investigation-for-alleged-obstruction-of-justice-in-hoa-probe/

112 Glenn Cook, Scherm Frederick, James Wright interviews

113 https://www.reviewjournal.com/local/local-las-vegas/four-found-guilty-in-massive-las-vegas-hoa-fraud-case/

114 James G. Wright interview

115 https://www.reviewjournal.com/business/las-vegas-*Review-Journal*-announces-newsroom-management-changes/ & *Review-Journal* Publisher Sherman Frederick, Editor Thomas Mitchell out—Las Vegas Sun Nov. 12, 2010, by Patrick Coolican

116 James Wright interview & https://www.reviewjournal.com/news/*Review-Journal*-rakes-in-awards-from-nevada-press-association/

117 https://www.reviewjournal.com/local/local-las-vegas/*Review-Journal*-parent-stephens-media-to-be-sold-to-new-media/

118 https://www.reviewjournal.com/business/casinos-gaming/las-vegas-sands-corp-steven-jacobs-reach-confidential-settlement-in-wrongful-termination-case/

119 Opensecrets.org and CRP provided data about the Adelson's federal and state political contributions to the author. Federal data showed contributions that went back to 1990 and state data to 1996.

120 https://www.forbes.com/profile/sheldon-adelson/?sh=473554b4a224 & additional background on Adelson from Mother Jones, Forbes, Bloomberg, New York Times.

121 https://www.reviewjournal.com/business/casinos-gaming/nevada-supreme-court-rejects-effort-to-remove-judge-from-las-vegas-sands-corp-case/

122 https://time.com/4168689/sheldon-adelson-judge-las-vegas-review-journal/

123   https://www.nytimes.com/2016/01/07/business/
media/a-publisher-puzzles-staff-with-his-role-in-las-vegas.
html#:~:text=When%20a%20relatively%20obscure%20
newspaper,appearance%20baffled%20journalists%20%E2%80%94%20
in%20Connecticut.

124   Interviews with Jim Wright and David Ferrara

125   Mike Hengel interview.

126   The author contacted Michael Schroeder on Oct. 21, 2023 but
he declined to be interviewed, saying "I don't want to participate."
When asked whether he wanted to know what was going in this book,
Schroeder responded: "I can't control it."

127   Mike Hengel and Jim Wright interviews and RJ news stories,
including https://www.reviewjournal.com/local/local-las-vegas/
controversial-manager-of-*Review-Journal*-parent-company-removed-
from-job/ & https://www.reviewjournal.com/local/local-las-vegas/
adelson-son-in-law-orchestrated-familys-purchase-of-las-vegas-
Review-Journal/ Additionally quote appeared in: https://www.cjr.org/
special_report/sheldon-adelson-metoo-las-vegas-review-journal.php

128   James Wright interview. Stutz declined to be interviewed for the
book and Robison and Dehaven did not return calls and emails.

129   The author was unable to find a phone number for Taylor as his
name is quite comment but contacted him through LinkedIn.

130   Mike Hengel interview.

131   https://www.medill.northwestern.edu/news/2016/las-vegas-
review-journal-reporters-awarded-2015-james-foley-medill-medal-for-
courage-in-journalism.html

132   https://www.reviewjournal.com/opinion/editorials/editorial-how-
adelson-might-change-rj-editorial-page/

133   Craig Moon did not respond to phone calls and emails
requesting an interview for the book.

134   The Vegas Columnist And The Newspaper Owner Who Once
Sued Him For Libel published on NPR.org on January 14, 2016 &
Court records in the libel lawsuit. Smith repeatedly refused to do an
interview with the author, claiming he was too busy and was concerned
about the author's journalistic persistence. He wrote on Twitter private
message: "I have written thousands of words on this subject, and will
write thousands more. As for not jumping at you're your (SIC) pushy
attempt to grab a quote from me, did you ever think the problem might
be you?"·

135   Author interviews with David Folkenflik

136   https://caselaw.findlaw.com/court/nv-supreme-court/1270461.html

137   Author interviews with David Folkenflik and Kelly McBride.

138   https://www.npr.org/2016/04/27/475913440/las-vegas-columnist-quits-after-ban-on-writing-about-adelson

139   https://www.politico.com/media/story/2016/04/las-vegas-*Review-Journal*-columnist-resigns-004502/ & https://www.nytimes.com/2016/04/27/business/media/another-journalist-quits-las-vegas-newspaper-bought-by-sheldon-adelson.html & https://www.npr.org/2016/04/27/475913440/las-vegas-columnist-quits-after-ban-on-writing-about-adelson & https://www.salon.com/2016/04/27/journalist_resigns_after_barred_from_writing_about_las_vegas_newspapers_right_wing_billionaire_owner_sheldon_adelson/

140   https://www.reuters.com/business/environment/pge-charged-with-manslaughter-sparking-california-wildfire-2021-09-24/ & https://www.linkedin.com/in/jenniferrobison/ & https://www.npr.org/2021/09/24/1040630538/pacific-gas-electric-manslaughter-charges-california-wildfire-zogg

141   Interview with Colton Lochhead, who after more than a decade with the paper resigned to take a job at the Las Vegas Valley Water District in October of 2023. He had been covering water at the paper.

142   https://www.cjr.org/special_report/sheldon-adelson-metoo-las-vegas-*Review-Journal*.php

143   Moyer interview 40 minutes in

144   https://www.reviewjournal.com/news/politics-and-government/nevada/pension-system-perks-cost-taxpayers-23-million-a-year/ & Moyer interview.

145   https://www.politico.com/blogs/media/2015/04/ralston-las-vegas-sun-editor-pulled-column-to-protect-reid-204868

146   https://www.reviewjournal.com/news/las-vegas-*Review-Journal*-killed-story-in-1998-about-steve-wynn-sex-misconduct-claims/#:~:text=%3E%3E%20News-,Las%20Vegas%20Review%2DJournal%20killed%20story%20in%201998,Steve%20Wynn%20sex%20misconduct%20claims&text=A%201998%20fax.&text=Claims%20that%20casino%20developer%20Steve,brought%20the%20issue%20to%20light.

147   https://money.cnn.com/2018/02/06/media/las-vegas-*Review-Journal*-steve-wynn-story/index.html

148   https://www.reviewjournal.com/local/local-las-vegas/lvcva-spends-millions-to-wine-and-dine-but-some-question-spending/

149   https://www.reviewjournal.com/investigations/lvcva-focused-on-damage-control-after-rj-investigation-emails-show/

150   Zobell and Wright interviews.

151   https://www.reviewjournal.com/local/local-las-vegas/las-vegas-convention-staff-fails-to-track-more-than-125k-in-gifts/

152   https://www.reviewjournal.com/local/local-las-vegas/lvcva-security-officers-diverted-to-drive-rossi-ralenkotter-oscar-goodman/

153   https://www.reviewjournal.com/investigations/las-vegas-tourism-executives-got-british-airways-comps-for-family-1635949/

154   https://www.reviewjournal.com/local/the-strip/las-vegas-strip-shooter-targeted-aviation-fuel-tanks-source-says/

155   Author interview with Neil Brown

156   https://www.reviewjournal.com/investigations/charged-with-felonies-tourism-boss-gets-sweetheart-deal-2102579/ (CASE NO LONGER SHOWS UP IN COURT DATABASE)

157   https://www.reviewjournal.com/business/judge-stays-state-court-joa-litigation-between-review-journal-and-sun-1906890/

158   Case No. 2:19-cv-01667

159   https://www.reviewjournal.com/business/court-filing-greenspun-sought-buyout-from-review-journal-suns-closure-2242017/#:~:text=Court%20filing%3A%20Greenspun%20sought%20buyout,the%20companies'%20joint%20operating%20agreement.

160   Larry Mir interview, audio outtakes Mir provided and German's scripts from the podcast.

161   Geoff Schumacher interview and interview with Glenn Cook

162   https://www.reviewjournal.com/news/politics-and-government/clark-county/170k-settlement-related-to-countys-legal-battle-with-rj-approved-2874135/#:~:text=Clark%20County%20will%20make%20a,the%20release%20of%20child%20autopsies.&text=Clark%20County%20is%20paying%20an,the%20release%20of%20child%20autopsies.

163   https://www.reviewjournal.com/investigations/sex-harassment-claims-accreditation-warnings-coroner-staff-still-got-

raises-and-bonuses-2467046/#:~:text=In%20July%2C%20the%20
Review%2DJournal,in%20the%20county's%20payroll%20system. &
https://www.reviewjournal.com/investigations/former-coroner-claimed-
iffy-degrees-did-outside-work-on-taxpayer-time-2463081/

164   https://www.reviewjournal.com/investigations/coroners-
generous-retirement-package-raises-questions-of-county-
oversight-2391026/

165   Author interview with Kevin Schiller

166   Author interview with Jeff Wells Dec. 19, 2023

167   Text message from Rita Reid with exact date on Oct. 25, 2023.

168   Author interview with Robert Telles in Clark County Detention
Center Dec. 5, 2023

169   Interviews with Rita Reid, John Cahill and Aleisha Goodwin.

170   https://www.reviewjournal.com/investigations/deputy-
clark-county-manager-on-leave-related-to-sons-employment-
2741230/#:~:text=In%202018%2C%20allegations%20surfaced%20
that,the%20allegation%20was%20not%20substantiated.

171   https://www.reviewjournal.com/investigations/former-
govs-daughter-others-accused-of-anti-police-culture-in-county-
office-2936394/ Investigative Reporter Briana Erickson broke the story
of the hiring and other allegations of Ashley Sisolak's conduct in a
story edited by the author if this book.

172   Author interview with Jeff Wells Dec. 19, 2023.

173   https://www.reviewjournal.com/investigations/henderson-
constable-indicted-faces-5-felony-counts-1544154/#:~:text=A%20
Clark%20County%20grand%20jury,property%20by%20a%20
public%20officer.

174   Author Interview with Jeff Wells Dec. 19, 2023

175   Author interview with Jeff Wells Dec 19, 2023

176   Author interview with Kevin Schiller

177   Rita Reid interview. Jeff Wells exchanged emails with the author
when he was researching issues with departments under his control and
the hiring of son, but he did not respond to emails requesting interviews
(his cell phone could not be found) for this book.

178   Author interview with Jeff Wells Dec. 19, 2023

179   Interview with Aleisha Goodwin

180   https://www.reviewjournal.com/investigations/telles-investigated-in-alleged-kickback-scheme-tied-to-house-flipping-2677470/

181   https://www.reviewjournal.com/crime/courts/robert-telles-says-he-was-under-surveillance-in-bribery-investigation-2804969/

182   Author's Dec. 5, 2023, interview with Robert Telles about corruption probe: "It doesn't take that long to investigate someone's finances. It doesn't take that long to, you know, to do any of the work necessary to bring up charges in a financial crime. It's clearly false."

183   https://www.reviewjournal.com/investigations/emails-telles-faulted-office-consultant-hired-to-manage-turmoil-warned-of-fraud-2689725/#:~:text=%E2%80%9CI'm%20not%20sure%20if,the%20next%20three%20months!!%E2%80%9D

184   Author interview with Jeff Wells Dec. 19, 2023

185   Interview with John Cahill. Author's email exchange with Jon Ralston.

186   Ralston email to author: "John is a good guy and would not lie. But that's not my recollection, and the email I have from John about Telles from last year and my response to him does not reflect what you said and it came after German was already working on the story. It's possible John and I talked, but I don't remember any conversation. If we did, I might well have told him we didn't have the bandwidth to cover Telles. So what? What relevance that has to a German bio is beyond me."

187   Interviews with Tom Dillard, Rita Reid and Aleisha Goodwin

188   Despite talking repeatedly at conferences and to the media about the case, Prast declined to be interviewed for this book. Her account is taken from her speech at an IRE event in April 2023.

189   Interview with Rita Reid

190   Lee-Kennett did not respond to requests for comment both when the author was researching stories after German's death and in the Fall of 2023 for the book.

191   County complaints provided to author by Aleisha Goodwin

192   Author interview with Telles Dec. 5, 2023

193   Author interview with Jeff Wells, Dec. 19, 2023

194   Interview with Michael Murphy

195   https://www.ktnv.com/news/contact-13/april-parks-others-plead-guilty-in-guardianship-exploitation-case

FROM GERMAN'S STORY: It has been stung by scandal periodically over the past 40 years. One administrator in the 1970s was convicted of fraud for attempting to overcharge a dead man's estate for storage.

Controversy followed the lengthy tenure of Jared Shafer, who ran the office between 1979 and 2003. That included the 1983 FBI arrests of an estate manager and an investigator charged with stealing from the estates of dead people.

For years, the office oversaw the much-criticized private guardianship system until the county spun off those duties into an appointed public guardian's office in 1999.

Shafer's tenure was marred by allegations of poor record-keeping and a failure to properly track estate possessions. He also was accused of paying neighbors and other friends for services performed for the estates he supervised. But he was never charged with any wrongdoing.

196   Interview with Lisa Mayo

197   https://www.the-independent.com/news/world/americas/crime/jeff-german-murder-rob-telles-las-vegas-b2162924.html

198   Telles case search warrants

199   Grand Jury testimony, power point and video taken from neighbor's camera.

200   Sept. 4, 2022 autopsy of Jeff German from the Clark County Coroner's office and testimony on page 49 of the grand jury transcript.

201   Security camera video from German's neighbor that was submitted to the grand jury in the case.

202   Grand Jury testimony and discussion with the neighbor shortly after the murder, who requested his name be withheld fearing retribution.

203   Rita Reid interview.

204   John Cahill interview.

205   Michael Murphy interview.

206   Arrest and Search warrants

207   Search warrants

208   Search warrants in Telles case.

209   David Ferrara interview.

210   https://www.reviewjournal.com/crime/how-jeff-germans-grieving-review-journal-colleagues-covered-his-murder-2640952/

211   Source with detailed knowledge of the investigation.

212   Police reports, Grand Jury records and photos, News reports.

213   Interview with Ozzie Fumo

214   Grand Jury testimony and photos.

215   https://cpj.org/data/killed/?status=Killed&motiveConfirmed%5B%5D=Confirmed&motiveUnconfirmed%5B%5D=Unconfirmed&type%5B%5D=Journalist&type%5B%5D=Media%20Worker&cc_fips%5B%5D=US&start_year=1992&end_year=2023&group_by=year

216   https://www.reviewjournal.com/crime/homicides/in-journalism-world-killing-of-rj-reporter-viewed-as-an-exceptional-case-2644245/ & https://news.google.com/newspapers?nid=897&dat=19520416&id=C-7JaAAAAIBAJ&sjid=CFADAAAAIBAJ&pg=6413,4578483

217   https://www.cnn.com/2019/03/04/media/att-time-warner-trump-gary-cohn/index.html

218   https://www.nytimes.com/2017/12/14/business/dealbook/disney-fox-takeover.html and author interview with NPR's media writer David Folkenflik.

219   Associated Press fact check Sept. 11, 2018 https://apnews.com/article/9d9a76067d5b47e5a290dc9832369c92

220   https://www.usatoday.com/story/news/politics/2019/04/11/julian-assange-six-wikileaks-most-memorable-revelations/3434371002/

221   https://theintercept.com/2018/11/16/as-the-obama-doj-concluded-prosecution-of-julian-assange-for-publishing-documents-poses-grave-threats-to-press-freedom/

222   https://news.yahoo.com/kidnapping-assassination-and-a-london-shoot-out-inside-the-ci-as-secret-war-plans-against-wiki-leaks-090057786.html

223   May 11, 2021 Veterans in Politics interview with Robert Telles: https://veteransinpolitics.org/2021/05/what-you-should-know-about-robert-telles-clark-county-public-administrator/ Telles declined to discuss his personal history in an interview with the author, saying he is saving that information for a different project. Additional information was provided in https://www.reviewjournal.com/crime/homicides/suspect-in-rj-reporters-killing-came-from-politically-powerful-family-2641145/

224   https://www.state.gov/following_fathers_footsteps

225   "The Making of a Mexican American Mayor: Robert L. Telles of El Paso" by Mario T. Garcia.

226   https://www.washingtonpost.com/archive/local/1977/01/19/ex-ambassador-pleads-guilty-of-illegal-aid-wages-to-alien/cdfa3b03-a580-4566-9625-7dbb87993d9d/

227   https://www.reviewjournal.com/crime/homicides/suspect-in-rj-reporters-killing-came-from-politically-powerful-family-2641145/

228   https://clerk.clarkcountynv.gov/AcclaimWeb/Search/OpenMarriageDocumentAvailable?transactionItemId=7967717

229   Veterans in Politics interview

230   Clark County divorce case D-08-397436-D | Robert Richard Telles, Plaintiff vs. Tonia Melendrez, Defendant.

231   Interview with Tonia Burton

232   https://clerk.clarkcountynv.gov/AcclaimWeb/Search/OpenMarriageDocumentAvailable?transactionItemId=6263203

233   Veterans in Politics interview

234   Author interview with Carlos Morales and another student who asked to remain anonymous. Also internal records of student bar activity.

235   Account is based on an interview with Carlos Morales, off-record interview with other students and internal records of student bar. Review-Journal investigative reporter Briana Erickson also wrote a detailed history of Telles after German's murder, providing details and leads for the book. https://www.reviewjournal.com/investigations/a-reporters-killing-revealed-a-decade-of-robert-telles-toxic-behavior-2679171/ Erickson is currently one of the author's reporters on the investigative team.

236   https://www.reviewjournal.com/crime/courts/telles-accuses-judge-of-badgering-him-in-recusal-request-2742138/

237   March 2, 2016 cease and desist letter from attorney Elizabeth Tullio to Telles. Tullio said she can't comment and hung up when reached by the author.

238   https://ballotpedia.org/Robert_Telles#:~:text=General%20election,-General%20election%20for&text=Robert%20Telles%20defeated%20Thomas%20L,Administrator%20on%20November%206%2C%202018.

239   https://transparentnevada.com/salaries/search/?q=Robert+Telles

240   https://www.reviewjournal.com/crime/i-am-a-public-official-new-video-shows-robert-telles-after-2020-arrest-2640522/

241   https://www.reviewjournal.com/investigations/911-call-to-police-from-robert-telles-wife-my-husband-is-going-crazy-2639098/

242   Dutro did not respond to an email seeking comment.

243   https://www.reviewjournal.com/investigations/a-reporters-killing-revealed-a-decade-of-robert-telles-toxic-behavior-2679171/ & Federal lawsuit 19-cv01660 & Settlement agreement from the county.

244   Interview with Jeff Wells

245   Interview with Nichole Lofton

246   Page 54 in the grand jury testimony.

247   Author interview with Robert Telles in the Clark County Detention Center December 5, 2023

248   Interview with Ben Lipman & statement to author from LVMPD attorney and district attorney

249   https://www.reviewjournal.com/crime/courts/da-robert-telles-charged-in-reporters-killing-a-danger-to-community-2638982/

250   Interview with Katelyn Newberg

251   https://www.reviewjournal.com/investigations/911-call-to-police-from-robert-telles-wife-my-husband-is-going-crazy-2639098/

252   https://www.reviewjournal.com/crime/courts/ive-certainly-made-mistakes-robert-telles-gives-jailhouse-interview-2641212/

253   https://en.wikipedia.org/wiki/David_Chesnoff# & Interviews with David Chesnoff, Ashley Kissinger and Ben Lipman.

254   https://www.reviewjournal.com/investigations/the-rise-and-fall-of-the-oath-keepers-born-in-las-vegas-2645040/

255   https://www.npr.org/2023/05/25/1178116193/stewart-rhodes-oath-keepers-verdict

256   https://www.reviewjournal.com/investigations/county-oversight-failures-didnt-start-with-murder-suspect-robert-telles-2645992/

257   https://www.reviewjournal.com/crime/courts/rj-asks-court-to-block-government-review-of-slain-reporters-devices-2646727/

258   https://www.reviewjournal.com/crime/courts/news-groups-support-rj-effort-to-protect-slain-reporters-devices-2647346/

259   https://www.reviewjournal.com/investigations/city-hall-video-of-fight-between-2-feuding-councilwomen-likely-deleted-2457300/

260   https://www.reviewjournal.com/investigations/michele-fiore-has-history-of-unreported-tax-business-problems-1621418/ & https://www.reviewjournal.com/investigations/fiores-campaign-pac-spend-6-figures-on-constituent-outreach-1619778/

261   https://www.reviewjournal.com/investigations/lvcva-board-member-michele-fiore-travels-far-at-agencys-expense-1581706/

262   https://www.reviewjournal.com/investigations/seaman-sues-fiore-for-assault-accuses-city-of-sweeping-conspiracy-2646606/

263   https://www.reviewjournal.com/investigations/murder-of-jeff-german-brings-historic-challenge-to-reporter-shield-laws-2653993/

264   https://www.reviewjournal.com/crime/courts/judge-grants-injunction-barring-search-of-reporters-devices-2655556/

265   https://www.reviewjournal.com/crime/courts/rj-seeks-sanctions-after-police-search-of-slain-reporters-phone-2715941/ & https://www.reviewjournal.com/crime/courts/judge-denies-rj-request-for-sanctions-against-metro-over-search-of-slain-reporters-phone-2718236/

266   https://www.reviewjournal.com/crime/courts/robert-telles-may-have-misappropriated-client-funds-high-court-says-2660415/ & November 28, 2023 email from Bar Counsel Dan Hooge: "We completed our investigation of his client trust account. We found minor violations. He had outstanding probate matters that he should have ended before becoming a public official. But we found no significant misconduct, such as misappropriation. Because Telles remains suspended on more serious murder allegations, we elected not to prosecute the trust account issues. Telles will remain suspended until his criminal case concludes. At that time, if he is convicted, then we will pursue discipline related to the criminal convictions."

267   https://www.reviewjournal.com/investigations/telles-investigated-in-alleged-kickback-scheme-tied-to-house-flipping-2677470/

268   https://www.reviewjournal.com/investigations/a-reporters-killing-revealed-a-decade-of-robert-telles-toxic-behavior-2679171/

269   https://transparentnevada.com/salaries/search/?q=Edward%20Kane & https://transparentnevada.com/salaries/search/?q=David+Lopez-Negrete

270   https://www.reviewjournal.com/investigations/telles-has-thousands-in-assets-but-taxpayers-pay-for-two-attorneys-2661026/

271   https://www.reviewjournal.com/investigations/telles-hires-private-attorney-to-replace-public-defenders-2663601/

272   Interview with Ozzie Fumo

273   https://www.reviewjournal.com/crime/courts/robert-telles-hires-new-attorney-in-jeff-german-murder-case-2717824/ & substation of counsel forms filed in the case.

274   Author interview with Ryan Helmick

275   Interviews with Ryan Helmick and Robert Telles. Damian Sheets did not respond to repeated requests for comment.

276   https://www.reviewjournal.com/crime/courts/suspect-in-reporters-killing-wants-to-represent-himself-2724747/

277   Author's interview with Robert Telles Dec. 5, 2023. Attorney Damian Sheets did not respond to repeated calls and emails to his office.

278   https://www.reviewjournal.com/crime/courts/telles-sells-4-rental-properties-in-arkansas-2965548/ & Author interview with Robert Telles.

279   Author interview with Helmick

280   Gary A. Modafferi declined comment when the author emailed him for an interview.

281   https://www.reviewjournal.com/crime/courts/telles-accuses-judge-of-badgering-him-in-recusal-request-2742138/

282   https://www.reviewjournal.com/crime/courts/robert-telles-wants-to-disqualify-judge-overseeing-murder-case-2741457/

283   https://www.reviewjournal.com/crime/courts/telles-motion-to-have-judge-dismissed-rejected-2753241/

284   https://www.washingtonpost.com/dc-md-va/2023/02/01/mormon-ponzi-scheme-vegas-fbi/

285   https://www.reviewjournal.com/local/local-las-vegas/national-press-club-honors-slain-reporter-jeff-german-lizzie-johnson-2880488/ & https://www.reviewjournal.com/local/local-las-vegas/review-journal-washington-post-honored-with-freedom-of-the-press-award-2922781/

286   Author interview with Jeff Wells.

287   Document from the DA's employment management software obtained under a state open records request.

288   Author interview with Jeff Wells.

289   https://www.reviewjournal.com/investigations/deputy-clark-county-manager-on-leave-related-to-sons-employment-2741230/ & https://www.reviewjournal.com/investigations/deputy-county-manager-who-oversaw-telles-other-embattled-officials-retires-2759618/ & https://www.reviewjournal.com/investigations/embattled-clark-county-official-retired-with-250k-in-payouts-2771481/ & https://www.reviewjournal.com/investigations/report-questions-deputy-county-managers-actions-in-sons-discipline-2799001/

290   https://www.reviewjournal.com/crime/courts/robert-telles-files-subpoenas-for-arrest-details-wants-judge-recused-2752510/ &

291   https://www.reviewjournal.com/crime/courts/suspect-in-reporters-killing-files-complaint-against-police-2778338/ & https://www.reviewjournal.com/crime/courts/metros-citizen-board-dismisses-robert-telles-complaint-against-department-2879982/

292   https://www.reviewjournal.com/crime/courts/telles-claims-he-wants-to-avoid-confrontation-over-newspapers-rights-2756810/

293   https://www.reviewjournal.com/news/politics-and-government/nevada/nevada-supreme-court-protects-phone-computers-of-slain-reporter-2916660/

294   https://www.reviewjournal.com/crime/courts/agreement-would-let-review-journal-look-over-slain-rj-reporters-devices-2940097/

295   Marquis Aurbach billings to LVMPD obtained under state open records laws and interviews with RJ counsel.

296   https://www.reviewjournal.com/investigations/selling-dead-peoples-homes-lucrative-for-some-but-what-about-the-heirs-2986851/

297   https://www.reviewjournal.com/crime/courts/telles-claims-he-was-framed-by-local-real-estate-firm-in-rj-reporters-murder-2982916/

298   https://www.reviewjournal.com/crime/courts/telles-second-request-to-recuse-judge-in-murder-case-denied-2988181/

299   https://www.reviewjournal.com/local/local-las-vegas/former-judge-sentenced-to-26-months-in-prison/

300   https://www.reviewjournal.com/crime/courts/former-las-vegas-nightclub-promoter-acquitted-in-rape-case/

301   https://casetext.com/case/in-re-draskovich-bar-no

302   Author interview with Robert Draskovich after he was hired by Robert Telles

303   Email exchanges between the author and Ralston as he repeatedly refused to do a phone interview about his interactions with

German and the media climate in Las Vegas during the decades he worked at newspapers, television and online.

For more news about Arthur Kane, subscribe
to our newsletter at *wbp.bz/newsletter*.

Word-of-mouth is critical to an author's long-term
success. If you appreciated this book, please leave a
review on the Amazon sales page at *wbp.bz/LastStory*.

ALSO AVAILABLE FROM WILDBLUE PRESS

https://wbp.bz/Ruin

I WILL RUIN YOU: The Twisted Truth Behind the Kit Martin Murder Trial delves into the complex circumstances behind Martin's story. It looks beyond the sensational headlines and legal turmoil into the heart of this controversial case.

ALSO AVAILABLE FROM WILDBLUE PRESS

https://wbp.bz/hha

This "riveting true life account" goes inside the life-or-death world of a Las Vegas police crisis negotiator: "a must read" (Gary W. Noesner, Chief, FBI Crisis Negotiation Unit, author of *Stalling For Time*).

ALSO AVAILABLE FROM WILDBLUE PRESS

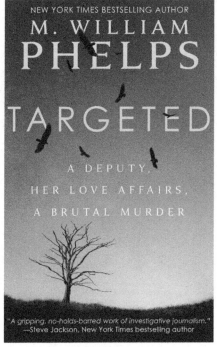

https://wbp.bz/targeteda

A *New York Times*–bestselling author's account of a Georgia deputy accused of murder: "A gripping, no-holds-barred work of investigative journalism" (Steve Jackson, author of *No Stone Unturned*).

Made in the USA
Las Vegas, NV
12 August 2024

93753761R00157